DRUGS, DAYDREAMING, and PERSONALITY:
A Study of College Youth

DRUGS, DAYDREAMING, and PERSONALITY:
A Study of College Youth

BERNARD SEGAL
University of Alaska, Anchorage

GEORGE J. HUBA
University of California, Los Angeles

JEROME L. SINGER
Yale University

LEA LAWRENCE ERLBAUM ASSOCIATES, PUBLISHERS
1980   Hillsdale, New Jersey

Lawrence Erlbaum Associates, Inc., Publishers
365 Broadway
Hillsdale, New Jersey 07642

Library of Congress Cataloging in Publication Data

Segal, Bernard.
  Drugs, daydreaming, and personality.
  Bibliography: p.
  Includes indexes.
  1. Adolescent psychiatry. 2. Adolescent
psychology. 3. Personality. 4. Drug abuse.
5. Fantasy. I. Huba, George J., joint author.
II. Singer, Jerome L., joint author. III. Title.
RJ506.D78S44   378'.1981   80-10094
ISBN 0-89859-042-6

Printed in the United States of America

Contents

Preface

This book presents a detailed account of a series of investigations that examined the patterns of resort to drugs and alcohol use in college youth, and how such substance uses are linked to personality characteristics and daydreaming patterns. We have chosen to emphasize the more "private" features of the personality, because these have often been ignored in earlier research, despite popular assumptions that there are close ties between fantasy, inwardness, "spacey" qualities (all suggesting permanent changes in mental organization), and substance use in youth. The plan for this study stemmed originally from the collaboration between two of us, Segal and Singer, who had the opportunity of examining a broad spectrum of college freshmen at such contrasting institutions as Murray State University, in a rural border region of Kentucky, and the more urban, affluent, nationally selected and academically competitive, Ivy League, Yale University. We were subsequently joined by Huba.

Supported by a 2-year grant from the National Institute of Drug Abuse (Grant #RO1-DA-00590), our plan was to study two annual cohorts of college students, males and females, from each institution, and to move beyond large-scale psychometric data analyses to specific processes through experimental procedures as well as intensive interviews. We hoped to not only gather basic data on substance use and abuse but to also examine patterns and reasons for such use and to see how the normal personality and daydreaming styles of college youth might predict differential degrees of resort to drugs or alcohol. Along the way we also wanted to examine basic theoretical questions about the stream of consciousness in young adults, the functional role of daydreaming in daily life, and the different patterns of daydreams and broader self-reported hierarchies of motivation.

Because of our effort to go beyond normative patterns of substance use toward explorations of personality and consciousness, we believe this volume will be of interest to a wider audience than just drug and alcohol researchers. We have attempted some novel applications of psychometrics and statistics that may be of interest to students of individual differences and to investigators in the area of the psychology of personality. We have not stinted on the technical details that critical scientists require, yet we have tried to recognize wherever possible the broader human interest of our subject matter, such as the initiation of 18-year-olds into the new life of a residential college with its special attractions and temptations. The clinical psychologist, the investigator of the psychology of consciousness, the college counselor and more general workers in the fields of substance use, psychiatrists, social workers, and drug counselors may also find material of interest in this volume.

The research we describe here involved a complex cooperative effort not only between the three authors but also between teams of assistants, some at Murray State University in Murray, Kentucky, some at Yale University in New Haven, and others, as the authors moved on professionally, to the University of California, Los Angeles (Huba) and the University of Alaska, Anchorage (Segal). Our study called for advanced research assistants with administrative skills and public sensitivity, for competent young people to help in group testing, individual interviewing, the conducting of experiments, recording, coding and punching of data, typing protocols and manuscripts, and so on. We have acknowledged these people in special government reports, some specific publications in professional journals derived from this work, and in a few cases in doctoral dissertations that emerged from this program of research. We shall therefore limit our formal thanks only to the major participants in the project at each setting.

At Yale University, Dr. Susan Frank took the major role in soliciting subjects, organizing group testing, running individual experiments and interviews, and keeping track of data. Drs. Anthony Campagna and Philip Powell also helped with some of the experimental studies and group testing. Mr. Irving Leon, an undergraduate at Yale, was very helpful in various phases of the study and in interviewing, as was Ms. Judy Pack. Other research assistants for extensive phases of the work at Yale University included David Diamond, Jon Douglas Singer, and George Rhenberg. Valuable clerical and research assistance was provided by Delores Hyslop and Audrey Klein, and Esta Schaefer aided in manuscript preparation, as did Cheryl Olson and Kay Wardlaw.

The work conducted at Murray State University could not have been done without the very able assistance of Sara Sterling, Russ Brethauer, and John Conboy. George Rhenberg, Stephanie Davidson, and Rebecca Stewart

Altfeld also contributed significantly to the project. The work could not have been completed without the very important contribution of Judith Beam's secretarial assistance. Her willingness to work over and beyond what was necessary made this research possible.

The additional assistance of Bill Horr at the University of Alaska, Anchorage, is also acknowledged. Grateful appreciation is also due to Rita Dursi Johnson, Mary Parker, Kathie McDonough, and Sandi Alger for their secretarial support.

At the Los Angeles end of the production, support in terms of administrative, computer, and clerical assistance as well as Huba's salary was provided in part by a program project grant (DA-01070) to Dr. Peter M. Bentler from the National Institute on Drug Abuse. Janel Hetland and Bonnie Barron produced the final version of the manuscript on an IBM System-6 text editor. Janel and Bonnie contributed humor, diligence, and the ability to face endless rounds of scribbled thoughts that we were trying to dignify as paragraphs. William Wong-McCarthy and Clyde Dent helped with final computer analyses. Byerly Woodward aided in the final aspects of production.

Several individuals in Los Angeles provided professional advice and consultation that added immeasurably to the quality of the final manuscript. Dr. Peter M. Bentler repeatedly acted as a sounding board for various ideas, helped us to refine our thoughts, and commented extensively on portions of the manuscript. He was also extremely supportive of the preparation of the manuscript when, at times, it seemed that the project was getting in the way of Huba's other research duties. Dr. Bentler made facilities at the *UCLA/NIDA Center for the Study of Adolescent Drug Abuse Etiologies* available for the writing of the results and provided an extremely stimulating environment for the study of drug use and methodology. Many interchanges between Bentler and Huba resulted in additional research, which is cited throughout. Dr. Carol S. Aneshensel read the entire manuscript and commented extensively on substantive issues. Dr. Aneshensel helped to find loose ends in our arguments, present our thoughts more clearly, and organize the diverse materials that make up the themes for this volume. Dr. Aneshensel followed the manuscript through several drafts over a period of 2 years and suggested improvements at many stages.

A special acknowledgment is in order for the support, guidance, and assistance provided by Dr. Dan J. Lettieri of the National Institute on Drug Abuse. We also wish to acknowledge four institutions: Murray State University, Yale University, the University of Alaska, Anchorage, and the University of California, Los Angeles. The administrative support that afforded us the necessary investigators' freedom despite the "touchiness" of our domains of inquiry was remarkable. Provisions of space and facilities were excellent. Our research was carefully scrutinized by committees of ethics of human investigation, and useful suggestions were received from them for protection of our student participants' rights.

Finally, of course, there are the more than a thousand undergraduates at Murray State and Yale who involved themselves in long hours of testing or experiments with remarkable grace and impressive candor. In addition to assigned code numbers to preserve anonymity, the participants were encouraged to use pseudonyms on all their test forms and communications with us. In our seemingly endless sorting of records and files of tests and interviews, we have developed sentimental feelings about those people who named themselves "Male Animal," "Hedda Gabler," "Kingman Brewster," "Martin Luther," "Marilyn Monroe," and dozens of other whimsical aliases. We thank them all for sharing a phase of their lives and private worlds with us.

BERNARD SEGAL
GEORGE J. HUBA
JEROME L. SINGER

DRUGS, DAYDREAMING, and PERSONALITY:
A Study of College Youth

1

A Perspective on
Youthful Drug Use

Daydreaming, drug use, and drinking are often linked together by an older generation as among the most besetting vices of late adolescent and college-aged youth in this final third of the 20th century. In this volume, we describe a systematic attempt to explain the relationships between a conceptualization we call the *private personality* and the use of popular and rarely used psychoactive biochemical substances such as alcohol, marijuana, amphetamines, tranquilizers, hallucinogenics, and narcotics. Rather than accepting the a priori assumption that youthful substance use is a manifestation of "deviance," "psychopathology," or "emotional disturbance," our objective was to determine if substance use can be part of a normal growth of private personality during the college years. In summary, the vast majority of the young people studied are characterized by considerable self-absorption and substance use without serious consequence.

In this chapter, we discuss the theoretical considerations and previous formulations that shaped our view of substance use during the current historical period. In subsequent chapters, we trace: (1) the theoretical bases of the private personality concept; and (2) present data that show the linkages between different types of private personality style, daydreaming tendencies, and substance use. However, before beginning a formal review of issues relevant to studying drug use, it seems appropriate to state briefly the scope of the volume.

In this volume, we describe a series of analyses conducted with two large samples of college students at an urban, northeastern university and at a regional state university in Kentucky. Using extensive questionnaires, we examined the nature of the inner life of the students from their reports of daydreaming tendencies and typical stream of consciousness. Additionally, the battery assessed self-reported hierarchies of needs and activity preferences. The different facets of private personality—inner experience, motivational structure, desired behavioral tendencies—were then related to patterns of substance use and the perceived motives for, and consequences of, using different psychoactive substances.

After probing the linkage of private personality and substance use, experimental studies were conducted to answer questions about the structural properties of the stream of consciousness, the determinants of ongoing thought, and possible adaptive consequences of the self-awareness of imagery and daydreaming processes.

It has often been assumed that extended daydreams or undue attention to one's ongoing thought and inner experiences may have pathological implications or, indeed, may actually be a precursor to emotional or social withdrawal. We infer, then, that if such pathological consequences of certain types of inner experience are true, it is quite possible that some individuals will turn to alcohol or other drugs in an attempt to self-medicate, or supplement, such inner reality. On the other hand, if certain forms of inner experience are adaptive for the individual, drugs may be used to induce desired states of consciousness. The data gathered for this volume represent the largest sampling to date of the private personality experience of college youth and concurrent drug taking. The primary questions asked in our various studies seek basic information about private personality processes and their importance for understanding substance use and potential abuse. We have also sought to examine more generally the nature of the daydreaming process and its tie to other facets of personality in young adults. The major questions guiding inquiry have been, "Is private personality closely tied to usage of drugs and alcohol among young adults?", "Is the capacity to enjoy inner experience a countervailing force against reliance on alcohol and other drugs?", and "To what extent is the private personality experience a determinant of substance use as a coping strategy?"

In the remaining pages of this chapter, we discuss the scope and nature of drug use in American society. We also review different theoretical viewpoints offered to explain youthful drug use, and we explore deficiencies in prevalent viewpoints that led to the theoretical perspectives presented here and in Chapter 2.

DRUG AND ALCOHOL USE: PUBLIC PASSION AND THE NEED FOR RESEARCH

Drug and alcohol use are not new to American society, nor are they new to any human society. In his classic book, Brecher (1972) shows that psychoactive chemicals have been ingested individually, as well as collectively, since the beginning of recorded history. Brecher carefully documents substance use since the American colonial period and shows that drugs have been used for recreational, as well as self-medicinal, purposes whenever a supply was available.

A relatively recent development in American society, however, is the increasing frequency and intensity of substance use among individuals of college and secondary school ages. The recent trend has been supplemented with the extensive publicity that substance use has received in the new "global village" media period. Media presentations have emphasized the size of the "drug problem" and have graphically portrayed the "junkie" in numerous movies and television series.

In examining research conducted on youthful drug use, it is necessary to remember the social context in which research is conducted. Illuminatingly, the concern expressed today over drug use, particularly in high schools and on college campuses, closely resembles similar concerns of 50 years ago about college drinking during the days of the "flaming youth" of the 1920s. As Suchman (1968) points out, studies of college students in the last generation found alcohol to be the major campus "vice" and "alarming reports were published about drinking problems of college students [p. 146]." Public concern not only prompted the classic study of Straus and Bacon (1953) on college alcohol use but has since motivated numerous other investigators to examine college drinking patterns (see Glatt & Hills, 1968; Globetti, 1972).

As was the case with the study of alcohol consumption, recent public concern about drug use and abuse has resulted in the development of a large body of research literature attempting to explain the phenomenon. A good part of this scientific investigation contains a statement to the effect that the research is important because of widespread drug use among youth of the time (1960s and 1970s). Furthermore, much of this research focuses on determining the causes of youthful drug use. Although not often explicitly stated, many investigations proceed from the assumption that *drug use—the ingestion of any chemical substance for nonmedical purposes*—is tantamount to *drug abuse.* Accordingly, it was considered quite appropriate for the socially concerned behavioral and medical scientist to adopt the role of a fireman and come rushing to extinguish the drug-abuse forest fire!

Unfortunately, many studies undertaken *in reaction* to the drug-use problem paid little attention to the effects of drug laws, policies, and attitudes on the implicit assumptions of researchers. Interest centered on stopping or decreasing the problem immediately, with the consequence that scholars tried to develop a single simple explanation, or a small number of closely related explanations, to account for drug use. Today, such approaches seem overly simplistic: There is probably *not a single explanation for drug use at any stage of development,* and the problem is further compounded by a recent realization that many forms of drug use may not constitute drug abuse (Richards & Blevens, 1977).

In any evaluation of the research literature on drug use, it is necessary to try to separate those studies primarily concerned with drug abuse from those in which drug use was the focus. The importance of this dichotomy is underscored by the conclusions of the National Commission of Marijuana and Drug Abuse (whose very title seems contradicted by the group's final report). That commission concluded that the term *drug abuse*, when used in reference to the use of any type of drug without regard to its specific pharmacological actions, is an eclectic concept with the only uniform connotation being *social disapproval*. The Commission (1973) further stated that "drug abuse" terminology should be deleted from official pronouncements and public-policy dialogue. In the words of the Commission, the term "has no functional utility and has become no more than an arbitrary codeword for that drug use which is presently considered wrong. Continued use of this term with its emotional overtones will only serve to perpetuate confused public attitudes about drug using behavior [p. 13]."

The emotional climate surrounding drug abuse during the last few decades clouded both public policy and research issues. With respect to research, reaction to public hue and cry has dominated the field and has almost precluded an approach oriented toward systematic scientific examination of the socialization patterns of various substance-user groups rather than an immediate solution to the perceived problem. Because of earlier public concern, there was a presumed need for explanation, particularly for drug use by the children of the majority group of voters. Not surprisingly, the explanations advanced often reflected the prevailing public attitudes. Consequently, concepts such as "alienation," "nonconformity," and a host of similar constructs (Sadava, 1975) have been suggested to account for youthful drug use and abuse. These earlier studies sometimes fail to contribute substantially to understanding the phenomena because of the presumed use–abuse linkage and the various methodological difficulties that were undoubtedly exacerbated by the "rush to put out the fire" ethos of the time.

The emotionality of prior years has moderated somewhat, and changes in political climate and research funding priorities have allowed research probes into drug-taking behavior to become more mature. More systematic research programs have been developed (see, e.g., Huba, Wingard, & Bentler, 1979; Jessor & Jessor, 1977; Kandel, 1978a, b; Kandel, Kessler, & Margulies, 1978; Lettieri, 1975; Platt & Labate, 1976; Smith & Fogg, 1977, 1978; Wingard, Huba, & Bentler, 1979), and more sophisticated design and data analysis strategies for conducting drug use research have emerged (see, e.g., Bentler, 1980; Bentler & Huba, 1979; Bentler, Lettieri, & Austin, 1976; Nehemkis, Macari, & Lettieri, 1976). Investigators now recognize that the use of drugs, including alcohol, is a complex multidimensional process influenced by a plethora of past experiences and aspects of the present environment as well as possible biological predispositions (Huba, Wingard, & Bentler, 1980; Kandel,

1978a). It is quite a positive sign that researchers have increasingly attempted to describe the interrelationships of different domains of causal factors in determining youthful drug use (Becker, 1974; Bentler & Eichberg, 1975; Gorsuch & Butler, 1976; Jessor & Jessor, 1977; Sadava, 1975).

Whereas significant progress has been made in systematically examining different clusters of causal factors for youthful drug use, there has been minimal effort to systematically differentiate types of use. Although certain alternate models for the phenomenon of drug use have been proposed—such as the stage theory of Kandel (1975a; Kandel & Faust, 1975), the multidimensional alcoholism structure of Horn (1977), the generalized smoking dimensions of Tomkins (1966a, b), and Carlin and Stauss' (1977) twofold table of polydrug use—it is fair to say that most studies still continue to treat the phenomenon as essentially unidimensional. Consequently, most investigations continue to contrast "users" with "nonusers" or "addicts" with "normals." As the recent work by Kandel (1975a) in overall general stages of drug use suggests, such contrasts do have their place in understanding drug taking.

Recently, a new conceptual framework for drug-taking behavior has gained increasing acceptance among behavioral scientists. Since it has been recognized that the term *drug abuse* may not be appropriate, the phrase has been replaced by newer, perhaps more tenable, concepts of "deviant behavior," "deviancy," or "problem behavior" now employed in sociological and psychosocial studies of drug-taking behavior (e.g., Jessor & Jessor, 1977; Johnson, 1973; Kandel, 1974, 1975a,b, 1978a). This newer perspective illustrates best the extent to which the existence of a social "problem" depends on societal definitions at a given time. Thus the emotional connotations of the term *drug abuse* have led to a shift toward a concept that may represent a more tolerant view but that, nevertheless, labels drug-taking behavior as being apart and deviant from the values of society. Two major questions must be asked about this new emphasis:

1. Is drug taking behavior actually apart from the cohort norms of current youth, or is such behavior an integral part of growing up in the late 20th century?
2. Does a concept of deviancy imply a general explanatory construct for drug taking behavior?

Stating these two questions another way, where does the concept of deviancy leave us with respect to developing an etiology of youthful drug-taking behavior and its consequences? We contend that the concept of deviancy is insufficient as an explanatory construct and present our rationale for this contention in subsequent sections.

A question arising at this point in our argument is whether an explanation can be derived to help to understand drug-taking behavior. While it seems apparent from the previous discussion that no single, comprehensive explanation is possible, it seems reasonable that we may partially understand patterns of drug use by considering the social context, motives for use, and psychosocial concomitants pointed out in previous work. A reasonable beginning for our investigation, then, is a discussion of some historical conceptions of drug use; the relationship between drug laws, policies, and attitudes; and the derivation of conceptual frameworks previously offered as explanations.

HISTORICAL PERSPECTIVE ON AMERICAN DRUG USE

It is intriguing to note that the apparent general attitude among the American public is that drug use is a new phenomenon destroying the fabric of American life and that something must be done to stop the decay. Hence, news of large-scale "busts" of drug suppliers and the interception of drug shipments by law-enforcement officials is given emphasis in the print and broadcast media. Such attitudes that drug use is abhorrent are not new, nor is the response that drug supplies must be controlled. Public outcry in America during the 20th century has generally given impetus to a politicization of the drug problem that places responsibility for controlling use into the hands of government, law-enforcement agencies, and the courts. This process is particularly evident with respect to narcotic or opiate use, but the furor during July 1978 resulting from reports that President Jimmy Carter's youthful White House staff used marijuana suggests continuing broad concern about a drug whose use is almost a normative behavior among those under 40 years of age.

The use of opium as a self-medicant for just about anything ailing the body was extensive during and after the Civil War. There was little popular support to ban opium use at that time, even though the intravenous effects and addictive potential of morphine had become apparent after the introduction of the hypodermic syringe in 1854. The byproduct of the analgesic value of morphine—addiction—was viewed as a medical problem, not as a deviant behavior (Goode, 1978). While the general public did not approve of addiction and the morphine-dependent individual was considered to be "sick," he or she was not generally discernible because of atypical appearance, membership in a subculture, or rejection of the majority culture's social standards. The addicted person, according to Goode (1978), was able to "live a more or less normal life, carry out ordinary, everyday functions—work, take care of family, attend school. There was no isolation or stigmatization of the addict before the turn of the century [p. 249]."

The change from the tolerant attitude of the past century and the current state of affairs appears to have originated in an attempt to control the widespread use of opium and its derivatives. Public interest in prohibiting opium use first started in San Francisco during the 1870s because of the belief that "many women and young girls, as well as young men of *respectable family* [italics added], were being induced to visit the [Chinese opium smoking] dens, where they were ruined morally and otherwise" [cited in Brecher, 1972, p. 42]. This first anti-opium legislative action was clearly a reaction to the social impact of the drug promoted by disapproval of the life style associated with (Chinese) opium use. Impetus for reform was also motivated by fear of the addict, especially when the drug-dependent individual was a minority member (Platt & Labate, 1976). Initial legislation in San Francisco was followed by a bill enacted by the New York State legislature in 1882 aimed almost exclusively at controlling the flourishing opium dens of New York City's Chinatown.

Although a multitude of significant national and international treaties and agreements attempted to control the opium-use problem around the turn of the century (see Brecher, 1972; Kramer, 1972), the major legislative consequence of the public concern was passage of the Harrison Narcotic Act in December, 1914. After enactment of the bill, unauthorized sale, possession, or purchase of narcotic drugs became a criminal offense, and nonmedical narcotic use was considered an illegal act. The social implications of the Harrison Act were further heightened by the stringent manner in which law-enforcement agencies chose to interpret the law. Most significantly, the United States Treasury Department (in a decision later upheld by the Supreme Court) decided that physicians could not prescribe narcotics to an addict for the purpose of maintaining an addiction, even though the Act included the statement that physicians could provide or prescribe narcotics in the course of professional practice. The courts ruled that providing an addict with opium merely sustained the addiction rather than constituting treatment for withdrawal symptoms. It was this interpretation of the Harrison Act that paved the way for a punitive orientation toward narcotic use and ingestion of other chemical substances such as cocaine.

After the Harrison Act became law, the climate was ideal for the development of an illegal drug market. Since medical treatment (through supply of the drug) was no longer available for the withdrawal syndrome, "underground" use became common. As the Harrison Act was modified through additional legislation and court decisions to include other chemicals used as substitutes by formerly opium-dependent individuals, users began to engage in illegal activities to pay the exorbitant prices charged for drugs in the underground market. Increased illegal activities, of course, caused high arrest and conviction rates for addicts, and it was not surprising that the public came to perceive the addict as criminal and deviant. Finally, narcotic users typically became confined to urban ghettos and invisible to the majority of Americans.

As long as the drug problem remained in the ghettos among poor and minority groups, the phenomenon posed no generalized threat to the public as a whole.

The "problem" of drug use, of course, did not long remain isolated in the ghetto away from mainstream America. Drug use leaped into the American consciousness in the 1960s after slowly trickling in after World War II. During the protest era of the 1960s, drug use became more blatant and visible, but the trend had started far earlier as the products of pharmaceutical research had become "miracle" drugs for the psychiatrist and general practice physician to prescribe for mental health problems. Barbiturates, amphetamines, LSD, minor tranquilizers, and antidepressants moved from the sophisticated laboratory to the physician's prescription pad to the street as drug abuse. Futhermore, drugs with long histories of use in America, such as marijuana, cocaine, organic hallucinogenics, and alcohol, began to be purchased illegally by an increasingly large and visible segment of the population.

Public reaction was swift, although well behind the peak of major increases in use. Once drugs began to invade the middle-class suburbs, there was again public outcry to combat the "epidemic" sweeping the country. Drugs long identified with economically disadvantaged and minority-group individuals were now used by an identifiable (by means of clothing and lifestyle) minority of suburban adolescents and young adults. Furthermore, psychoactive "prescription" drugs such as amphetamines and barbiturates could now be obtained rather easily. The state of affairs and perceived threat of invasion from the minority ghettos paralleled the situation with respect to opium use encountered almost a century earlier. Additionally, the drug use of the 1960s and 1970s was associated, in the public mind, with unconventional life styles and political views; broadcast media of the time frequently portrayed the protestor against international and domestic policies as "high on drugs." Once again the public demanded federal intervention. And once again the government responded with major legislation.

The Comprehensive Drug Abuse Prevention and Control Act of 1970 brought control of all drugs, whether involved in interstate commerce or not, under federal jurisdiction. In superseding previous laws, the act established federal enforcement and prosecution for any illegal activity involving controlled drugs. Surprisingly, the law, for the first time, called for the reduction of penalties for "onetime" users, particularly for those possessing marijuana. Emphasis was directed primarily toward drug distributors. Provisions were also provided for treatment and prevention of drug abuse as well as the rehabilitation of drug addicts, but much more money was spent on the law-enforcement aspect of drug use than on treatment and prevention (Lewis, 1976).

The major accomplishment of the severe legislation and "tough talk" of the early 1970s, apart from a temporary decline in overt, visible drug use, was an assuagement of public demands. This political approach, for as long as the society continues to view drug use as a form of deviant behavior, only ensures that the government will continue to play an important role in the response to drug use. A significant effect of the punitive approach to drug use is that: (1) reliance on treatment programs to rehabilitate drug abusers is lessened; and (2) the intervention that is provided is sometimes coercive. More importantly, however, the federal government, through its control over access to psychoactive drugs and funding, determines (sometimes benevolently, other times not) what forms of treatment will be provided. Society has come to equate drug use with criminal behavior and mental illness and has correspondingly demanded that the government be compelled to regulate both drug availability and conditions of treatment (National Commission on Marijuana and Drug Abuse, 1973). Treatment is thus equated with punishment, which not only potentially minimizes treatment outcomes but also limits the development of innovative strategies for combating chemical dependency. As long as basic treatment decisions rest primarily with law-enforcement agencies with power to place users in facilities, it becomes difficult to conclude that progress has been made in the "war" against drugs. As Lewis (1976) reports, "That such tactics fail is confirmed by the figures released by NACC in 1971 showing that for the $345 million spent since its inception, fewer than 200 addicts have been released as cured (i.e., totally drug-free) and stayed cured from a civil commitment population in excess of 20,000 [p. 32]." From being regarded as deviant, the drug user was then regarded as a criminal, then a diseased person, and now a criminally diseased deviant (Lewis, 1976).

The foregoing comments, of course, are not meant to imply that there is not such a phenomenon as drug abuse, or more properly, maladaptive patterns of substance use that can lead to physical, psychological, and social damage for the individual and others. Staggering numbers of individuals are killed each year in automobiles driven by intoxicated drivers, millions of worker hours are lost due to drugs, and various criminal activities are committed under the influence of alcohol and other drugs. On the other hand, socially maladaptive behaviors (which might be called substance *abuse* behaviors) are committed by a small number of the total group of users of substances. Consequently, while there is a definable and "real" substance abuse "problem," the maladaptive consequences of drug use for some individuals must not be equated with the use of drugs by all individuals unless it can be *empirically* demonstrated that use and abuse are synonymous.

Also, we should point out that we do not mean to imply that public concern about maladaptive drug use is unfounded; in the current historical era, private citizens have taken the positive step of becoming increasingly aware of the potential damage of food additives, asbestos, industrial pollutants, and radiation. Given the wide concern about the danger of physical substances, it is not surprising that there should be concern about the potentially dangerous effects of psychoactive substances. What we are pointing out is that while alcohol use is frequently differentiated from alcoholism, marijuana use is not as often considered separate from drug abuse; this lack of differentiation is apparent in the criminal laws that still cover the use of marijuana at the federal and state levels.

We have little doubt that public reaction to drug use and legislative response have, over the decades, combined to affect the attitudes and approaches taken by behavioral scientists—particularly psychologists, psychiatrists, and sociologists—toward developing an explanation of drug use and corresponding methods of alleviation. Furthermore, the attitudes and results of respected professionals studying drug use have then served to reinforce more general public beliefs and appeals for legislative action. The following sections explore some of the approaches taken toward drug use.

THEORIES OF DRUG USE

With all the past and present public outcry over drug use, the question arises why drugs continued to be used. That is, what is there about the drug experience that perpetuates drug use, particularly among nonaddicted individuals, in the face of disapproval from the majority of society? Drugs are used, it would appear, to obtain desired effects—to help the individual to feel or experience something uncommon, to change a mood or alter one's experiences and state of consciousness. Each of these two themes is discussed more fully in later chapters, as one of our primary interests in this volume is to probe the relationship between personality and self-reported motives for drug use.

The Psychopharmacological Model

The reasons for using drugs are not unrelated to their specific pharmacological effects, although, as attribution theory (see Schachter & J. E. Singer, 1962) has pointed out, the situation of use partially determines the individual's subjective response. While the pharmacological and physiological properties of most chemical substances are fairly well known (Julien, 1975), the psychological experience involves significant individual variation contingent on many factors such as: (1) individual physiological intolerance; (2) expectations of drug effect in the dosage consumed; (3) the setting for use; (4) the purity of the chemical combination and level of potency; (5) susceptibility at the time of use; (6) method of administration; and (7) previous experience with the drug. Although all of these factors contribute to variations in how drugs are experienced, it is nevertheless possible to discuss drugs in terms of their chemical actions and describe generally what the psychological effects are. In the study of drug use, knowledge of chemical actions is valuable in attempting to understand and infer the relationship between personality and the motivation behind ingesting the drug. At this point, we characterize briefly the typical effects of the group of drugs that are discussed further in subsequent chapters:

1. *Opiate narcotics.* Included in this group of drugs are opium, heroin, morphine, codeine, and other opiate deriatives. The principal therapeutic use of opiates is for the relief of pain, but they also alleviate coughing and diarrhea. The use of opiates seems to cause a subjective experience characterized by an extremely pleasant euphoric state, warmth, well-being, peacefulness, and contentment. A pleasant dream-like state of consciousness can also be induced. Not all reactions to opiates are pleasant, but narcotics seem to be primarily used in anticipation of the relaxed state they produce and the euphoric experiences of the drug.

2. *Generalized depressants.* These drugs are chemical agents that depress the central nervous system. Among the generalized depressants are barbiturates, alcohol and the "major" and "minor" tranquilizers. Although both alcohol and barbiturates are similar chemical compounds, the social and legal aspects involved with alcohol necessitate that they be treated separately; because alcohol is used so widely in American society, it deserves special attention.

a. *Alcohol.* As with other types of depressants and narcotic agents, alcohol is potentially addicting. Alcohol is capable of producing clinical effects such as sedation or sleep, but it is used more typically for its intoxicating effects. Among the well-known effects of alcohol consumption are a lessening of restraints on speech and behavior, mild euphoria, self-confidence enhancement, and a disruption of motor coordination. The behavioral reaction to the state of disinhibition engendered by the drug is not uniformly predictable; amount of alcohol consumed, setting, and expectations play a major role in determining the exact reaction.

b. *Barbiturates.* The most commonly used barbiturates are short-acting agents such as Nembutal, Seconal, and Amytal. All of these compounds are potentially addictive and induce calming and sleep. Barbiturates are widely used as "downers" to bring oneself down from a normal state of consciousness or from a condition brought about by stimulant drugs. Barbiturates are also known to induce a behavioral state that is virtually indistinguishable from alcohol intoxication, including behavioral disinhibition, and a mild state of euphoria might be experienced at that time. Negative or violent reactions are also not uncommon. High doses lead to behavioral depression and sleep.

c. *Nonbarbiturate tranquilizers.* Nonbarbiturate tranquilizers are relatively recent pharmacological products developed for alleviating mild anxiety and depressive states. Among the minor tranquillizers are the well-known drugs Librium and Valium, whose use, both with and without prescription is rampant in the society. Minor tranquilizers produce slightly euphoric states with slightly less behavioral disinhibition than that experienced while using barbiturates or alcohol. It is not unusual to find individuals who regularly mix the use of alcohol and minor tranquilizers. Major tranquilizers include the behavioral straitjacket drugs, such as chlorpromazine, that are used for the treatment and control of psychosis.

3. *Marijuana.* This controversial drug has been known about for thousands of years, and arguments still persist as to whether it is harmful or not. The effects of marijuana are also quite diverse, ranging from reports of "good highs" to "bad trips." Very generally, the inhalation of marijuana is followed by a feeling of well-being, relaxation, and tranquility. There is a heightened state of awareness, in which visions seem sharper and sounds more distant. There are also frequent reports by marijuana users that a novel profundity of thought and insight is achieved, as well as reports of a greater feeling of the awareness of others.

4. *Psychedelic drugs,* including LSD, mescaline, psilocybin, phencyclidine, and others all have the capacity to induce visual, auditory, or other hallucinatory experiences and to separate the individual from reality. Although marijuana can also be included in the drug classification category, it has been treated separately because of the popular current focus and its more widespread use. The principal use of psychedelics is to induce an altered state of consciousness, the specific nature of which varies with the user's drug experience, the nature of the drug itself, and many other factors. The experience can be summarized as "mind expanding," but individual reactions vary greatly.

5. *Stimulants.* Drugs classified as stimulants—such as amphetamines, cocaine, caffeine, and nicotine, among others—work to increase behavioral activity. These compounds, in moderate doses, elevate mood, induce euphoria, increase alertness, and reduce fatigue. Of the illegal stimulants, cocaine's behavioral effects are much shorter than those produced by amphetamines.

In summary, we have attempted to present a very brief overview of the behavioral or psychological effects of the various chemical substances on which we focused in our series of studies. Although we have presented five major categories, each with similar or contrasting effects, it is possible to reclassify the present drug categories in several different ways. For example, we can use seven categories to reflect behavioral effects (see Julien, 1975): (1) relief from anxiety; (2) achievement of a state of disinhibition or euphoria; (3) achievement of altered states of consciousness; (4) expansion of creative abilities; (5) attempt to gain interpersonal or external insight; (6) escape from uncomfortable or oppressive surroundings; and (7) experience of altered states of mood.

The Medical Model

A parallel need in addition to examining the use of narcotics and other drugs is the task of developing a body of knowledge from which psychological understanding can be derived. Such knowledge can then presumably be utilized to develop treatment methods for those users who seek help for drug-related problems as well as prevention strategies. Along with the popular views of addiction and drug use, medical theories have developed in the clinic and private practice. Unfortunately, many of the treatises on medical formulations of drug-taking behavior are vague as to whether the author is discussing drug use or drug abuse. Nonetheless, it seems fair to state that a dominant position in the medical profession is that drugs such as alcohol and heroin produce a condition of physical dependence resulting in a process of withdrawal when drug use is discontinued abruptly. Recent writings have tended to extend the concept of withdrawal and dependency from the physical domain to the psychological as well. An important implication of the major reliance on the dependency model is that treatment should focus on helping the addict through the period of withdrawal or drug-use cessation. A major concern among treatment professionals who hold the dependency model as valid has been whether the withdrawal of the drug should be sudden or gradual; this issue is still largely unresolved. It also seems explicitly assumed that for the treatment to be effective, it is necessary for the user "to be 'in earnest' and 'strongly motivated', and to have 'will power'; moral weaklings failed" (Brecher, 1972, p. 66). The impact of these expectations by medical professionals has been mirrored in subsequent explanations offered by behavioral scientists.

About the time that the notion of physical dependency was gaining acceptance among medical practitioners, medical models of drug addiction tended to define the phenomenon as a disease state in which usage was an aberrant behavior of a sick individual. As a consequence, attention was focused on which drugs were taken rather than on individual or environmental factors that might contribute to, and sustain, drug use. The current emphasis on methadone maintenance is a reflection of the medical-model approach to the treatment of narcotic addiction.

Even if a medical model is true, it leaves several questions largely unanswered if it does not invoke psychological concepts. For instance, why would a person not under the influence of a drug take the drug, and why have individuals been able to quit using such drugs as heroin without intervention (Robins, 1978)?

Over time, the simple, early medical model of drug use has become more refined. The concept of symptomatology was introduced; and drug use, drug abuse, and addiction were seen as being merely symptomatic of some underlying *psychological* disturbance. Primary support for the psychological disease concept came from the infusion of psychoanalytic theory in the early

20th century. Although the disease model provided a basis for psychiatry to begin to address the problem of drug use, the concept still did not resolve the controversy over whether drug use, drug abuse, and addiction were crimes or manifestations of disease. Each choice has inherent implications that govern the nature of research, treatment, and public attitude toward drugs. Whatever approach is selected, moreover, often involves "covert or even overt rivalries and clashes of interest among the adherents of particular approaches and therapeutics" (Schur, 1969, p. 502).

The recent draft of the *Diagnostic and Statistical Manual of Mental Disorders* (*DSM III;* January 15, 1978, printing) from the American Psychiatric Association represents an effort to develop a new diagnostic nomenclature that moves beyond the traditional medical model. The term *substance-use disorders* is employed. Alcohol and caffeine are cited as normal substances to use under most circumstances (based on majority use!), while cannabis (marijuana) use is presented very sketchily. The terms *abuse* and *dependence* are reserved as dimensions of dysfunction for substance users. Continued use for a month serves as a criterion for the abuse of various substances. Much emphasis is placed on psychological and behavioral manifestations of dependency, which is defined for cannabis as "impairment in social or occupational functioning (e.g., marked loss of interest in activities previously enjoyed, loss of friends, missed work) or legal difficulties" (*DSM III,* 1978). Unfortunately, the increased elaboration of behavioral criteria framed within a medical classification system may be seriously confusing the issue, because many kinds of stress from marital discord through persisting disagreements among co-workers can potentially be fit into this category of medical disorder if drugs are concomitantly taken to control emotional upheaval. Many of the behavioral indicators used to diagnose "dependency" are directly confounded with the fact that the individual is known to use the drug. The "revised" classification system, accordingly, still makes a very explicit value judgment about the personality of the drug user.

Pathological and Trait Emphasis

Largely synonymous with the psychoanalytic disease model is the psychopathological orientation toward substance use. Both views follow that Brecher (1972) calls the old "weakness-of-will" approach in that the drug user is perceived as having a personality prone to drug use and abuse. Psychoanalytic interpretations of drug use have traditionally relied on such assumed causal factors as early childhood disturbances, with current drug-taking behavior symbolically representing underlying, unresolved conflict. Thus, as Wurmser (1977) summarizes the position, "Before the beginning of compulsive drug use there are clear signs of a serious emotional disorder, one of which may be called the 'addictive illness' or the signs of an addictive career [p. 42]."

Within the psychoanalytic tradition, more radical theorizing has focused on psychosocial mechanisms that incorporate the role of environmental forces in shaping ego development. In the new conceptualization, drug use may be an adaptive function that helps to "overcome crippling adolescent anxieties evoked by the prospect of facing adult role expectations with inadequate preparation, models, and prospects" (Khantzian & Treece, 1977, p. 13).

The psychoanalytic view, contemporary or traditional, has generated a large body of psychological research that attempts to delineate specific traits or profiles of personality attributes associated with drug use. Although proponents of trait theories of psychology will undoubtedly argue that their conception is quite different from that of psychoanalytic theorists, in practical matters of research the two are virtually indistinguishable. Aside from debating whether basic dimensions of individual differences should be derived theoretically or empirically, classical forms of both approaches generally agree that all forms of drug use, including alcohol and marijuana ingestion, should be investigated from the perspective that the use of drugs is potentially related to underlying personality dimensions. In the case of the psychoanalytic and psychopathological trait theories, the assumption is made that the underlying differences are along dimensions of psychological deficiences or emotional problems. Other trait theories may value underlying dimensions of psychological growth or health. To the extent that the trait systems are explicitly linked to traditional medical concepts of medical health or illness, however, it is likely that drug use will be perceived as unhealthy simply because of the implicit assumptions in the assessment instrument for personality.

It is interesting to note that implicit assumptions of psychological deficits have most frequently been made in the study of heroin use, in which the labels *psychopath* and *psychopathic personality* have been used extensively (see Ausubel, 1948; Clausen, 1957; Platt & Labate, 1976). Unfortunately, the psychopathy assumption has not always been limited to this case. Other diagnostic labels used to describe the drug user in general have included *psychotic, borderline psychotic, psychoneurotic, emotionally unstable, latent schizoid, paranoid, inadequate personality,* and even *sexual deviate* (Sadava, 1975). Similar assumptions have been made about alcoholism (NIAAA, 1971).

Against this background, it is probable that studies based on the general disease model would have implicit self-fulfilling prophecies. This problem is further exacerbated when a disease model that might be relevant for grossly dysfunctional individuals, such as those who regularly ingest a drug like alcohol or heroin, is applied to individuals who experiment mildly with the "harder" substances and confine most of their substance use to recreational marijuana smoking and drinking. When the disease model is accepted as relevant for the whole area of drug use, rather than confining the theory to only dysfunctional forms, investigators typically choose instruments that are measures of psychopathology to administer to groups of users and nonusers. Unfortunately, the effects of precision error (such as low validity and reliability measurements, bad distributions of dependent measures, statistical tests that are far too liberal for multivariate data) may lead to false rejection of the statistical null hypothesis of no difference between drug users and nonusers. To the extent that the dependent measures are measures of psychopathology, the observed differences will tend to be attributed to differences in underlying psychopathology, and differences that show that nonusers are more pathological will either be rationalized or not published.

A concrete example of the problem of applying disease constructs in a general way is given by the research literature that contrasts users and nonusers on the clinically derived scales of the Minnesota Multiphasic Personality Inventory (MMPI). The MMPI scales presumably measure types of psychopathology. Brill, Compton, and Grayson (1971) found that frequent marijuana users, based on MMPI profiles, were somewhat hostile and rebellious. The marijuana users were described as having emotional problems and less respect for the law within a *research context* in which the focus was on psychopathology. In contrast to the Brill et al. results, Steffenhagen, Schmidt, and McAree (1971) found that marijuana users could not be meaningfully differentiated from nonusers using the MMPI. Further work by McGuire and Megargee (1974) further confirmed the notion that individuals with marijuana-use histories are not pathological in their MMPI profiles. Consequently, it appears that the original Brill et al. results may have falsely rejected the null hypothesis. Because the study was conducted using MMPI psychopathology measures, the attribution was made that marijuana users have higher levels of psychopathology. In their recent review, Pihl and Spiers (1978) conclude that while there is still a controversy over whether or not *alcoholics* and *addicts* have higher levels of psychopathology on the MMPI than control subjects, moderate marijuana and hallucinogenic users do not appear to be any more pathological than control subjects. These results, considered in their totality, then seem to indicate that recreational drug use among nonaddicts is not significantly associated with psychopathological tendencies. Kandel (1978a) generalizes this statement to other types of studies of the consequences for personality functioning of other types of substance use.

In opposition to those studies attempting to quantify the disease approach to drug use, many other trait investigations have been carried out without explicit or implicit assumptions that drug (particularly marijuana) use is associated with psychological deficiency. Many of these additional studies, conducted within the framework that there might be differences on traits indicative of normal psychological functioning, have shown quite a different picture of the marijuana user. For example, one set of results suggests that student drug users are more poised, sociable, flexible, creative, and aesthetically sensitive than nonusers (Grossman, Goldstein, & Eisenman, 1971; Hogan, Mankin, Conway, & Fox, 1970; McAree, Steffenhagen & Zheutlin, 1969; Steffenhagen, McAree, & Zheutlin, 1969; Zinberg & Weil, 1970). Grossman et al. (1971) summarize their results and the previous literature as follows: "The personality dynamics of the marijuana smoker are becoming increasingly clear. Explanations of marijuana use based on character defects or psychopathology seem to be inadequate. Marijuana use, in the present sample of college students was associated with personality characteristics which many would tend to value [p. 336]."

The conclusion of Grossman et al. is not surprising if drug use is viewed as providing beneficial short-term gain, such as a more positive feeling or a decrease in discomfort (Ray, 1972). In this respect, Tart's (1970) description of the experiential effects of marijuana may be the desired gain sought by cannabis users. "... sense perception is often improved, both in intensity and scope. Imagery is usually stronger but well controlled, although people often care less about controlling their actions. Great changes in perception of time and space are common, as are changes in psychological processes such as understanding, memory, emotion, and sense of identity [p. 704]." Tart's description of the marijuana experience should be considered in the context that individuals of college age are developmentally seeking to explore and understand themselves and the role of society as they plan for their futures. Consequently, such changes as identity and understanding may be perceived as highly desirable even though emotional effects gained from the drug are transient.

A more recent group of studies have shown that a dimension that might roughly be labeled as "rebelliousness" or low respect for conventional rules is associated with adolescent drug use (Jessor & Jessor, 1977; Kandel, 1978a; Smith & Fogg, 1978; Wingard, Huba, & Bentler, 1979). Typically, those individuals who start using marijuana and other drugs at an early age score more highly on scales that measure tendencies toward disrespect for current social norms or lack of conventionality. Some investigators (Jessor & Jessor, 1977; Kandel, 1978a; Smith & Fogg, 1978) take this result at face value and perceive rebelliousness to be a trait that manifests itself in drug-taking behavior for many youth with high tendencies; other workers (Mellinger, 1978; Wingard et al., 1979) believe that Suchman's (1968) interpretation of rebelliousness as a *value,* rather than a trait, might represent an important alternative orientation. Mellinger (1978) points out that such "values, of course, are not conducive to a highly competitive academic life-style in which the major goal is a high paying, nine-to-five job at Standard Oil [p. 261]," and he emphasizes throughout his work that values must be differentiated from traits. In summarizing his own work, Mellinger (1978) notes that:

Nevertheless, in retrospect, the uproar surrounding drug use at [the University of California at] Berkeley [during the early 1970s] seems to have been largely unwarranted. And our [longitudinal] study showed, as have many others before and since, that the major differences between drug users and nonusers have to do with the extent to which one accepts or rejects some of the basic values of traditional society [p. 262].

The points emphasized by Mellinger (1978), Wingard et al. (1979), and Suchman (1968) have direct bearing on this discussion of the traits that might be related to substance use; many dimensions that might be characterized as *values* or *life style* may be interpreted as traits if the observer disagrees with the values and life style being expressed. Consequently, from our perspective, it appears necessary to use personality trait systems in contrasting users and nonusers of various drugs that are free of either traditional or contemporary disease concepts. Tending to disagree with tradition may or may not be a trait, but the label *nontraditional* in itself carries less of a value judgment than terms such as *psychopathic deviant* or *rebellious*. Furthermore, if a concept such as rebelliousness is to be elevated to the level of a trait, it must be shown that such a construct also predicts milder forms of turning from tradition, such as dressing unconventionally, expressing nontraditional political views, and disregarding social rules of etiquette. If, indeed, it is then the case that the current concept of rebelliousness can be construed to be such a concept of being free of tradition or generalized autonomy, it is possible to conclude that drug-taking behavior might be so attractive to nontraditional, autonomous, "rebellious" individuals precisely because the society has branded the behavior as "rebellious." While such a conception hinges on the notion that current definitions of rebelliousness are primarily negative evaluations about the values of those individuals who behave nontraditionally, we would be willing to accept the notion that a more generalized dimension including many different forms of nontraditional values can be shown to be a trait. After such a demonstration, however, we feel that it is the burden of those individuals who currently label *rebelliousness* negatively to show that it is expressed in maladaptive rather than adaptive behaviors independently of the constraints of the society.

Sociological Theories

While the trait and psychopathology theories of drug use seek to place responsibility for drug use and abuse within the individual, the alternate sociological approach offers an explanation of drug use which professes that elements outside the person are highly related to substance use. Accordingly, the despair of slum dwelling, the social pressures of friends, a sense of frustration and anger about social conditions, racism, and poverty are all factors that contribute to initiate and sustain substance use. In effect, then, whether or not an individual or class of individuals becomes involved with substance use or abuse depends on the situation in which they are exposed to possibilities, role demands, or contextual support for such behavior.

Research conducted within a sociological or sociocultural framework has focused on the identification of the characteristics of drug users attributable to impinging social forces. For example, such studies have resulted in the delineation of specific drug subcultural norms (Johnson, 1973) and estimates of risk for individuals from different racial and socioeconomic backgrounds (see Austin, Johnson, Carroll, & Lettieri, 1977). The recent NIDA volume, *Drugs and Minorities* (Austin et al., 1977), indicates that numerous studies have been conducted to assess risk rates for individuals within definable groups presumably influenced by various social conditions.

While it is apparent that sociocultural contexts are related to patterns of drug-taking behavior, the nature of the relationship becomes muddied when such pressures are attributed to motivational qualities (Sadava, 1975). Stated another way, do sociocultural factors motivate drug use, or do they act concomitantly to shape and modify personality so as to heighten the probability of drug use? If the latter point is the case, then drug use is primarily a psychological phenomenon with sociocultural processes contributing to mediate the pattern of drug use. In the absence of any consistent theoretical structure, however, sociocultural factors "while providing some useful empirical information, lack explanatory and predictive power; they stand as raw empirical data" (Sadava, 1975, p. 33).

The true significance of the sociological approach, it seems to us, is in emphasizing how the behavior fits within a given sociocultural context. Becker (1963) has made an important distinction between deviance as a characteristic of the individual and as a social construction. Deviance, as Becker (1963) suggests, "is not a quality of the act the person commits, but rather a consequence of the application by others of rules and sanctions.... deviant behavior is behavior people so label [p. 9]." This definition of deviance, as Schur (1969) argues, implies that the term itself has to be conceived as shaping the very nature of the condition labeled as *deviant* and the meaning the behavior holds for the individual. Consequently, if the sometimes arbitrary dichotomy between legal and illegal drugs is discarded, it may be useful psychologically to consider the use of marijuana and other drugs as nondeviant behavior except when consistent patterns of chronic use, *having dysfunctional* effects, are developed. If such a framework is considered valid, it then becomes likely that different etiological explanations are necessary to account for different patterns of general drug use not confined to any categorization of drugs as licit or illicit. Additionally, since the current social context labels drug use as *deviant,* this perspective underscores the need to examine different etiological explanations within that social context. These premises are further explored in subsequent chapters.

Within different societies, drug use has different functional types of significance. As noted earlier, there were periods in America when drug use was not punished and there was no widespread disapproval of the behavior. Within those sociocultural contexts, needs to rebel probably could not be met by taking drugs. Furthermore, since the individual drug taker was not labeled as a *deviant,* a "problem," or a potential criminal, certain pressures and attendant consequences associated with being excluded or ostracized, from groups and activities would not be brought to bear on the individual. Undue amounts of stress generated by being labeled "different," of course, may be manifested in more general behavioral disorders, and it is therefore possible that, within a society more tolerant of drug use, a much lower number of "drug-related problems" would be seen in emergency rooms or crisis-treatment centers.

In our society, marijuana use and experimentation with other drugs can serve many different purposes for the individual:

1. It is quite possible that by using drugs, individuals can become part of a rather tightly cohesive group. The fact that marijuana possession is still illegal, but not often a prosecuted offense, has engendered a cult around the drug. It is almost axiomatic that any center of a town catering to youth will have several stores that carry a complete line of supplies and literature for the marijuana smoker and nonaddicted drug user. Various publications such as *High Times* and *Head* magazines provide news about drug supplies, articles about drug experiences and producing substances, and advertisements about the latest in drug paraphernalia. Indeed, a cursory inspection of these glossy publications is sufficient to convince the most skeptical that certain aspects of drug (particularly marijuana, but also cocaine and hallucinogenics) use can become almost a hobby.

2. The use of marijuana and other drugs is a behavior that is still perceived as rebellious by a sizable number of adults. During the normal explorations of late adolescence, when the individual must confront the decisions inherent in becoming an adult and take increasing responsibility for all aspects of life, a typical response seems to be the rebelling against and discarding of influences from adults. Consequently, the symbolic protest function of marijuana (see Kohn & Annis, 1978) is important. In a society in which the majority of adults approved of marijuana and other drug use, it is likely that substance use would not have this psychological significance among normal young adults.

3. Within the current culture, and seemingly particularly within the youth culture cognizant of drug use, there are certain expected effects for various types of drug intoxication. For instance, counterculture magazines often equate the use of a particular drug (such as marijuana) with enhanced enjoyment of some activity (such as sex). When Peter Bourne resigned as President Carter's expert on drug abuse because he allegedly wrote a

fraudulent prescription for Quaaludes, there was speculation in the popular press that the prescription had been written because of the assumed aphrodisiac qualities of the drug. Given different cultural expectations about the effects of drug ingestion on behavior, it is quite possible that a drug would not be used for the same reasons as it is in our society. Individuals who are intoxicated on alcohol are often treated differently by the people around them while inebriated, and particularly aggressive and irritating behavior is sometimes discounted.

4. There seems to be some tendency in the youth culture to lionize the individual who can supply peers with various drugs. Again, we refer here to printed stories abounding in counterculture publications and certain cinema representations (such as *Easy Rider*) that have portrayed the supplier as something of a modern Robin Hood who outwits the hapless law-enforcement agencies. To the extent that drugs are in demand at a particular time, the individual who can supply friends with desired substances assumes a role that is reinforced both monetarily and socially. Interestingly, it would thus seem possible that the drug supplier may be able to express and satisfy various achievement and social approval needs that may be frustrated in other situations.

5. Within the standards set by a particular culture, drug use must be considered in the context of what the society expects from its members, as well as how drug users are rebelling against the demands of the society. Certain drug-use patterns (such as high levels of drinking at weddings and other special occasions) are condoned even for the very young, and various rituals (pairing, discussing work, celebrating) of the majority culture are frequently performed in establishments that sell liquor. Modeling effects of drug use from both parents and peers have been well documented (see, e.g., Huba et al., 1979; Jessor & Jessor, 1977; Kandel, 1978a; Kandel et al., 1978), and it seems axiomatic that the extent to which the parents and other adults are perceived to use drugs and alcohol will influence the substance-use pattern of the youth. Although there have been no detailed studies of the phenomenon, it would also appear likely that the youth learns how to use substances to cope with different types of stresses from adults and valued youthful peers.

In summary, then, the major importance of the sociological perspectives on drug use has been to emphasize the social context of drug use and the consequences of drug use faced by the user. It would seem quite naive to assume that the same psychological theory of drug use will fit different societies with the same degree of utility, and almost as naive to assume that even within a society a psychological theory should have the same level of validity at different time periods or for all groups. Consequently, we have tried in the following chapters to interpret our results within the current context of drug use and do not argue that our psychological theories are equally applicable to future cultural milieux.

Behaviorist Orientation

Current psychological theories of learning have also been applied to the phenomenon of drug use. Rather than blindly asserting that a particular behaviorist viewpoint such as social learning, modeling, operant reinforcement, or classical conditioning is relevant in a global way to drug use, it seems most fruitful to consider how these different perspectives serve to explain different aspects of the phenomenon.

The effects of modeling influences and social reinforcements upon the initiation of youthful drug-taking behavior seem indisputable (see e.g., Huba et al., 1979; Jessor & Jessor, 1977; Kandel, 1978a). While such influences are significant causal factors in the development of drug taking, however, these influences explain no more than 15–20% of the variation in several forms of substance use measured concurrently (Huba et al., 1979) and longitudinally (Kandel et al., 1978). Consequently, it would be impossible to argue that modeling influences and social reinforcements are *the* unitary causes of substance use initiation (Gorsuch & Butler, 1976). Nonetheless, there is sufficient evidence to indicate that the presence of adult and peer models for the ingestion of *particular* substance will predispose the individual to experiment with that drug (Huba et al., 1979). Furthermore, it seems reasonable to assume that the mechanisms for the modeling to be translated into action on the part of the observer are the familiar ones of developing expectations about the consequences of the act and gaining acceptance from valued models.

Classical and operant conditioning principles are probably most applicable to the maintenance of drug-taking behavior and the possible development of either psychological dependence or physiological addiction. By continuing to use a drug, an individual may gain membership within a group, which serves to reinforce the behavior as a requisite for, and identification with, membership: Such subcultures provide reinforcements for the behavior (Johnson, 1973; Kandel, 1978c). As noted earlier, the typical effects of various drugs as categorized by Julien (1975) may be directly reinforcing by either enhancing positive experiences or tending to alleviate and inhibit negative ones. Wikler (1953), for instance, has hypothesized that drug use is initially dependent on reinforcement from social forces but that such reinforcement loses importance as the drug taking continues, and the effects of the drug themselves become rewards.

The behavioral approach to drug taking, then, seeks to perceive the contingencies in the environment that serve to initiate experimentation with substances and to maintain use. Such an approach, in and of itself, can be sobering; to the extent that scientific explanations are possible through an examination of the reinforcers of the behaviors, such theories tend to be rather parsimonious and relatively value-free. On the other hand, the available data on youth seem to indicate that while a behaviorist orientation can serve to explain a small chunk of drug taking, it cannot explain most of the differences between those individuals who do or do not engage in the behavior. Several questions left largely unanswered by the various behaviorist perspectives are: "What types of individuals might be most responsive to peer reinforcements for trying drugs?", "What types of individuals will find themselves in situations where there are many models for substance use?", "What types of individuals will perceive the effects of a particular drug as positively reinforcing rather than aversive?", and "What types of individuals can discount the reinforcing properties of certain drugs and substitute alternate activities to gain the same reinforcements?" In answer to these questions, we would pose the possible answer that perhaps drug use will occur in responsive social context only when the use of the chemical substance is seen as enhancing a basic need for the person taking the drug. Or, perhaps a personality characteristic predisposes an individual toward undue reliance on the approval of others for her or his actions. Or, perhaps certain personality properties of an individual may be changed in desirable and predictable ways under the influence of a particular substance and then allow the individual to satisfy basic needs. Such personality characteristics need not be "deviant" or psychopathological but may, rather, be those positive personality characteristics, such as a strong need to be creative, that can be enhanced by the drugs.

Our conclusion about the utility of the behavioral viewpoint for explaining adolescent drug taking is therefore twofold. On the one hand, it cannot be denied that there are sufficient demonstrations of the positive effects of models as well as social and pharmacological sources of reinforcement to conclude that all three are significant factors in the initiation and maintenance of drug taking. On the other hand, the concepts of behavioral positions, not robust enough in themselves to be considered the major causes of drug use, also leave several questions largely unanswered. A logical conclusion is that in spite of the clear relevance of behaviorist positions, personality factors clearly play a complementary, and perhaps dominant, role in the explanation of drug taking.

Social–Psychological, Interactionist Approaches

The bulk of current attempts to study youthful drug use may be subsumed under a label of the *interactionist* approach. In recent personality work, there has been an increasing emphasis on the interaction of traits and the actual and perceived environment of the individual in determining specific behaviors (see Endler & Magnusson, 1976). This interactionist position has reached a position of ascendancy in the study of youthful substance use; the majority of individual studies described by Kandel (1978a) and represented in her edited collection (Kandel, 1978b) are particularly representative of this approach. The Boulder study (Jessor & Jessor, 1977) and the New York State study (Kandel, 1978a; Kandel et al., 1978) are probably the dominant exemplars of the position.

The interactionist position may be stated briefly as postulating that stable personality characteristics of the individual place her or him at risk when certain situational conditions are present for initiation of drug use and subsequent assimilation into a drug-using culture (Jessor & Jessor, 1977; Kandel, 1978a). Consequently, the position tries to integrate sociological, trait-psychopathology, and behaviorist approaches to the phenomenon. This brief statement should not be construed, however, to imply that all inter-tionist studies are the same. For example, quite different domains of personality are assessed in the studies ranging from Jessor and Jessor's (1977) emphasis on values and needs to Kandel's (1978a) emphasis on affective measures to Smith and Fogg's (1978) use of social behavior dimensions to Bentler's (see Wingard et al., 1979) psychometrically based inventory. Different interactionist studies also define the environment quite specifically: Jessor and Jessor (1977) assess the individual's perceptions of *distal* and *proximal* influences, whereas Kandel (1978a, Kandel et al., 1978) has agents from the environment rate themselves and the participant. Intermediate to this position, Bentler (see Huba et al., 1979) has defined the adolescent environment as primarily that involved in home and schooling and has sought ratings from the individual as well as a matched best friend since perceived and actual environments may be quite different.

At the present time, major results from interactionist studies have not filtered into the field primarily because most of these projects have been longitudinal in nature and much of the data has yet to be analyzed. From the summaries thus far presented (Huba et al., 1979; Jessor & Jessor, 1977; Kandel, 1978a; Kandel et al., 1978; Smith & Fogg, 1977, 1978; Wingard et al., 1979), it is possible to conclude that both personality and environmental influences must be considered important *causal* determinants of adolescent drug use. In general, the results have indicated that the major personality variables causing drug use cluster into constructs that might be called rebelliousness, autonomy strivings, liberalism, the willingness to try new experiences, and independence. Most of the studies also converge in suggesting that proximal influences (such as the drug-taking behavior and attitudes of peers and friends) are more important than distal influences (such as the drug-taking behavior and attitudes of parents and other adults). Some workers have suggested (Jessor & Jessor, 1977; Johnston, O'Malley, & Eveland, 1978; Kandel et al., 1978) that drug use is but one of a series of problem or deviant behaviors emitted by these individuals, but a careful analysis of the work of Jessor and Jessor (1977) may be interpreted as arguing strongly for the notion that individuals recently of college age are engaging in normative experimentation behaviors that are not highly predictable from a deviance framework.

In general, the interactionist approaches will probably dominate the field of substance use within the next decade because of their relative completeness and complexity (Huba et al., 1980). These approaches do have several difficulties, and it would be inappropriate to completely abandon traditional trait and sociological approaches until the problems are solved. Among the major problems with these interactionist conceptions are that the most relevant predictors from the individual domains of personality and environmental influences may not be assessed because of a lack of understanding about the dynamics of the domains. Within the major interactionist studies, there is no strong emphasis on the tendencies of the individual to manipulate levels of arousal or to supplement inner experiences, which, as is shown later (Chapters 6 and 7), are crucial to understanding the phenomenon from within the personality domain. Similarly, within the interactionist studies, there has been little emphasis of the differentiation of types of deviancy, whether individually or socially caused (see Becker, 1963), or very general types of typical interaction between parents and youth or peers and youth (see Huba et al., 1979). Consequently, it would appear to us that the adoption of interactionism as a dominant position within the study of substance use does not preclude further investigation primarily within a personality or sociological framework; on the contrary, further explorations of the individual domains are necessary to guide interactionist studies designed to link major influences from each of the areas.

A further problem of interactionism is the manner in which personality and social influences work together to determine the drug-use history of the individual. As Dunnette (1975) has suggested, many of the influences from the different domains may not be additive; rather, it may be necessary to apply traditional nonadditive, interaction-term models to the study of substance use. Furthermore, there must be work on disentangling the personality and environmental influences (Bentler, 1978). It seems quite likely that personality influences primarily predispose an individual to certain social environments, although it is also possible that belonging to a subculture with different norms will influence personality development over time. Although both types of influences may be operable, it is also possible that one or the other is much more important for predisposing the individual to use of one or more psychoactive substances.

ASSUMPTIONS UNDERLYING OUR STUDY
OF DRUG USE

From our review of the relevant literature presented earlier, we have formed some conclusions about the phenomenon of substance use among youth. These assumptions guided various stages of the study, and more recent theories and findings influenced interpretations of the results reported. So that our assumptions are clear, let us briefly restate some points made in preceding sections:

1. *Drug use in the current society is a normative behavior for college-aged youth.* The bulk of recent studies of adolescent and early-adult drug use show that a sizable percentage of individuals have at least tried marijuana (Abelson and associates, 1972, 1973). Furthermore, many of these individuals regularly use that drug or alcohol. While the legal process still makes drug taking a behavior that may be heavily punished if the individual is caught and prosecuted, the typical student knows other individuals who use many different types of drugs and is liable to use them him- or herself. Consequently, it appears to us that it makes little sense to try to understand the phenomenon by invoking the scare that drug taking is a behavior engaged in by a deranged minority who are a burden on the general society.

2. *Approaches that have made explicit negative evaluations of drug users have rarely contributed significantly to understanding the phenomenon.* In general, contrasts in the general population of *noninstitutionalized* drug users with noninstitutionalized nonusers have rarely been able to demonstrate that more than a small amount of the variation can be explained by invocation of a disease model. "Contrasted groups" studies using instruments such as the MMPI do occasionally uncover differences, but when such differences do occur they can frequently be attributed to falsely rejecting the null hypothesis or to a conceptual slippage in the meaning of the difference due to low reliability and validity measurement. The postulated differences between drug users and nonusers have an ephemeral quality: Now you see them, now you don't. Furthermore, since the bulk of drug users are not institutionalized, it is not valid to contrast institutionalized drug users with noninstitutionalized nonuser control subjects and then argue that the drug use made the drug users more pathological.

3. *Previous trait studies without explicit evaluation go about halfway.* Many of the studies that we have reviewed have little theoretical context, and even when they do it is sometimes difficult to argue that the assessment instruments used to quantify personality follow directly from the theoretical viewpoint. In some cases, it is possible to point to a particular study and argue that differences were not found because the measures lack reliability, or that the measures were not really measuring the construct the investigator (rightly)

thought should be theoretically related to substance use or nonuse distinctions. Furthermore, in most studies reviewed, there is no explicit evaluation of the amount of variance that the personality measures contribute in predicting substance use. While large samples can often promote the rejection of the null hypothesis, many significant findings within the field of psychology have little predictive utility or robustness across different sampling plans. At minimum, it seems necessary to moderate theories based on statistically significant findings by the amount of variance that the theoretical constructs account for in explaining the phenomenon under study. This attitude is of further importance when a reviewer is faced with the reality that many psychological constructs are neither conceptually nor statistically independent, or when faced with a choice between constructs that are logical subsets of one another; a consideration of the predictive utility and theoretical meaningfulness gained (or lost!) by a wideband versus a narrowband construct must be made.

4. *The social context of drug use must always be considered even when the attempted explanation is from within the personality domain.* Drug use will have a different functional significance within different social systems. In a society where the use of a drug is normative behavior, drug use will probably not be chosen by an individual as a means of expressing autonomy or disapproval of the rules of society. Conversely, disapproval of the behavior by a majority of adults may make an illicit behavior attractive to the young adult who wishes to express a heightened level of autonomy or disapproval with the rules of the adults. The specific social context and consequences for the individual must also be considered in conjunction with personal characteristics of the user. For instance, in our current social situation, in which drug use may be punished with incarceration, individuals who are fearful about disapproval or coming to psychological harm will avoid drugs at the same time that individuals wishing to throw off the influence of the society will flaunt their independence through illicit behaviors such as drug use. Similarly, in those situations in which there is little opportunity to experience new and different things, it is possible that drugs, with their purported consciousness-altering properties, will be tried as a way of overcoming boredom and altering affects.

Within the social context, then, it must be remembered that certain rules and constraints will influence the drug user, because the consequences of drug use are what they are. We must also remember that the lore of the time is about the supposed effects of the substance, who is supplying it and how easy it is to get, and how the *use* of the drug (as opposed to its effects) will satisfy needs of the user. The notion of how the drug satisfies needs is particularly important: Entrance into a tight "clique" of users may satisfy a need for social membership and affiliation for an individual who cannot find social membership and a sense of belonging within traditional social institutions.

5. *The domain of personality must be studied intensively so that we can design effective interactional studies and develop suitable interactionist theories for the phenomenon.* Once we abandon traditional methodologies and move toward the procedures necessary to develop either models with trait–situation interaction terms (see Dunnette, 1975; Wiggins, 1973) or complex interrelationships among environmental demands and structures and personality dimensions (Bentler, 1976; Bentler & Huba, 1979; Jöreskog, 1969), it will be necessary to focus attention on a few salient and important variables. Simply "shot-gunning" measures into confirmatory methodologies in an attempt to develop a comprehensive theory of the interaction of traits and situations in determining substance use is, at best, a self-defeating strategy that does little to explain the phenomenon and provides fuel for critics. Rather, it is necessary, through careful selection of theoretically and empirically meaningful indicators, to limit modeling attempts to those aspects of the total psychological domain that are important. It has been our belief that this project is best accomplished by carefully studying each of the domains separately and then trying to integrate them through careful introspection before large amounts of data are collected.

A careful exploration of the personality domain can help to select those variables that are critical for explaining the substance-use phenomenon among youth. Various procedures such as factor analysis, multiple regression, canonical correlation analysis, and discriminant analysis allow us to determine relationships between personality variables and substance-use domain and then select theoretical constructs for further consideration. We are, then, advocating a truly multivariate study of the relationship of personality to substance use; the sampling of measures as well as the sampling of subjects is critical and will determine what models for the process can be developed. Throughout our studies, we have tried to be multivariate psychologists and to study simultaneously a large number of relationships in order to determine which ones are truly important.

On the other hand, statistical analysis without theoretical interpretation is a barren enterprise, and we have tried to use heuristics for interpreting the multivariate analyses throughout. Furthermore, we believe that it is important to interpret isolated results in terms of their robustness across different samples of subjects and power in explaining variance. A large number of isolated results on a single construct can point out the relationship between the construct and drug use, but all the isolated results ever generated cannot tell the scientist what the appropriate model for a phenomenon should be. Consequently, we believe that it is imperative to try to predict drug use from a wide domain sampling of seemingly relevant personality constructs and determine which of these constructs should be integrated into a larger model of substance use such as that presented by Huba, Wingard, and Bentler (1980).

SUMMARY

We have attempted to present an overview of some major theoretical approaches that have sought to provide an explanation for drug use and abuse. Other taxonomies of drug-use theories have recently been suggested (see, e.g., Ginsberg & Greenley, 1978; Lettieri, 1978; Pihl & Spiers, 1978), but the concepts are similar to those expressed here. Regardless of the theoretical constructs invoked, it seems that none of the perspectives definitively answers the question of whether drug use, drug abuse, or drug addiction constitute coping behavior or mental illness. Furthermore, for the nonaddict drug user it is unclear if the drug use is simply social–recreational behavior free of any implications of deep-seated emotional disorder. Yet, if we are to seek to determine why individuals come to use and abuse drugs as well as what sustains such use, it is essential to focus on the relationships of drug use and emotional distress and coping behaviors in addition to such other factors as the family environment, role expectations, social settings, and interpersonal relationships. For those individuals who use drugs in a social–recreational, or possibly a coping, manner, a key to understanding such linkages may be in examining the relationships of drug use to more normal dimensions of personality functioning.

It is from within this "normative" perspective that we will base our approach to seek an understanding of the use or nonuse of various substances by youth. The following chapter provides a theoretical rationale for our overall orientation and a description of those facets of personality investigated within a nomological network we term the *private personality*. Subsequent chapters detail the procedures undertaken, the results obtained, and interpretations of the findings.

2 The Private Personality

THE COGNITIVE MOVEMENT AND PRIVATE EXPERIENCE

To anyone but the most doctrinaire behaviorist, it is obvious that a major feature of what we view as our "personalities" derives from a set of private self-communications, interior monologues, and sequences of images, reminiscent or future-oriented, which we typically call *daydreams* or *fantasies*. This ongoing stream of consciousness seems so uniquely our own since, even in the case of identical twins, no one else can have had quite the same set of memories or the same dreams or fantasies. The thought stream thus represents a special and important part of how we define ourselves as human beings.

Within this private sector of human existence, one can also include sets of short- and long-range goals, the hierarchy of needs so elaborately developed by Henry Murray and his collaborators and followers (Murray, 1938). Sometimes these needs are themselves expressed in the form of guiding images or fantasies in which we see ourselves accomplishing certain tasks, winning certain prizes, attaining certain types of material goods, engaging in particular forms of sexual practice, or winning particular kinds of approval from others. Often we are not necessarily constantly conscious of the way our needs are organized, and we understand them only when given an opportunity as in the case of an extended psychotherapy or when we take psychological tests. Inventories such as those of Edwards (1959) or Jackson (1967), which pit needs for affiliation against needs for achievement or measures where we are asked (as in the case of the Thematic Apperception

Test) to make up stories about ambiguous pictures and find ourselves using certain themes in a recurrent fashion (Murray, 1938; Tomkins, 1947), all provide methods for establishing hierarchies of motives.

The special feature of the kinds of experience we are describing here is their *privacy*. With the rare exception of a young child or of an occasional paranoid individual, most people recognize that their thoughts are purely their own (in James' 1890/1950 phrase). They realize that there remains an elaborate sector of their experience that can be held apart through life and not shared at all except under special circumstances. Indeed, the importance of this privacy is apparent in the fact that voluntary self-disclosure, when it occurs either in efforts at loving exploration with intimates or in situations of psychotherapy, is regularly associated wtih greater feelings of closeness and warmth, willingness to cooperate with the other, as well as occasional backlashes of defensiveness (Janis, 1969).

It is not clear to what extent our daydreams of organized private wishes or other features of the stream of consciousness have any direct impact on overt behavior or on the personality style we show to others. Psychodynamic theory places its greatest emphasis upon private expectations (conscious and unconscious) concerning human relationships. The so-called Object-Relations theory that has emerged in the last decade as a dominant direction for psychoanalysis makes the basic assumption that the way in which the extremely young child organizes his or her picture of the boundaries between self and others, or the benignity or malevolence of particular kinds of individuals in the environment, will determine over the long run whether or not psychopathology will emerge in the life course or the particular types of interactions, sexual orientations, and social competencies that are manifested in adult life. By contrast, the social learning theory that emerged in the 1960s and early 1970s presented an alternative emphasis primarily on overt behavior and on the interaction between situational demands and consistencies in public behavior patterns. A text on personality such as that by Mischel (1971), while lucid and responsible in its efforts, omits almost any reference to human fantasies, daydreams, emotions, or other experiences that fall within the purview of what we have called the *private personality*.

A major paradigm change took place in psychology toward the latter part of the 1950s and emerged full blown in the 1960s with the shift from a stimulus–response view of behavior toward the cognitive orientation, which now continues on the upswing. A major feature of cognitive conceptions involves the view that human beings are not only *moving* actively in their environments but also *surveying* their milieu and indeed anticipating new situations constantly by the formation of private plans or images that are then checked and rechecked as novel information is encountered. Important presentations of this cognitive emphasis on private organization of experience, on the development of centrally generated plans and anticipations, and on the fact that motivation of behavior can be generated by cognitive tendencies for clarification, reduction of ambiguity, and assimilation of complex novelty (in comparison with earlier behaviors and psychoanalytic emphasis on reduction of particular drives such as sex, thirst, or hunger) emerged in research and theory by Hebb (1960), Miller, Galanter, and Pribram (1960), Tomkins (1962–1963), and Neisser (1967).

From the cognitive paradigm perspective, images are of increasing importance. They involve the reduplication of direct experience, the constant replay in memory of earlier situations, matching them against new ones presented to the senses or against other material drawn from long-term memory as we see so clearly in our dreams but also in frequent waking fantasies. This complex ongoing internal processing heightens the significance of the private sector of the personality as an area for potential research. McClelland's (1958, 1961, 1975) extensive work on motivation that employs the expression of private fantasies of *achievement* or *power* through storytelling procedures has indicated that private experience does influence behavior in important ways. Much of this work did not study self-reported magnitudes of various needs or motives or the *ongoing* private fantasies of individuals. Relying as he did on stories or on projective techniques, McClelland remains somewhat outside the mainstream thrust of the cognitive movement.

A major step was taken by Tomkins (1962–1963), who proposed an elaborate theory (to this day not fully assimilated into mainstream personality research) to show how human motivation and the emotional or affect system of the personality is closely intertwined with the information procession or cognitive system. Thus, according to this view, the matching of newly presented information to established schema evokes particular differentiated affective responses depending on the degree of novelty in material presented, the rapidity of presentation of the novel material, the *availability* of easily retrieved schema that can assimilate new material, or on the *persistence over time* of new material that cannot be readily assimilated into established schema. Our emotions of fear or terror, anger, sadness or joy are dependent to some nontrivial degree on the extent to which we have anticipated situations and have the capacity for experiencing or assimilating new ones. The positive emotions of interest and surprise are evoked by novel stimulation that is only moderately complex. It is apparent that our private world of fantasies, daydreams, and short- or long-term expectations may turn out to be more significant than psychologists believed during the 50-year period between 1910–1960 (Holt, 1964; Singer, 1966, 1975a).

Measures of Private Experience

Because the thrust of the present volume is directed toward the role of drug or alcohol use among youth, it seems worthwhile to examine in greater detail the role that private experience may play in predisposing one to substance use. It may be asked whether drug or alcohol experimentation in youth alters the structural pattern of such private experience. We proposed to examine four instruments for tapping inner trends. At the most central or private level, we have the range and variety of human daydreams and fantasies—next, the hierarchy of self-described needs. A third major dimension is one of cognitive style, the Locus of Control. Here we deal with whether reinforcing events are believed to be generated by one's own actions or by circumstances derived from the actions of others or from fate. The Internal–External Locus-of-Control dimension has been so extensively discussed and researched (Lefcourt, 1976; Rotter, 1966) that it scarcely requires further elaboration here. Rotter's scale was employed in most of the actual research carried out within the project reviewed in this monograph. Finally, we include the personal report of an orientation toward different types of sensation seeking (Zuckerman, 1974, 1975).

Our emphasis on four measurement approaches—daydreaming, need hierarchies, locus of control, and sensation seeking—is of theoretical significance, because current evidence strongly supports the important role of *situational* or *peer-group determinants* in youthful substance use or abuse. The research work of Jessor and Jessor (1977) has gone beyond pure situationism to show that a set of measures of motivational facets of personality reveals consistencies over time in high-school and college students and also relates to the likelihood of drug use or the development of other "problem" behaviors. The model of Jessor and Jessor also includes another sector of personality labeled *belief systems,* which in their research failed to indicate a strong relationship to the overt behaviors they used as their criteria. Ultimately, the Jessors were able to show that the best prediction of their cluster of so-called "problem" behaviors came from combinations of motivationally oriented personality variables with the situational variables, particularly those "proximal" to the problem area, such as *relative influence of friends.* We have some question about the Jessors' linkage of sexual behavior or relatively minor use of drugs and alcohol as "problems" on the same dimension of seriousness as criminal acts or aggression. It is, nevertheless, especially important that these investigators have found support for certain kinds of relatively private motivational structures as being related to complex overt behaviors. The approach described in our report represents a further effort to explore more extensively the degree to which a variety of private orientations, whether involving elaborate fantasies and daydreams, the self-described organization of needs, Internal or External Locus of Control, and various forms of sensation seeking may relate to a significant pattern of overt behavior and drug and alcohol use in youth.

The examination of this private-personality sector seems especially important, as suggested in the previous chapter, because many recent inquiries about the significance of drug exploration, in particular, have emphasized that part of the need and interest in drug use has been to attain "altered states of consciousness" or to generate more complex and elaborate private experiences. In other words, it has been argued that substance use in youth (which may occasionally also become substance abuse) is motivated to some degree by desire to produce a variety of enriched fantasy and related altered or (in Zinberg's, 1977 phrase) "alternate" states of consciousness. Much of the literature that links drug use to a search for an enriched consciousness or as an expression of excessive "in-dwelling" was based essentially on anecdotal reports of relatively few individuals. Without any more extensive research base, it has become almost a part of accepted scientific understanding, as well as popular folklore, about the nature of substance use.

The present approach therefore places much greater emphasis on a particular sector of the personality that has typically been ignored in systematic research concerning drug or alcohol use in youth. Our focus is on daydreams, the need hierarchy, locus of control, and self-reports (as measured by the Zuckerman scales) of sensation seeking. We examine each of these dimensions in turn in the balance of the chapter, placing the greatest emphasis on the area of daydreaming because this facet of human experience has been most ignored in the systematic research on substance use, even though anecdotal accounts such as those by Tart (1977) and Weil (1977) emphasize their significant role as a part of the drug experience. Singer (1977b), however, has put greater emphasis on the normative role of daydreaming and of its possible alternate significance to reliance upon drug use. Therefore the bulk of the balance of this chapter emphasizes the background of a growing literature on the psychology of daydreaming— definitions, theory, and research orientations.

Daydreaming: The Inner Experience of Youth

The passage from adolescence to young adulthood known as youth (Keniston, 1970) is perhaps best characterized as a time of the *possible*. The physical and intellectual development of the individual in this period, the lack of long-term commitment and entanglement, all come together to create a mood of anticipation when the subjunctive "might" and the conditional "would" or "could" are dominant *motifs* of experience. By the age of 17 or 18, most young persons in our society are fully grown, sexually mature, and have reached the peak of their intellectual capacities for abstract thought, memory, and the other variables assessed by intelligence testing. Spread before the youth of this period are a multitude of possible directions in which it appears they can move in terms of career and social, sexual, or physical development.

It is no wonder, then, that the human capacity for daydreaming, for exploring the range of the "possible" through private imagery, reaches its peak in this period. Literary reminiscences of adolescent experience are replete with examples of adolescent fantasies. Curiously, however, with the exception of clinical anecdotes based on emotionally disturbed youngsters in treatment, psychologists and other behavioral scientists until fairly recently have almost completely ignored the subject of daydreaming as a topic for systematic research and theory. Since the 1960s, however, with psychology's rediscovery of private experience and human imagery capacities as part of what has been called the "cognitive revolution" (Dember, 1974; Hebb, 1960; Tomkins, 1962–1963), there has been an increasing effort to find the technical means for studying in systematic fashion the phenomena of anticipation, explorations freed of time and space, which adolescents carry on privately in so much of their spare time. Some of the literature and discussions of beginning approaches to the study of daydreaming and related phenomena of the stream of consciousness are available in earlier books (Singer, 1966, 1974a, 1975a). In this chapter, an attempt is made to examine in more systematic fashion specific approaches to the definition of daydreaming and related phenomena in operational terms that permit replication and related systematic research. In the next chapter, we examine specific findings from research that opened the way for the explorations described in this volume of the relationships between daydreaming, personality need structure, and drug and alcohol use as part of the life style of the youth who make up the samples under study here.

TOWARD A DEFINITION OF DAYDREAMING

Stimulus-Independent Mentation

The continuous nature of human thought so aptly characterized by William James (1890/1950) as a stream of consciousness presents serious problems for any attempt at defining subproperties of ongoing cognition. Generally speaking, in the attempts at finding a reasonable delimitation within thought for describing daydreams, most investigators from Freud (1908/1962) to Klinger (1971) and Singer (1966, 1975a,b) have viewed the phenomenon as a shift of attention away from some ongoing task to the processing of material in effect derived from one's own long-term memory system. Such material may involve not only "vertical" reproduction of earlier events but may be reshaped often into novel and original combinations that represent the future as well as the past. If someone is mowing the lawn and thinking about being careful not to hit any rocks, then that person's thought could be described primarily as task-relevant or defined pretty clearly by the external stimulus context. Suppose that the same person who is mowing the lawn finds himself suddenly shifting into images of a far off sandy beach against which long breakers roll from a blue sea while tall coconut palms sway in the background. One can describe such thought as being characterized by a daydream.

Indeed, the shift of attention need not be quite so far-removed from the life situation of the grass-cutter as he goes about his task. Simply thinking about supper for that evening or a recent altercation at the office or the possible outcome of a forthcoming championship football game also meets the definition of daydreaming. All of these thoughts involve a shift of focus away from an ongoing task defined by immediate stimulus contexts.

The definition is particularly useful in laboratory studies of daydreaming, where they can be even more precisely operationalized. In day-to-day life situations, there are times in which it is more difficult to specify a clear-cut task. Someone sitting in a waiting room of a bus terminal is likely to engage in quite far-ranging thoughts with no other immediate cognitive task than to keep on the alert for announcement of the bus departure or possible changes in schedule. When preparing for bed at night, a time when most adults and adolescents report the greatest frequency of daydreaming activity (Singer, 1966; Singer & McCraven, 1961), there is clearly no defined task other than one's conscious intent to sleep. One might stretch the definition a bit to argue that in the waiting room one's main task is to stay alert, to observe one's physical surroundings, to watch out for one's baggage lest it be filched or mislaid. Thus, any sequence of thoughts involving a future rendezvous with an attractive member of the opposite sex or any reminiscences about painful experiences with the family at Thanksgiving dinner all could qualify as shifts of attention and as daydreams.

Indeed, even at night if one really wants to get to sleep, then it is best to try to exclude sensory awareness by shutting one's eyes, reducing movement or other tactile sensation through snuggling under a blanket, and trying to reduce thought as much as possible. In extreme cases where the would-be sleeper has gone through a day with still much unfinished business, or where the next day holds in store some unusually important event, it is hard to fall asleep because of the upsurge of thoughts about this material. Under such circumstances, one may experience insomnia. Some people cope with such situations by introducing very specific types of thought-reducing activities such as counting sheep or reviewing mildly interesting but repetitive events such as sports or ballet routines.

Fantasy and Daydreaming

Applying the definition of daydreaming loosely as task-irrelevant or stimulus-independent mentation, we have developed questionnaires (supplemented where possible with interviews) to sample from fairly sizable groups in the population information about the range of content and relative frequency or structural patterns of daydreaming. Large-scale studies suggest that day-dreams are clearly more than "castles in Spain" or purely "make-believe" or "fantastical" types of thinking. Indeed, the words *daydreaming* and *fantasy* still need to be better understood. The terms represent very private experiences and have not in the past ever been defined with sufficient precision. One might therefore propose that *daydreaming* be regarded as that aspect of the stream of consciousness that involves a shift of attention away from an ongoing task or externally derived stimulus context, and that *fantasy* be considered a specific type of daydream that introduces new combinations of material from the past to an especially probabilistic or even impossible private context.

We do not attempt to deal with the notion that fantasies may be unconscious, a viewpoint that is of course very important within psycho-analytic theory. It has been extremely difficult to establish operational definitions for concepts such as unconscious fantasy. One might, for example, conceive of the possibility that certain types of daydreams or specific fantasies formed by children, partly on the basis of their limited capacity for assimilating experiences in their modest range of cognitive schema, might have been played and replayed mentally so many times as to become automatized. Thus, much as we have automatized the complex motions and other cognitive aspects that make for driving a car or riding a bicycle, these fantasies may have also been internalized in the form of *programs* that, in an appropriate context, run themselves off rapidly without conscious awareness. A child who had frequent frightening fantasies about a threatening father may, as an adult, experience frequent discomfort in dealings with "father figures" or authorities but do so automatically without recognizing the link to earlier "practice" of such fantasies. The even more complicated notion of unconscious fantasies that have *never* been part of conscious daydreaming activity seems too speculative to be testable at all and to have little scientific potential.

In effect, then, daydreaming is represented as a general pattern of thought that can be identified by the fact that it represents a shift of attention away from an immediate motor or cognitive task or stimulus context. A fantasy is probably best viewed as a subtype of daydream that usually involves somewhat greater speculation, somewhat more of a thrust toward future possibilities, or a juxtaposition of elements from long-term memory that may have much less probability of occurrence in the external life of the individual.

Distractibility, Mindwandering, and Daydreaming

Terms such as *reverie* may be viewed from this framework as descriptions of conditions or external appearances of the individual, which suggest to observers that the person they're watching is involved in daydreaming or some extended thought-like activity. It must be stressed, however, that simply because an individual shows a shift of attention away from somebody else's conversation or from the ongoing activity in a classroom does not mean that such a person is engaged in daydreaming. It is important to notice that *distractibility* and *mindwandering* are not the same as daydreaming. A person can be distractible and unable to concentrate not only by moving away from an immediate task, such as a homework lesson or the teacher's lecture, into private ruminations, fantasies, memories, interior monologues, or replaying of melodies from popular songs. A diversion from such externally demanded tasks may take the form of looking around the room at other persons, involvement in reviewing scenes in nature, obsessional types of activities such as counting the number of separate strips on the Venetian blinds, or engaging in some other rhythmic activity such as humming a song or whispering or talking to another child.

Our research using questionnaires has made it quite clear that mind-wandering, distractibility, boredom, and related experiences are not necessarily associated with carrying on extensive interior thought processes whether in the form of fantasies, interior monologues, or reminiscences. Instead, it seems likely that persons who report themselves to have great problems of distractibility or mindwandering activities are drawn to the external environment and do a great deal of looking around a room or become involved in motor activity, *constantly changing their environment,* rather than dipping into their own stream of long-term memories and "playing" with those.

Research by Isaacs (1975) indicated that those subjects who scored high on the factor of Mindwandering derived from the Imaginal Processes Inventory (Singer & Antrobus, 1970, 1972) were quite discriminable from subjects scoring high on a measure of Positive-Vivid Daydreaming. The mind-wanderers while sitting in a room alone showed a great deal more response to the physical characteristics of the setting. When they were interrupted every 15 seconds, very little reference was made by them in their self-reports to private thoughts or interior monologues. By contrast, subjects who scored high on the Positive-Vivid Daydreaming scales reported much more trans-formational activity—that is, responses in which specific aspects of the room or specific thoughts were compared with other material from memory—and much metaphorical thought activity characterized their response pattern. Daydreaming clearly involves thinking, whereas mindwandering can also involve perceiving or acting upon the environment.

Within the framework of the definitions suggested, it should also be clear that there is no attempt to prejudge daydreaming with respect either to its wish-fulfilling nature or with respect to its positive or negative emotional implications. It turns out that when one carries out empirical studies on a large scale with a variety of questions within this definitional framework, many people produce daydreams that are either extremely planful or primarily reminiscent. Some daydreams involve fearful anticipations rather than wishful or emotionally positive fantasies such as those implied in a term like 'castles in Spain" (Singer, 1966, 1975a; Singer & McCraven, 1961, 1962).

As Huba (1980) has pointed out, the effort to characterize the individual's inner life requires consideration of some of the following features:

1. *predispositions toward organized inner experiences,* which include imagery in the various modalities, controls over such imagery and specific abilities as represented in spatial manipulation or in repetition of verbal or auditory passages;

2. *representation of typical thought styles,* controlled or impulsive, diffuse or analytic, simple or complex;

3. the *relative emphasis* in thought on the self, on others, or on the inanimate objects of the environment;

4. the *realistic possibility* of occurrence of the content of thought—that is, its relative improbability; and

5. the *emotional states manifested* during spontaneous mentation—the strength and variety of emotions produced by particular thoughts and the extent to which various fantasies are designed to augment, enhance, or reduce particular emotional reactions.

The *Imaginal Processes Inventory* (IPI) developed by Singer and Antrobus (1963, 1970, 1972) represents one of the few available instruments designed to measure the various dimensions cited previously. The 28 subscales of this self-report measure of ongoing thought predisposition attempt to sample various domains of mentation style (such as propensity for boredom or distractibility, rate of mentation, degree of visual or auditory imagery during daydreaming), orientation toward daydreaming more generally (for example, the degree to which an individual can become totally absorbed in fantasy activity, the degree to which daydreaming is accepted as relatively "normal and even desirable"), and specific fantasy patterns (such as sexual content, hostile-aggressive content, or fantasies of guilt). The scales have been developed in a Likert form and have attempted to take into account the possibility of acquiescence sets by keying items within a subscale in opposite directions. The scales have respectable degrees of internal consistency (Singer & Antrobus, 1972). Oakland (1968) has shown that the pool of items from which these scales were drawn seems relatively free of association with a measure of social desirability, a frequent problem for self-report inventories.

In summary, the general emphasis on daydreaming in the research reported in this volume eventually focuses on the use of a very specific instrument, the *Imaginal Processes Inventory,* which is essentially a large-scale self-report measure comparable in its way to the Personality Research Form designed to measure the needs of the individual or the Locus of Control and Sensation-

Seeking Scales. There are, of course, other methods of thought sampling that might be considered, and some of these are described in the review of research and daydreaming in Chapter 3. Indeed, in the present project some techniques like these were used in smaller experiments with limited numbers of subjects, but it is obvious, of course, that for the large sample study that is the focus of this volume, such methods are not practical at this time.

MOTIVATIONAL CONTENT AND STRUCTURE IN PERSONALITY: MURRAY'S LIST OF NEEDS

In developing a list of major human needs, Henry Murray (1938) and his collaborators at the Harvard Psychological Clinic tried to move beyond the restricting reductionism of Freud's emphasis on sex and aggression as primary motivating forces in human existence. The Murray group recognized that human behavior is subject to direction by a supraordinate group of perhaps a dozen to 20 major organizing intentions, which came, perhaps somewhat unfortunately, to be called *needs*. To represent the total theoretical position that has an important interactionist emphasis (see Jessor & Jessor, 1977, for an attempted test of the interactionist view), Murray also emphasized the role of *press,* or in effect, demands from others or from environmental characteristics made upon the individual. External *press* necessarily interacted with the needs of the individual to produce ultimate overt responses or particular sets of expectations. Murray's needs included affiliation, achievement, harm-avoidance, aggression, nurturance, sex, play, autonomy, and so on. It could be presumed that individuals place different priorities on needs of these kinds, so that some people may put affiliation, sex, play, harm-avoidance, and nurturance at the top of their list of motives, whereas other may be more characterized by groupings such as achievement, autonomy, orderliness, power, or dominance.

Murray's list of needs has generated a relatively fruitful pattern of research that employs both projective methods and personality questionnaires. The most extensive projective test research that focuses particularly on needs such as achievement and power has been carried out by McClelland (1958, 1961, 1975) and various collaborators with variants of the Thematic Apperception Test or other storytelling procedures. The extensive research by McClelland and dozens of others on achievement motivation using these procedures need not be documented here any further. McClelland, Davis, Kalin, and Wanner (1972) have examined various organizations of power motivation, as represented in fantasy behavior, that are tied to different approaches to drinking in adults. Their major conclusion (based on a study of males) is that men's striving for power is a major motive for alcohol consumption in a variety of cultures and settings. This effect is, however, less strong in college samples. McClelland (in McClelland et al., 1972) comments that "men drink...to feel stronger...[Alcohol] in larger amounts, in supportive settings and in impulsive people...leads to an increase in thoughts of personalized power—of winning victories over threatening adversaries. Among younger men...thoughts of personal power are often expressed in terms of sexual and expressive conquests [p. 334]."

This finding suggests a possible close tie between fantasies of heroism, hostile-aggression, and sexuality and drinking. The tie between motives and content of fantasy as it bears on substance use is clearly worth pursuing, therefore. This position is further strengthened by an admittedly preliminary study reported by McClelland and Steele (1972) as an appendix to the drinking volume. They found that heavier marijuana use in college students was linked to personalized power fantasies (much as in older men who drink heavily) rather than to socially oriented power motives. The heavier users showed a rebellious power orientation, whereas light pot smokers were more achievement oriented. The heavier smokers showed an alienated, impersonal aggressive trend in thought and, to some extent, in behavioral preference. Heavy drug users (LSD) show a comparable rebellious, anti-achievement orientation but less of a risk of violence orientation. Clearly these data point the way for more extensive studies of the role of private fantasies, need structure, and sensation-seeking in substance use (see Chapters 5, 6, and 7).

Because the focus of the study described in this book has been on objective questionnaires, it is important to note that a number of inventories have made extensive use of the Murray needs as a basis of organization. The *Edwards Personal Preference Schedule* (EPPS) was an important first step in this direction (Edwards, 1959). More recently, the Personality Research Form (Jackson, 1967), which also made use of Murray's list of needs, has been developed. The PRF is, as of this date, one of the most psychometrically sophisticated instruments because of the careful way in which the scales have been developed to maintain relative independence. The PRF has also been validated rather carefully not only against self-descriptions of behavior by individuals but also against descriptions of their behavior by their peers.

The PRF (in the standard shorter forms, A and B, employed by us) consists of 15 scales that measure 14 Murray needs (e.g., Achievement, Affiliation, Aggression through Social Recognition and Understanding) and one validity scale, Infrequency. Although the scales can be grouped (with statistical justification from factor analyses) into broader categories such as Impulse Expression and Control, Orientation to Work and Play, Degree and Quality of Interpersonal Orientation, etc., there is sufficient justification for their employment as individual scales (Jackson, 1967). Detailed descriptions of high scorers and defining trait adjectives are supplied. Thus, Autonomy, a need we shall see is strongly emphasized by certain groups in our study, bears the following description for a high scorer:

Tries to break away from restraints, confinement, or restrictions of any kind; enjoys being unattached, free, not tied to people, places, or obligations; may be rebellious when faced with constraints.

A list of adjectives such as "free ... rebellious ... nonconforming, uncompliant ... lone wolf" is also appended to aid in understanding the scales. Attaining a high score on a scale involves answering appropriately items such as: "I would like to wander freely from country to country," and "my greatest desire is to be independent and free." Of special importance in the development of these scales is the fact that they are keyed for both "yes" and "no" answers to avoid acquiescence sets; the scales have also been "purified" to minimize social-desirability response sets. The manual, a model of careful presentation, elaborates on the development and statistical analyses of item pools, evaluations of scale separation, internal consistency, reliability, and so on. Validity was achieved by a number of careful studies on peer ratings and by multitrait, multimethod factor analyses (see Chapter 4).

In general, the PRF is perhaps the single most sophisticated "normal" personality measurement instrument now available. For the purposes of our present study, it provides a measure of motivational orientation through self-description that moves from wish and fantasy toward overt behavioral description.

The reasonably good validation material for the Personality Research Form indicates that this self-report measure describes not only personal orientation but actual overt behavior. We are emphasizing in this study the fact that it is, however, a self-description and indeed essentially a list of preferences for types of behaviors, or *a private ordering* of the individual's motivational structure. In keeping with the general cognitive point of view, motivational structure is expressed in part through a series of conscious intentions and anticipations, many of which may take the form of fantasies or daydreams about future events or about courses of action necessary to attain particular goals. Thus the daydreaming scales of the IPI provide a more general indication of the individual's orientation toward fantasy, awareness of different patterns of styles of fantasy, and an indication of some of the particular directions these fantasies take. The PRF measure represents a more specific and focused feature of the private personality against the more diffuse background of a general ongoing stream of consciousness.

COGNITIVE STYLE: INTERNAL VERSUS
EXTERNAL LOCUS OF CONTROL

The third measure employed as a representation of the private personality in this study was the extremely well-known and widely used Rotter Locus of Control scale (Lefcourt, 1976; Rotter, 1966). Essentially this measure attempts to indicate the relative emphasis an individual places on anticipation that reinforcing circumstances will come either from one's own actions or from environmental circumstances or the effects of chance. This scale has been so extensively employed and studied from so many angles that it seems unnecessary to elaborate on the research literature here. Again the Locus of Control represents in a sense a kind of even more delimited orientation of the private personality so that one's anticipation of events in the form of interior monologues or fantasies may reflect either expectations that "I will do so and so; if I try the thing out this way or that way it might work out" versus a kind of interior monologue or fantasy about "let's go for broke, it doesn't make a hell of a lot of difference how I do it anyway!"

Similarly, it might be argued that an individual who has developed an extensive and differentiated fantasy orientation, who has delineated carefully a precise set of needs, will possibly feel less necessity for relying on external substances to provide stimulation. Such an inner-differentiated person might feel less urgency to reduce negative affects or enhance positive affects by drinking or drug use. In general, this was the point of view adopted in incorporating the Rotter Scale into a battery for measuring the relationship of private personality to substance use.

Of course, the reader can sense by this time a general theme or overarching hypothesis of our approach. This position reflects an orientation that individuals who have in effect developed a complex set of self-communications are perhaps more likely to be able to find reinforcement in their own activities or indeed through other forms of self-stimulation rather than by relying on external stimulation. It is conceivable that persons who are especially prone to using substances to provide certain kinds of experiences that might normally be available to all of us are perhaps excessively dependent on external stimulation and cues. There is an increasing body of research that suggests that persons who are overweight or who find themselves indulging in a variety of activities involving immoderate reliance on food, drink, or external stimulation may have failed to develop adequate internal resources as an alternative form of stimulation and reinforcement (Rodin & Singer, 1977; Singer, 1975a, b,). This approach leads quite naturally into the choice of the next instrument.

SENSATION-SEEKING SCALES

An extremely interesting series of scales was developed by Zuckerman and various collaborators to estimate the degree to which individuals are drawn to a variety of risky or externally challenging activities in order to maintain what might be called an "optimal level of stimulation" (Zuckerman, 1974, 1975, 1979; Zuckerman, Bone, Neary, Mangelsdorff, & Brustman, 1972). The origin of these scales in studies of tolerance for sensory deprivation has been extensively documented in the references cited previously. Essentially the findings indicate that while these scales have been of little value in predicting ability to remain in restricted environmental stimulation chambers, they have shown a remarkable network of correlates with other behavioral and attitudinal measures.

The scales eventually developed include *Thrill Sensation Seeking*, a measure of interest and fantasy about risky undertakings such as sky-diving, mountain-climbing, etc., and *Experience Sensation Seeking*, a series of items about a quest for novelty or external stimulation for its own sake. The kind of items reflected in this latter scale emphasize the various forms of interest in travel without any fixed aim, in unusual dress, or in forms of exhibitionism. Items include, in a sense, a taste for the unconventional in people and in artistic forms, an interest in conduct that flouts irrational authorities. Specific items about the use of marijuana and hallucinatory drugs are included. As we shall see in subsequent analyses presented in this book, the use of this scale for correlations with actual reports of drug and alcohol use necessitated the elimination of specific items on the scale dealing with self-reported interest in drugs and marijuana because this would obviously contaminate our findings.

The third scale employed is called *Disinhibition*. This scale focuses on an apparent searching of opportunities for freeing oneself of the ordinary conventional limitations on sexual or social behavior. It includes items that represent interest in impulsive activities, varieties of sexual partners, wild parties, gambling, and so on. Again, in our use of this scale, a specific reference to drinking was eliminated.

A fourth scale involves *Boredom Susceptibility*, which represents a tendency toward easy association with activities, constant concern about the possibility that repetitive activities will be boring or unpleasant, a preference for encountering new people, and so on. This scale seems less clearly related to the others, according to Zuckerman (1975), although it does seem in general to represent an orientation not unlike that reflected in the third factor (mindwandering or attention control), which generally emerges from the Imaginal Processes Inventory. Finally, there is a *General Sensation-Seeking scale* that combines the four scales to attempt to measure a more general propensity.

Some of the psychometric properties of the scales are discussed in more detail in the methods section. While these measures are of satisfactory internal consistency and reliability, there are some significant problems about their use since they overlap in items and therefore are not really completely independent scales. Despite some reservations we have concerning their psychometric purity, however, the fact remains that they have developed out of a theoretical approach to the notion that all individuals seek what is for them an "optimal level of stimulation" and that some individuals require far more stimulation than others and are constantly seeking either thrills or danger, or new types of reinforcing experiences generally through outlandish actions, or through the expected consequences for them of the ingestion of substances such as drugs or alcohol.

Zuckerman (1975) has documented an extensive network of correlations between these scales and a variety of other measures of personality, of drug and alcohol usage, and indeed of certain neurochemical and genetic patterns. It seems reasonable to believe, therefore, that the types of individual differences reflected in responses to the items of these scales have pervasive implications for overt behavior as well as for private expectations.

What is less clear, however, is whether the notion of sensation seeking as a search for "optimal levels of stimulation" is entirely satisfactory. Most of the items on the scales seem to reflect a need for *externally derived* stimulation and place relatively little emphasis on the possibility that some individuals can generate extremely interesting and novel environments through private experience. Thus the scales emphasize interests by the respondents in either extremely risky activities such as fast driving or gambling, interests in outlandish external situations, or travel and exposure to continuously novel physical environments. The fact that the scales consistently correlate with measures of *extraversion* (Zuckerman, 1975), particularly of the type that seems to reflect opposition to thoughtfulness and private enjoyment of thinking, reading, or intellectual activity, suggests indeed that we are dealing here with an externalization orientation particularly in the Experience Sensation-Seeking scales.

Although Zuckerman (1975, 1977) is inclined to view sensation seeking as a generalized trait, there seems little basis for such a statement from the psychometric data he has available. There seems little doubt that there is a generality to the self-description presented by subjects in response to these items, but their value as a specific trait with unique variance cannot be supported either from the data he presents or, as we shall see, from the evidence found in our present study, which indicates that almost 75% of the variance of a scale like Experience Sensation-Seeking can be predicted from subscales of the IPI or the PRF. Nevertheless, the value of these scales as possible predictors of drug and alcohol use was apparent from the literature available at the time we began our research, and it seemed important to include them in our battery of self-description measures.

Our approach has been to assume that the SSS may be regarded as a self-report indication of an interest in certain types of "life style." In other words, just as we have documented general patterns of daydreaming and structural variations in these patterns or in the content of fantasies, and have included measures of a variety of fairly specific directional motives and a measure of cognitive style reflecting an orientation toward internal or external Locus of Control, it seemed useful to include *an orientation within the individual toward experiencing certain types of life style that involved different degrees of thrill seeking, externalization of stimulus requirement, or the search for disinhibitory experiences.* Indeed, we felt there might be some important differences between Experience Sensation Seeking and Disinhibitory Sensation-Seeking with respect to the role they play for college students and the relative resort to drugs versus alcohol. Some specific hypotheses with regard to these differences were partially tested by our procedures. In effect, the sensation-seeking pattern or life style would be to some degree quite different from a life style or private set of attitudes and wishes in which one valued thoughtfulness and emphasized a particularly positively oriented approach to daydreams and fantasies. It could be argued that there are indeed individuals who satisfy their need for "optimal levels of stimulation" through more extended and elaborate private experience, and that they have learned early to accomplish this without the necessity for external substance. Many people who make a point of remembering their night dreams or who plan to dwell at length upon vivid and elaborate daydreams may be capable of generating a tremendous range of novelty that is satisfying irrespective of the complexity or novelty of the external environment.

Obviously, a person who restricts *public* experience drastically would develop fewer stored memories, which might then lead to fewer complex and original possibilities. One must go out in the world to obtain some experiences that can later become the basis for a rich and varied "internal" environment. People like Marcel Proust who became near recluses at periods in their lives nevertheless had spent a considerable amount of time "in society" and then elaborated the experience in their private fantasies, ultimately expressing this material in fine literature.

A reading of the items of the sensation-seeking scales suggests that people who score high on these scales are expecting a great deal more from externally generated stimulation, and the scales say relatively little about the possibility that such individuals will take the time or effort to use their memories and fantasies about such experiences to generate comparably high levels of stimulation in private. At any rate, it was deemed likely that at least with respect to the Experience and Thrill Sensation-Seeking scales, we might find more reliance on substance use with particular emphasis on drugs, which would generate seemingly novel private experiences in lieu of the individual's having developed a capacity for providing these experiences without external assistance. In the case of the Disinhibitory scale, we felt that this orientation was not necessarily out of keeping with the awareness of fantasies and daydreams but, rather, that it might reflect the possibility that private fantasies and daydreaming were excessively guilt-ridden or dysphoric and that the use of alcohol, in particular, as a means of reducing awareness of one's own thoughts and fantasies might cut down self-consciousness and self-awareness and permit freer socialization and seeming enjoyment. In addition, the linkage of drinking to power fantasies and to a general "macho" syndrome characterized by heroic, sexual, and hostile daydreams might be demonstrable.

AFFECTIVE EXPERIENCE

An important implication of the new developments of cognitive-affective theory and a theory of differential emotions (Izard, 1977; Tomkins, 1962–1963) has been the indication as suggested at the outset of this chapter that information processing and the emergence of specific positive or negative affects such as joy and interest, surprise or anger, distress, sadness, or terror depend on the rates and persistence of presentation to the organism of novel stimulation. Since an important feature of this research was to use large samples and to focus on normative aspects, it was felt that no really suitable instruments had as yet been developed to measure systematically the differential affects in relation to this kind of theoretical orientation. Nevertheless, as is seen in Chapter 7, we have attempted to obtain some indications through the pattern of responses to the alcohol- and drug-use questionnaire, concerning the likelihood that substances were employed either to reduce negative affective experiences or to enhance positive affective experiences. Ideally, it would have been more useful if we could have been more specific and looked more closely at enhancing particular subcategories of affects such as anger, fear, or sadness versus joy or interest and curiosity. We do have some clues with respect to at least the affect of interest and the reduction of fear or distress in relation to the use of substances, and these are presented in Chapter 7, but a more careful analysis of substance use in relation to the newer forms of cognitive-affective theory and with appropriate emphasis on the differential affect system still remains to be carried out. Ikard and Tomkins (1973) have shown, with respect to smoking behavior, that some important differences in patterns of smoking and in potential response to control of the habit may depend on which affects are involved and whether smoking is carried out to enhance positive affect or to reduce negative affect. We deal with this issue in Chapter 7.

SUMMARY

The overall approach of this study has been to focus on a number of dimensions of the private personality with respect to how these are reflected in various overt behavioral situations and in particular with respect to the relative dependence on the use of drugs or alcohol by youth in college. The basic dimensions of private personality we explored include first of all the range and the frequency of daydreaming patterns as measured by the IPI, the more specifically focused self-described needs or motives of the individual as measured by the PRF, the cognitive style of direction of expected reinforcement from either internal or external sources as measured by the Locus of Control scale, and finally, the expectation about desirable life styles as measured by the SSS, which focuses primarily on externally oriented sources of stimulation. In general, then, we are proposing to ascertain the extent to which measures of sets of self-descriptions and self-expectations about private fantasies, private hopes and wishes, and related aspects of cognitive style, or expectations about desirable sources of stimulation, will predict the relative reliance on substance use by youth.

In part, we anticipated identifying those young people who have been living comfortably with a rich and varied private fantasy life that has been visually vivid, oriented toward the future and composed primarily of positive affective experiences. We expected that those who have seen themselves as capable of self-reinforcing activities and who may show other forms of motivation oriented toward self-development and achievement, toward orderliness or organization in their lives, would be less inclined toward the use particularly of hard drugs or toward extensive resort to alcohol. We felt on the other hand that those youth who have not been living comfortably with inner experience but who have either found their inner fantasies associated with guilt, or who have found themselves unable to catch hold of their fantasies and develop them (as in the case of those who might be high on scales of mindwandering and distractibility), might perhaps be less capable of self-entertainment and self-reinforcement. Such individuals might therefore find themselves increasingly aware of the desire to find novel stimulation from external sources and might be the same individuals in general who score high on some of the Sensation-Seeking Scales, who seek to find disinhibitory experience through the nullification of guilt fantasies through alcohol. Some might in general try to enrich private experience, seemingly a barren area for them, by the use of hallucinogenic drugs.

Clearly, in this orientation, we are not paying attention to the environmental determinants of drug and alcohol use that have of course already been shown in many studies to be significant factors. Nevertheless, since our focus is on an understanding of personality variation in youth and in enhancing our awareness of a neglected facet of personality research, private experience, we have taken the risk of placing our emphasis on these essentially internal features. It remains to be seen whether private personality measures such as daydreaming and need organization are consistent and whether we can determine if the use of substances modifies drastically such factors. Can we demonstrate statistically a persistence and continuity of private personality structure that will support our intuitive sense that our experiences are in effect continuous however much they may change from moment to moment? In William James' famous metaphor of the stream of consciousness, he likened ongoing thought to Heraclitus' notion of the river that continues to be a river despite the fact that the water passing through is always different. In a sense, we are proposing that continuities in private personality organization can be demonstrated and may indeed turn out to be systematically related to certain critical overt behaviors in youth such as the relative resort to drugs or alcohol as part of a life style.

3 Research Approaches to the Psychology of Daydreaming

The major focus of the research described in this volume was on relationships between drug and alcohol use and various measures of the private personality; a secondary objective was a more general examination of patterns of daydreaming in college youth. A long-standing research program (Singer, 1966, 1975a,b) has evolved that uses a variety of approaches to study daydreaming and the more general problems of ongoing thought. The research to be described in this chapter follows up on some issues raised in the earlier studies and points, we believe, toward further useful research directions. Since the variety and extent of systematic psychological studies of daydreams and ongoing thought are not widely known, this chapter is designed to review the basic issues and methodological innovations that have emerged recently. Furthermore, since there are no obvious external referents against which to validate the questionnaire measures of imaginal processes used in our large study, the assessment of the validity of the self-report scales must hinge largely on the basis of the nomological network (Cronbach & Meehl, 1955) of the construct. The demonstration of the robustness of the contructs through laboratory studies as well as indirect validation of the questionnaires through correlations between laboratory and paper-and-pencil measures (Huba, 1980; Singer, 1975a,b) support general theoretical expectations. A theoretical orientation to the nature of ongoing thought and the relevance of this phenomenon to the life style of college youth follows.

OVERVIEW OF RESEARCH QUESTIONS AND METHODS

Emerging from the attempt to define daydreaming more precisely has been an extensive series of specific systematic studies and experiments designed to delineate more precisely the various facets of this essentially private form of human experience. Some of the research has attempted to answer questions such as:

- "How widespread is daydreaming?"
- "Does everybody daydream and under what circumstances?"
- "Are there sex or age differences in frequency and content of daydreaming?"
- "Are there sociocultural group differences in frequency and content of daydreaming?"
- "Does daydreaming fall into fairly specific patterns, or is it a single general dimension along which all people vary?"
- "What are the personality and cognitive correlates of patterns of daydreaming, if the latter can be identified?"

Answers to these questions require, in part, an approach that involves the gathering of large-scale data using questionnaires and the methodology of psychometrics in order to provide reasonably systematic information. At one time, great hopes were held for the use of projective techniques—that is to say, ambiguous stimuli such as the Rorschach inkblots or the Thematic Apperception Test cards for producing daydream-like material (Singer, 1968). It seems more reasonable, nowadays, to rely as much as possible on the direct self-reports of individuals without interposing stimuli whose properties themselves may present technical difficulties. From the beginning of this research, therefore, following the earlier tradition of work by Shaffer (1936) and Seeman (1951) or the work of Page (1957), a series of questionnaires and eventually a series of separate scales (see Chapters 2 and 5) evolved. Thus one whole segment of the research on daydreaming has involved large samples and psychometric procedures, such as factor analysis and related correlational analyses, to study patterns of daydreaming and their correlates in normal populations.

A second major thrust of the research has been the use of laboratory experiments to examine daydreams as part of the ongoing stream of consciousness. Here one attempts to answer questions such as:

- "Can we determine how much of the time a person is daydreaming when he is actually also involved in gathering information from the external environment?"
- "To what extent does daydreaming interfere with or facilitate information processing?"
- "To what extent can one increase or decrease the occurrence of thought processes unrelated to an immediate task or information from the immediate external environment?"
- "Is there any evidence that daydreaming takes place at the same time as externally derived information is processed, or must there always be an

alternation, a sequential pattern, of external information processing and daydreaming?"

- "Are there particular or specific psychological concomitants of day-dreaming?"
- "Can one detect daydreaming through measurement of eye movements, shifts in heart rate, or other physiological indicators?"
- "Does daydreaming bear any relationship to newly discovered differences in the information-processing patterns associated with the two hemispheres of the human brain?"
- "Are there relationships between daydreaming (as manifested through ocular activity and the electrical activity of the brain) and nocturnal dream activity?"

Approaches to these questions have necessarily involved more direct experimental interventions. Indeed, precise and careful laboratory studies have, in some instances, made it possible to actually make mathematical statements about the relative relationship or likelihood of occurrence of daydreaming (stimulus-independent mentation) and the information load borne by an individual in performing a particular task (Antrobus, 1968; Fein & Antrobus, 1979).

The use of signal-detection experiments has made it possible to control the information environment of a subject rather precisely. Periodic questioning of the subject (every 15 seconds for example) generates a large number of data points during a single half-hour session and permits one to ascertain the number of stimulus-independent thoughts produced. Furthermore, pretraining subjects to a common definition with the experimenter of stimulus-independent mentation (Antrobus, Singer, Goldstein, & Fortgang, 1970) makes it possible to use relatively automated means of recording the occurrence of such thoughts. A simple Yes–No button-press by the participant can come every 15 seconds, while he or she is detecting signals at the rate of one per second, without interfering with the natural flow of the task. Periodic direct inquiries about the content of stimulus-independent mentation make it clear that even in these rather artificial laboratory settings young adults and adolescents are having thoughts such as, "I wonder who'll be at my cousin's party? I hope Sonja shows up again. I'd like to *really* have a chance to talk with her more this time."

Laboratory studies also involve work on eye movements related to daydreaming or consideration of the psychophysiological correlates of thought. More recently there has been an attempt to move out of the rigid confinement of sterile laboratory booths toward more naturalistic settings. Within the past 3 or 4 years, a number of studies have allowed individuals to move about more freely and interrupted them with electronic "beepers" during normal daily activities. Some studies that utilized these approaches, from our own laboratories as well as from laboratories of Klinger (1978),

Rychlak (1973), and Csikszentmihalyi (1978), are discussed below and in Chapter 9.

A third major focus of daydreaming research has explored relationships between fantasy and the arousal of drives or emotions. An important early influence from psychoanalysis had suggested that daydreams or fantasies are attempts at dealing with frustrated drives or conflicts. Fantasy was thought to represent a partial gratification of a drive leading to a temporary reduction of drive pressure. A series of experiments during the late 1950s and 1960s examined this conception of daydreaming. In general, the results indicated that daydreams are as likely to increase incentives as to reduce them and that the hydraulic energy model of psychoanalysis is not useful. Instead, experiments that examined the role of daydreaming following frustration or the arousal of different emotions give additional support to a cognitive-affective model (Tomkins, 1962–1963).

From the perspective of Tomkins' model, daydreams serve as stimuli or inputs drawn from memory similar to information presented by the external environment. When fantasy material is moderately novel (representing accidental or voluntary new combinations of material from memory), the positive affects of interest-surprise may be aroused. As material from fantasy is assimilated by being matched against better established schema, one experiences joy or responds with a smile or a laugh. When fantasy material represents a very high level of novelty that cannot be easily assimilated (as in a nightmare that a monster is pursuing you), one experiences anger or fear or terror. For example, a widow or widower goes about a familiar environment and constantly anticipates in fantasy that the deceased person will be in this or that room or imagines different situations of joint activity only to realize the other person is no longer alive. These fantasized interactions produce a high level of unassimilable information and may thus arouse the negative affects of distress, weeping, or depression.

For the adolescent or young adult, as suggested in Chapter 2, the future contains a greater range of possibilities than it does at almost any other life period. Thus one might expect a relatively larger emphasis on the positive affects, such as interest and joy, as imagined scenes produce new hypotheses that are not yet easily disconfirmed. Experimental studies are, however, sparse in this area. We do have increasing evidence from experimental studies of emotional arousal that suggest that the psychoanalytic view of fantasy as drive-reducing is too limited and that fantasy is better regarded as potentially arousing or as a general stimulus context whose relative ease of matching or assimilability determines affective value or recurrence of thoughts. Daydreams, or other forms of stimulus-independent mentation, may be regarded as part of that same process of establishing plans or guiding images or other "mental structures" that help us to organize the complex information that surrounds us or to orient ourselves in the ambiguities of the physical or psychosocial environment. The possible link of daydreaming to cognitive constructs such as "plans" was noted some years ago (Singer, 1966, 1970); more recent research on the "nitty-gritty" of the perceptual process has strengthened the empirical basis for assuming that comparable "mental structures" operate in various levels in dealing with ongoing information processing (Dember, 1974).

Additional facets of the overall research program on daydreaming may be cited briefly here as they have less direct pertinence to the studies described in this volume. Considering the sources of daydreaming and related imaginal processes, we can ask when fantasy first appears. The evidence suggests that the make-believe or pretending of the preschooler represents the first measurable indication of what will become adult fantasy (Piaget, 1962; Singer, 1973). A series of studies have examined the spontaneous play of preschoolers and have also employed intervention or training procedures to explore the parameters of make-believe play (Singer, 1977a). Implications for imaginative development of extensive exposure to television are also being examined.

More directly related to the fantasy of the young adult have been explorations of the role of imagery and daydreaming in psychotherapy and adaptive behavior (Singer, 1974a, 1978). It is increasingly clear that certain uses of imagery or directed fantasy can be helpful in psychotherapy to alleviate fear, reduce stress, or control unwanted behavior by the use of noxious imagery. The possible constructive functions of fantasy awareness and sensitivity to one's imagery have also been examined in research described later in this volume (see Chapter 9). It seems evident from recent work that imagery and extended fantasy capacity (if brought under systematic control) can facilitate other coping skills in adults (Meichenbaum, Henshaw, & Himmel, 1979).

A THEORETICAL ORIENTATION: DETERMINANTS OF ONGOING THOUGHT

A general point of view presented here is that daydreams are those features of the ongoing stream of thought at any given time at which a person attends. We are just beginning to develop a significant body of scientific literature that addresses the theoretical basis and experimental approaches to the stream of consciousness (Pope & Singer, 1978a). Pope and Singer (1978a,b, 1979) have gradually been formulating a grouping of the basic determinants of the ongoing stream of thought as the basis for integrating our understanding of this phenomenon with more general questions in psychology. Here, briefly, are some of the determinants of ongoing thought and some examples of research approaches to studying the phenomenon:

1. *Continuous activity of the mind.* The brain is not viewed as a passive repository of the tremendous amount of information it has stored. Rather, the storage process itself may involve continuous replay and interchange of information. This becomes evident when the degree of external input is reduced and an upsurge of private associations and images becomes apparent (Antrobus, Singer, Goldstein, & Fortgang, 1970; Klinger, 1978; Singer, 1966).

2. *Sensory input.* For the most part, awake individuals are continuously taking in new information and then replaying this new material in a short-term memory system before some form of effective labeling enabling efficient storage and retrieval takes place. Since it is increasingly clear that individuals also engage in a matching process of new input against long-term memory schema, the sensory intake process is far more complex than was once thought (Neisser, 1967). There may be a bias in processing toward externally generated material as Rapaport (1960) long ago noted—that is, we generally give priority to novel material from the environment over our own memories, wishes, or fantasies. Were we not to do so, we would risk bumping into objects or falling off precipices as we moved about in our environment.

To the extent that alert senses continuously receive stimulation from the environment, the more private material from long-term memory has less opportunity to appear and find "free channel space" within consciousness. There is increasing evidence that visual imagery produced by external stimulation involves the same processing pathways as private, internally generated imagery (Antrobus, Singer, Goldstein, & Fortgang, 1970; Segal & Fusella, 1970; Shepard, 1978). Consequently, a reasonable explanation is that the sensory processing of an active waking individual will generally monopolize much of the available channel space of consciousness. It also seems likely that individuals learn very early in their lives to ignore a good deal of private stimulation just as they must learn not to attend to their nose, muscle twitches, flickers of pain, or gassy gurglings that characterize continuously active body machinery. An experiment by Pope (1978) discussed further in Chapter 9 has attempted to systematically examine directions of attention in ongoing thought and shifts in sequence of thought.

3. *The continuum from external to internal poles of stimulation.* In an earlier work (Singer, 1966), an attempt was made to formulate a dimension of stimulation ranging from the extremely public (physically measurable, socially observable stimuli) through the most private. Our fleeting daydreams still remain beyond objective measurement. Even though the occurrence of night dreams may be grossly estimated by phasic Rapid Eye Movement (Emergent EEG Stage 1 Sleep), much of our private materials remain inaccessible. It is becoming increasingly clear, nevertheless, that in many situations we are as likely to make response to the most private sources of stimulation as to grossly observable external cues. Our consciousness reflects

the processing of stimuli from (a) the most public end of the continuum, (awareness of flashing lights, of ringing bells, sharpness of the wind) through (b) the somewhat measurable proprioceptive stimuli from within the physical body (twitchings and pains or awareness of heartbeat) to (c) the internal dimensions, which may include short-term memory and replaying of recently experienced stimuli, and then ultimately to (d) a deeper internal dimension that involves rehearsal and review or reworking of material from long-term memory.

A man driving to work may be extremely attentive to traffic ahead and to curves in the road or to signal lights, but he may also be processing material from recent memory (such as the fact that his wife has not been well) or from old memories (a recollection of the death of his mother or favorite sister). Suddenly, without any gross external cue observable to anyone else, he swings his car off the highway and heads back home. The linkage of early recall of a death in the family evokes a more personal and deep-feeling concern about his wife and therefore stimulates him to return to spend more time with her.

4. *The selectivity of attention.* The stream of consciousness is also influenced by the breadth or narrowness of our attention at any given moment. The reaction to a pressing danger may lead to actions that involve ignoring bodily experiences of pain or other cues from the environment including perhaps terror on the faces of others in a group. The child at play in an absorbing game with friends or even in a private make-believe activity can ignore the external signals of a mother's calls or the more private signals of habitual hunger pangs for the time of day. There is increasing research evidence that some people systematically learn to ignore environmental cues or even bodily reactions that might have threatening implications. These more extraverted individuals continuously process new material much like Broadbent's (1958) *short processors.* Others who are more willing to ignore new material in favor of the more elaborate processing of information presented from the environment in relation to other patterns of private association may be termed *long processors* (Broadbent, 1958). The relationship of these patterns to basic dimensions such as extraversion and introversion or to repression or sensitization as personality styles is worthy of much more extensive exploration.

In the present volume, we have approached this problem through the use of questionnaires that involve different patterns of daydreaming. Thus it is likely that individuals who in general show a good deal of acceptance and attention in relation to their own fantasy activity may represent more of the general attitude of attentiveness, whereas individuals who score higher on measures that tap mindwandering and distractibility may have little capacity for attending at length to their own private thoughts or with an internally generated sequence.

5. *Predictability or barrenness of the environment.* There is good reason to believe that one becomes especially aware of one's ongoing stream of consciousness when the external environment is not characterized by a great deal of variety, novelty, and perhaps also risk or danger. At one extreme, we find situations in which, because of the nature of physical challenge or danger or of the importance of direct and immediate response, one engages in activities that are perhaps grossly observable to others but which leave little self-consciousness. Csikszentmihalyi (1975) has indicated in some extremely valuable research that the extent to which one becomes aware either of the processing of elaborate external cues or of one's own ongoing thought stream may depend on the balance between the difficulty of tasks confronted and one's own inherent skills and capacities. In challenging situations within one's capacity but not invoking a well-established habitual response, a person may experience an almost completely consciousness-free blending of movement and experience. These states of "flow" are relatively rare and do indeed represent some of those few situations in which our minds are truly "blank." Only in retrospect can the details of the activity be recalled. As Czikszentmihalyi's (1975) data indicate, the surgeon confronted with the challenge of ligatures in a difficult case may be completely absorbed momentarily and unaware of anything except the fact of his performance, as contrasted with the few minutes before and afterward while others are performing their duties in the operation and he finds himself drifting into elaborate fantasies of social encounters or great golf games.

For most of us, a great many situations and environments contain redundant information. We can rely on established motor patterns to carry us through these phases, and under such circumstances, we may drift into daydreaming and fantasy.

6. *Central matching processes.* The exploration of both the external and internal environment (that generated by the awareness of long-term memory) is partially determined by initial sets of expectations and established schema previously generated. Presumably, we repeatedly form new organizational structures of codings or image representations (or some combination of images and codes) that are more efficiently retrievable schema (Miller, Galanter, & Pribram, 1960; Neisser, 1967; Paivio, 1970; and Tomkins, 1962–1963). In a sense, we come to each new situation with a moderately well-established script (Schank & Abelson, 1977; Tomkins, 1962–1963) that, along with the novelty of the situation, guides action. Thus our own projected sets of expectations may themselves determine to what degree an environment is viewed as "exciting and novel" or "dull and barren."

7. *Affect and emotion.* There are increasing reasons to view the affects or emotions of the organism as the major source of human motivation (Izard, 1977; Tomkins, 1962–1963). It is also clear that the affect system is closely tied to the rate and complexity of processing new information. Thus our emotions

are aroused not only by information processed from the external environment but also from our memories and established expectations or scripts. In addition, the very nature of ongoing thought processes may occasionally focus attention on unexpected possibilities which themselves generate affects such as startle, surprise, or the more pleasant experience of interest.

The evidence for a differentiated affective system linked to information processing has been extensively reviewed by Izard (1977) and is not discussed in detail here. It is important to recognize, however, that there may be important differential implications and subsequent behavioral responses depending on whether the individual engages in activities to enhance the positive affect or to reduce negative affect (Tomkins, 1962–1963). This distinction has already been proven relevant to cigarette smoking (Tomkins, 1966a, b; Ikard & Tomkins, 1973). As we shall see in our analysis of the various forms of substance use by young adults, it can be argued that for some people the awareness of one's own thoughts and of one's own private guilts and discomforts may necessitate some effort to shut down thinking or to reduce awareness of self by the ingestion of various substances.

Alcohol and other forms of drugs may perform this result permanently, or at least temporarily, although as Gray (1979) recently suggested, the alteration has some cost in continuing alertness and recognition of real dangers. The use of drugs like marijuana with the intention of simply enhancing the positive affect of curiosity or surprise may have very different implication for the individual as contrasted with use of barbiturates or alcohol to reduce the experience of dysphoric ongoing fantasy and recurring mental images of guilt or fear of failure.

In effect, then, the frame of thought is in itself a stimulus or a kind of environment that can generate moderate or extreme rates of novel information (leading to affects of interest or fear) or persistent unresolved thoughts (leading to anger, distress, or sadness). Important individual differences in the ability to recognize and control the rates and persistence of such material may be tied to patterns of daydreaming and cognitive styles. Evidence of recurring styles in which individuals over- or underemphasize the extent of their own emotional response to stress has been provided in a study of repressors—low-anxious and high-anxious individuals—carried out by Weinberger, Schwartz, and Davidson (1979).

8. *The role of current concerns, unfinished business, and unresolved stress in the stream of thought.* Freud's emphasis on the unfulfilled wish as the key to the night dream is now being understood in broader terms as a way of grasping the recurrence of contents in the ongoing stream of thought, which includes both awake and sleeping mentation. Lewin (1922, 1935) early saw the necessity for broadening the psychoanalytic concept of wish to include intentions and unfinished business. More recently, considerable theorizing and research evidence supports the importance of the notion that recurring

thoughts are related to current concerns, activities initiated but unfinished, and unresolved current or impending stressors (Breger, Hunter, & Lane, 1971; Klinger, 1970; Singer, 1975b).

The adaptive potential of the recurrence of such incompleted efforts or explorations of possible outcomes of current concerns has been increasingly recognized (Antrobus, Singer, & Greenberg, 1966). Since there are, after all, many pressures for immediate action stimulated by the specific environment, it is essential that long-term memory bring back to consciousness recollections of incompleted acts and intentions in order for us to take more clear control over the direction of our movements.

Ambiguity and difficulty in assimilating material into established schema may also be an important component of the recurring thoughts that characterize the ongoing stream of consciousness. Horowitz (1976) has dealt especially with more traumatic or unpleasant experiences and how these recur in the form of "unbidden images." In a study described in Chapter 8, Zachary (1978) has examined more closely the relationship of cognitive ambiguity and emotional intensity of a particular experience and its likelihood of recurrence in the ongoing thought stream.

9. *Structural chracteristics of stimuli.* A relatively ignored aspect of the ongoing stream of thought is the *form* of material drawn either from external or long-term memory stimulus sources. Some material may have special qualities of organization or *gestalt properties* that lend themselves to recurring ideation. Rather attractive rhymes or song lyrics as well as melodies may reverberate in the conscious for long periods of time and, indeed, are sometimes quite difficult to eliminate. A phrase like "How now, brown cow?", "You asked for it, you got it, _____!", "You deserve a break today!", or "We do it all for you!" may keep coming back to someone for no discernible reason other than the fact that it was first presented under circumstances that called special attention to the neat balance of lyrics and melody or the mixture of rhythm and rhyme.

10. *Stylistic priorities for internal or external processing.* As suggested earlier in connection with the discussion of attention, there may be long-standing patterns that emphasize the processing of material from long-term memory. Thus some individuals may have developed a special value in remembering their dreams and daydreams, in replaying past events at length, or rehearsing future real or improbable activities. Factor analyses of self-reports about mentation suggest that we can indeed identify at least three general and fairly stable patterns of daydreaming: (1) a guilty and dysphoric pattern in which considerable attention to material from long-term memory accentuates with a negative emotional quality; (2) positively oriented, wishful or planful content with relatively vivid visual and auditory images; (3) a pattern that consists of an inability to sustain long sequences of thought and a combination of fearful imagery with distractibility and a lack of control over

mentation. It seems likely that such styles of processing material from long-term memory may have been established relatively early and are pervasive as well as persistent. This volume addresses in considerable detail the evidence for the occurrence of such styles in young adults and their possible relationship to patterns of drug or alcohol use as well as to other personality dimensions.

Within an immediate situation, the nature of task demands may emphasize one or another style of processing the new material from the environment or material from long-term memory. Miller (1972) showed that one could measure the differences between: (1) attention to a recording with a focus on scientific analyses; and (2) listening with the intention of experiencing and appreciating the prose itself. Klinger (1974, 1978) has examined the various kinds of temporary sets that individuals adopt when approaching different kinds of situations such as the solution of simple motor-coordination puzzles, problems in pure logic, sustained fantasy or reverie, and nearly dream-like-type thought. Klinger distinguishes between directed, problem-solving thought, which he terms "operant," and non–problem-solving thought, which he terms "respondent." It might be argued, however, that even when confronted with an immediate task that requires thought, deviations from focusing on that specific task reflect recurrent intentions or wishes as well as unresolved ambiguities for the individual. Ultimately, these seeming distractions or daydreams may be problem solving even though they are not useful in solving the immediate task. In this sense, much of the stream of consciousness can be viewed as rehearsal or practice for later action.

THE STREAM OF CONSCIOUSNESS
AND THE YOUNG ADULT

In summary, the stream of consciousness is multiply determined and represents an alternative stimulus configuration to the external environment. It has already been suggested that the period of late adolescence is one in which the individual is likely to be especially sensitive to the ongoing stream of thought. Indeed, this notion is supported in literature by many novels of adolescence and young manhood, in which the stream of consciousness plays a particularly prominent role.

Especially for college students, who make up the largest group studied in the present report, the very nature of their role as students enhances the likelihood of awareness and involvement with their own ongoing thought stream. Contemporary college education repeatedly requires reading and examining issues mentally, analyzing questions, organizing one's thoughts, and setting ideas on paper. Most students are expected again and again to examine academic material in relation to their own lives and their own experience and futures.

In effect, therefore, the college experience creates an atmosphere of introspection and generates, at least temporarily, a strong set toward internal processing and daydreaming. It is no accident, therefore, that the major impetus for the national movement toward heavier use of a variety of drugs came from college students and got its major notoriety from the emphasis placed by Timothy Leary at Harvard on greater self-realization through LSD. One of our major objectives, as has been suggested, is the examination of the various manifestations of the stream of consciousness in college populations and the test of at least some issues relating to the determinants of the stream of consciousness. Our primary focus is on the more generalized style of processing as measured by the Imaginal Processes Inventory and related procedures. We also describe a series of studies, some employing questionnaire data and others more experimental methods, to examine relationships between patterns of ongoing thought and other personality characteristics or behavioral trends in college students and related groups of special interest.

SOME SPECIFIC RESEARCH ISSUES
TO BE EXPLORED

1. *Dimensions of daydreaming and their relation to substance use.* We have already mentioned that a number of factor analytic studies support the notion that we can identify at least three major styles of daydreaming. Nevertheless, it remains to be seen whether these findings can be replicated with samples larger than those previously employed and also whether there are different patterns to these dimensions for contrasted intact groups of American students.

We can next also ask whether these patterns relate in any systematic fashion to levels of drug or alcohol use. Still, further, we can look for any indications that individuals making long-term, heavier use of substances, which presumably could alter ongoing conscious experiences, will reflect very different motive and daydream patterns than nonusers.

2. *General implications for young adults of daydreaming patterns.* A second area of concern relates to other characteristics of ongoing thought in college students apart from the specific relationships to substance use. Can we identify more precisely the conditions that determine shifts in sequencing of thought or in recurrence of certain ideation in thought for college students?

It has already been suggested that contrary to earlier popular belief, a certain amount of what we experience as the stream of consciousness may have longer-term adaptive value. Some of the research to be described in a subsequent chapter deals with the possibility that the nature of attention to inner processes may also play a part in enhancing an individual's social awareness and social skills. At first, this notion seems contradictory since it implies that the introverted person, someone presumably paying more attention to long-term memory than to external events, may be capable of more effective social action. It is possible, however, that taking the trouble to examine in detail potential actions may actually be an effective means of preparation for social behavior. In addition, we can ask whether, from the standpoint of affect and emotion, awareness of one's fantasies and night-dreams may actually enhance empathy. Indeed, it may be possible that specific training in self-awareness may actually enhance certain forms of social competence. As suggested in our brief reference to the psychotherapeutic use of imagery and fantasy, there seems at least some reason to believe that such training may be useful in general for young adults (Singer, 1974a, 1975a,b).

3. *Daydreaming and psychopathology.* Currently, there is relatively little knowledge of the pathological aspects of daydreaming despite many popular or clinical assumptions concerning the presumed inherently self-defeating nature of the fantasy process. Research will be described studying individuals with gross emotional disturbances and chronic histories of alcohol and drug use. We examined patterns of fantasy and daydreaming among an institutionalized group to determine whether or not these dimensions correspond to what is found in presumably normal samples of youth. It seems fairly likely, for example, that those individuals whose predominant style of daydreaming involves either inability to control private experience or whose inner experiences are predominantly unpleasant in affective tone might be especially susceptible to broader emotional distress, maladaptive behavior, or reliance on alcohol and drugs for that control and avoidance. Although our research was not designed to emphasize gross pathology, we do have some results from the overall project that address these questions.

In conclusion, it seems possible to say that just as the first two-thirds of this century focused primarily on the extensive exploration of overt behavioral characteristics of human beings and outlined major dimensions of behavior, we are now into a phase in which it is increasingly possible to use scientific methods of psychology for explorations of private experience. The focus through much of the rest of this volume is on specific studies of the interrelations of overt behavior to various aspects of private experience. We stress the structural characteristics of such private experience rather than the content of fantasies or a whole array of behaviors controlled by a specific motivational tendency. Thus the work of McClelland and his various collaborators has offered a good deal about various specific fantasies and their relationship to drinking patterns. These researchers have dealt less, however, with the broader structural characteristics of the fantasizing process itself or of the nature of ongoing thought. In this sense, the present research opens the way for a view of a continuing process of thought and its relationship to the variety of significant features of behavior of young adults during a major period of transition.

4

Participants, Sampling, Measures, and Descriptive Statistics

OVERVIEW

The overall research plan was to obtain representative samples of primarily freshmen at two dramatically contrasting educational institutions, Yale University and Murray State University. Yale attracts students from all states who are, to a large extent, a predominantly white, mixed sample of Protestants, Catholics, and Jews. These students are primarily from middle- and upper-class social strata with well-educated, professional parents. Murray State University, a small regional university, enrolls students mainly from western Kentucky and those states immediately adjacent to the southwestern part, known as the "Jackson Purchase" area. These states are (Central) Tennessee, (Southeastern) Missouri (the "Bootheel" area), and (Southern) Indiana. Almost all students are white; most come from rural or semirural areas, many from farming families. The dominant religious orientation is Fundamentalist Protestantism with a Baptist denomination prevailing. Few Catholic or other religious persuasions are represented. A majority of the students at Murray State come from working-class or farming backgrounds, although middle-class backgrounds are also represented. The university is located in a county (Calloway) that bans the public sale of liquor. This "Jackson Purchase" area is a region of Kentucky that under Kentucky local option law is basically "dry," on a county basis. The official, county-wide attitude toward alcohol presents a sharp contrast to the atmosphere at Yale, where cocktails may be served to the students in their residential colleges. The use of alcohol by students (and faculty) on campus or in the dorms is not legal at Murray State, whereas there are no legal prohibitions against alcohol use at Yale.

Two independent samples at each of the two colleges were obtained in consecutive years. The first wave of data was collected in the fall of 1973; the second was obtained during the fall of 1974. All students volunteered to participate in large-scale testing sessions, for which they were paid ($5.00) with the understanding that they would also have the option of continuing to participate in follow-up studies with additional payment. Students were assigned code numbers and asked to make up fictitious names for the purpose of the follow-up studies. All respondents completed informed consent forms for their participation in each phase of the research.

Data-collection procedures at the two universities were virtually identical and conducted simultaneously. There were no systematic differences present in the two samples that can be attributed to questionnaire administration.

A total of 1095 college responses were obtained in the extensive assessment. Of the total, 588 were received in the first year (1973), and 507 in the second (1974). Murray State participants included 254 males and 447 females; 244 males and 150 females were from Yale. Table 4.1 shows the major demographic characteristics of the sample.

In most major respects, the four samples formed by sex and year of testing are roughly comparable to one another in basic background variables. This finding is especially important because in our replication strategies in later chapters of the volume, we have subdivided the total sample into these four groups to provide for robustness studies of the multivariate results. For instance, there are no detectable differences among samples in the average age of the participants ($F_{3, 1091} = 1.62$) or marital status ($\chi^2_3 = 4.02$). While there are statistically significant differences in racial composition ($\chi^2_6 = 14.81$, $p < .05$), class at time of testing ($\chi^2_9 = 25.15$, $p < .01$), and religion of upbringing ($\chi^2_{12} = 61.43$, $p < .001$), inspection of the relative percentages of occurrence indicates that the samples are generally the same. Consequently, the later analyses that use the four sample breakdowns to provide replication should be interpreted as being conducted on essentially the same population of individuals.

As a general sample, the individuals we studied are Caucasian (92.6%), single (95.1%), freshmen and sophomores (91.4%) with Protestant (62.9%), Catholic (18.6%), or Jewish (7.9%) religious backgrounds. It should also be remembered that all participants had passed through the several states of selection required for enrollment in college and that the Yale students had college-entrance credentials among the highest levels.

Since the inferential population for the analyses is college students as a general class of youth, we have consistently combined the respondents from the two colleges in the analyses to be discussed in later chapters. The results of pooling groups was to improve the univariate frequency distributions on most major personality variables by making the distributions better approximations to the normal. College differences are indirectly treated in the more

TABLE 4.1
Descriptive Statistics of the Total Sample Population[a]
1973-1974

Characteristics[b]	1973 Male	1973 Female	1974 Male	1974 Female	Total
Sex	267	323	231	274	1095
Age Range	16-27	17-21	16-29	16-33	16-33
Race					
White	245 (92.1)	308 (95.3)	211 (91.4)	249 (90.9)	1013 (92.6)
Black	7 (2.6)	11 (3.4)	10 (4.3)	18 (6.6)	46 (4.2)
Other	14 (5.3)	4 (1.2)	10 (4.3)	7 (2.5)	35 (3.2)
Marital Status					
Single	255 (95.9)	305 (94.4)	224 (97.0)	255 (93.4)	1039 (95.1)
Married	10 (3.7)	14 (4.4)	6 (2.6)	15 (5.5)	45 (4.1)
Divorced	1 (0.4)	4 (1.2)	1 (0.4)	3 (1.1)	9 (0.8)
Class Status					
Freshman	202 (76.5)	269 (83.7)	166 (72.2)	220 (80.3)	857 (78.8)
Sophomore[c]	39 (14.8)	39 (12.2)	29 (12.6)	31 (11.3)	138 (12.6)
Junior[c]	15 (5.7)	10 (3.1)	26 (11.3)	14 (5.1)	65 (6.0)
Senior[c]	8 (3.0)	3 (1.0)	9 (3.9)	9 (3.3)	29 (2.6)
Religion of Upbringing					
Protestant	148 (55.6)	237 (73.6)	89 (46.8)	151 (69.8)	625 (62.9)
Catholic[d]	61 (22.9)	53 (16.4)	40 (21.1)	31 (14.4)	185 (18.6)
Jewish[d]	26 (9.8)	11 (3.4)	29 (15.3)	12 (5.6)	78 (7.9)
None	19 (7.1)	15 (4.7)	18 (9.5)	12 (5.6)	64 (6.4)
Other	12 (4.5)	6 (1.9)	14 (7.4)	10 (4.6)	42 (4.2)

[a]Numbers given are number of respondents; numbers in parentheses are percentage of respondents.
[b]Totals will not always equal the total number of subjects because of omitted responses.
[c]These individuals were all from Murray State University.
[d]These individuals were all from Yale University.

general analyses reported in Chapter 8. College differences have also been explicitly treated by Segal and Singer (1976).

It should be noted, however, that while it seems desirable to generalize to college students in general, the sample certainly was not a national cross section of college youth. In the interests of "trading-off" between the desirability of a mixture of rural and urban students and the generally exploratory orientation of the present work, the mixture of the two colleges seems reasonable as long as it is recognized that major results should be replicated in a more totally representative group of college youth.

INSTRUMENTS

A major concern of the research was to combine a purely empirical research approach, focusing on determining personality characteristics associated with use or nonuse of alcohol and other drugs, with the development of a theoretical model suitable for experimental verification. Accordingly, potential assessment instruments were evaluated using the twin criteria of theoretical meaningfulness and technical soundness (Bentler & Eichberg, 1975). The criteria used in instrument selection were: (1) the scales should be derived from one of the accepted personality theories discussed previously; (2) each measure should have demonstrated construct validity and reliability; and (3) the instrument should have demonstrated utility for replication or validation of specific results about youthful drug use. Thus we are attempting to use theoretically derived personality constructs with demonstrated validity and reliability, with the specific intent of studying psychological processes inherent in the use or nonuse of substances.

The psychological domains studied were: (1) *needs;* (2) *daydreaming and mental style;* (3) *optimal level of stimulation;* and (4) *perceived source of reinforcement.* The first domain—needs—was chosen due to its long-standing relationship to deviancy of which drug and alcohol use are presumably exemplars (McClelland, 1975; McClelland, Davis, Kalin, & Wanner, 1972). Jackson (1967) has developed a psychometrically sound inventory, the *Personality Research Form,* which assesses an individual's levels on many of the needs in Murray's (1938) theoretical system.

The second domain, daydreaming and mental style, was selected because there has been increasing re-recognition of the role of the cognitive realm of experience as a legitimate area of psychological study (Paivio, 1971; S. Segal, 1971; Singer, 1966, 1974, 1975). Since the altering of conscious states may be an important aspect of drug use (Tart, 1971; Zinberg, & Weil, 1970), it seems essential that the relationship between an individual's typical spontaneous thought content and mental style and drug-use patterns be studied. Singer and Antrobus (1972) have undertaken an extensive scaling effort resulting in the development of the *Imaginal Processes Inventory,* which assesses many different aspects of spontaneous thought and mental style.

The concept of optimal level of stimulation has been utilized by Zuckerman (1975) to construct personality scales that have been found to be related to many general phenomena. The Zuckerman *Sensation-Seeking Scales* are measures of an individal's tendencies to seek out stimulation of various types. Since drugs and alcohol affect level of arousal, it would seem that these personality dimensions should be related to alcohol and drug use.

Rotter (1966) has discussed the importance of an individual's perceptions of the source of the reinforcements in his or her environment for specific behaviors. Rotter's theoretical dimension, called *locus of control,* has implications for self-reinforcement and interpersonal behavior (Lefcourt, 1976), and has been empirically studied in relationship to drug and alcohol use.

It is quite likely that the four domains, singularly, will each be related to drug and alcohol use. Furthermore, as each domain is theoretically distinct from the other domains, it is quite conceivable that substance use can best be concurrently predicted from a combination of constructs unique to each of the theoretical systems. Each of the four scale domains is described in more detail in succeeding sections.

Personality Research Form (PRF)

The Personality Research Form (PRF; Jackson, 1967) assesses a set of personality needs "broadly relevant to the functioning of individuals in a wide variety of situations" (Jackson, 1967, p. 4). The inventory limits itself to normal rather than abnormal processes and presents a generally comprehensive description of personality based on Murray's (1938) categories of basic motives. Briefly, Murray postulated a basic set of human motivational discharge tendencies that push a person to certain types of behavioral action. The individual's level of a particular need is typically inferred (in most assessment procedures based on the system) from a set of disparate behaviors and from wishes presumably partially controlled by the particular need. Murray certainly never argued that needs completely control behavior (a theory of situational presses was carefully developed in conjunction with the needs system), and we concur with that viewpoint.

Individuals tested in 1973 were given the short version (Form A) of the PRF, which measures 14 needs and one response tendency; individuals tested in 1974 were administered the long version (Form AA), which includes six additional content scales and one additional response-style scale. For the analyses presented here, only the 15 scales given to all subjects were used. The 15 scales and a brief definition of each are as follows:

1. *Achievement:* strives to get things done, goal oriented, sets high standards;
2. *Affiliation:* likes associating with people, desirous of friends, maintains relationships.
3. *Aggression:* assertive to the point of hurting others who get in the way, argumentative, vindictive;
4. *Autonomy:* free from obligations, dislikes any restraints, enjoys personal freedom;
5. *Dominance:* seeks leadership, self-expressive, controlling;
6. *Endurance:* shows perseverance, overcomes obstacles, has steady work habits;
7. *Exhibitionism:* likes to be noticed by others, seeks active recognition;
8. *Harm-avoidance:* avoids risk taking or dangerous situations, seeks to avoid personal injury;
9. *Impulsivity:* acts on the whims, emotionally self-expressive;
10. *Nurturance:* considerate and emphatic toward others, provides assistance;
11. *Order:* strives to maintain personal organization, likes organized surroundings;
12. *Play:* enjoys recreational activities of many types, derives great pleasure from recreation;
13. *Social Recognition:* concerned about how others perceive him or her, needs to be viewed positively;
14. *Understanding:* values knowledge, has intellectual curiosity and orientation;
15. *Infrequent Responding:* This scale is used by Jackson (1967) to check response tendencies: High scores reflect "responding in impulsive or pseudo-random manner, possibly due to carelessness, poor comprehension, passive non-compliance, confusion, or gross deviation [p. 7]." Since only four respondents (.04%) had scores on this scale that would be interpreted by Jackson as invalidating the set of inventory scores, this scale was retained in the data analyses as a possible measure of lack of careful responding.

As an operationalization of Murray's theoretical system, Jackson's (1967) inventory possesses excellent psychometric properties. Internal consistency statistics for the PRF content scales are generally above .7 and in many cases above .8 (Jackson, 1967; Stricker, 1974). Similarly, short duration test–retest reliability indices are at state-of-the-art levels (see Bentler, 1964; Jackson, 1967). Furthermore, the individual PRF content scales appear to be relatively independent of the social desirability response style (Jackson, 1967; Stricker, 1974), and the instrument is balanced for acquiescence (Couch & Kenniston, 1960) as well as eliminating the extreme response tendency (Hamilton, 1968).

Previous investigations have found strong evidence for the convergent and discriminant validity of the PRF scales studied in conjunction with peer- and self-ratings (Jackson & Guthrie, 1968), behavioral checklists (Jaccard, 1974), the Edwards Personal Preference Schedule (Edwards & Abbott, 1973; Edwards, & Abbott, & Klockars, 1972), the Edwards Personality Inventory (Edwards & Abbott, 1973), the Strong Vocational Preference Inventory (Siess & Jackson, 1970), and Cattell's 16 Personal Factor Inventory (Nesselroade & Baltes, 1975). For instance, using a multitrait/multimethod principal components analysis of PRF scales, peer-ratings, and self-ratings, Jackson and Guthrie have demonstrated strong support for the contention of construct validity through a converging operations strategy.

Additionally, the pattern of correlations among the Murray needs measured by the PRF appears to be comparable to that found in several other inventories constructed from Murray's theoretical system (Huba & Hamilton, 1976). Moreover, factor-analysis evidence to date on the PRF (Nesselroade & Baltes, 1975; Stricker, 1974) indicates a fairly stable factor pattern of between six and eight factors underlying the 20 content scales of the total PRF. This final result is discussed in more detail in the next chapter.

Imaginal Processes Inventory (IPI)

Singer and Antrobus (1963, 1970, 1972) developed a battery of 28 self-report scales, which they titled the Imaginal Processes Inventory (IPI). The IPI scales sample broadly from the interlocking domains of style of thinking (e.g., tendency to become bored, distractibility, rate of thinking, visual and auditory imagery), attitudes toward daydreaming (e.g., absorption in daydreaming, acceptance of daydreaming as a "normal" adult activity), and the content of spontaneous thought (e.g., guilt daydreams, hostile daydreams, curiosity about the lives of other people, curiosity about the nature of mechanical devices). The IPI scales have respectable levels of internal consistency (Singer & Antrobus, 1972) as measured using coefficient α and fairly minimal correlations with social desirability responding (Oakland, 1968).

The Imaginal Processes Inventory was administered to all subjects. All but one of the 28 IPI scales consist of 12 items answered in a Likert format; the Absorption in Daydreaming scale has 20 items. Items within each scale are keyed in both directions to control for acquiescence. Detailed descriptions of the 28 IPI scales and item statistics are given by Singer and Antrobus (1972).

Several studies (Giambra, 1974, 1977; Huba, Segal, & Singer, 1977b; Isaacs, 1975; Singer & Antrobus, 1963, 1972; Starker, 1974; Starker & Singer, 1975a) have identified at least three *second-order* factors underlying the 28 IPI scales. Following the terminology suggested by Huba et al. (1977b) and discussed in Chapter 5, these factors may be called Positive–Constructive

Daydreaming, Guilt and Fear-of-Failure Orientation in Daydreaming, and Attentional Control. In each of the studies cited, the three factors have emerged in substantially the same form. Support for the meaning of these factors has come from different measures developed from studies of imagery, reflective thought, night dream patterns, and thought-sampling laboratory studies (Singer, 1974b). The characteristics of the IPI have been recently reviewed by Huba (1980).

The 28 subscales of the IPI, together with a brief description of each, are as follows:

1. *Daydreaming frequency* presents a list of specific daydreams to which the respondent indicates the frequency of their occurrence. High scores on this scale are reflective of a good deal of daydreaming over a wide variety of content.
2. *Night dreaming frequency* is an index of how frequently the individual recalls night dreams.
3. *Absorption in daydreaming* assesses indications of frequent *intense* daydreaming with considerable absorption in the content of one's fantasies.
4. *Acceptance of daydreaming* was constructed to record information about how accepting or tolerant one is about daydreaming, and how much the individual accepts daydreaming as a "normal" adult activity.
5. *Positive reactions to daydreaming* taps indications of positive emotions occurring as a consequence of daydreaming.
6. *Frightened reactions to daydreaming* reports indications of anxiety or fearful reactions provoked by daydreaming.
7. *Visual imagery in daydreaming* measures the degree to which visual imagery components are important in one's daydreaming.
8. *Auditory imagery in daydreaming* assesses the role of verbal imagery in fantasies.
9. *Problem-solving daydreams* measures the extent to which daydreams play a practical role in problem solving, and how often the individual seeks to find alternative solutions to problems through daydreaming.
10. *Present-oriented daydreams* measures how often the individual daydreams about current events.
11. *Future-oriented daydreams* measures the incidence of daydreams that are future oriented.
12. *Past-oriented daydreams* assesses the degree to which an individual's daydreams are focused in the past.
13. *Bizarre-improbable daydreams* measures the frequency and intensity of daydreams clearly divorced from practical, realistic, or probable occurrences and problems in the respondent's lives.

14. *Mindwandering* measures the extent to which one's attention shifts to other perceptual responses or thoughts when the person is trying to concentrate.

15. *Achievement-oriented daydreams* represents a major class of daydream content, achievement of difficult tasks or outstanding accomplishments.

16. *Hallucinatory-vividness in daydreams* reflects a degree of vividness in daydreaming that makes the experience seem almost real.

17. *Fear-of-failure daydreams* measures the amount of daydreaming featuring self-doubt and lack of achievement.

18. *Hostile daydreams* assesses the frequency of aggressive themes in daydreams.

19. *Sexual daydreams* is a scale of the frequency of heterosexual erotic daydreams.

20. *Heroic daydreams* measures the extent of daydreams or fantasies about being brave and courageous and about receiving public recognition for heroic feats.

21. *Guilt daydreams* assesses daydreaming tied to obsessional recrimination, self-doubt, and guilt.

22. *Interpersonal curiosity* assesses the amount of curiosity about people and their relationships.

23. *Impersonal–mechanical curiosity* measures introspection or interest about natural or mechanical structures.

24. *Boredom susceptibility* assesses whether an individual is easily bored, loses interest quickly in tasks, and lacks perseverance at long tasks.

25. *Mentation rate* measures the degree of active thoughtfulness or awareness of considerable ongoing mental activity.

26. *Distractability* measures concentration difficulty, distraction by noise, and inability to concentrate fully.

27. *Need for external stimulation* scales the degree to which an individual needs outside stimulation.

28. *Self-revelation* was designed specifically to assess the degree to which reporting or talking about daydreaming or inner experience is viewed negatively (low score) or positively (high score) by the respondents.

Sensation-Seeking Scales (SSS)

The Sensation-Seeking Scales (SSS; Zuckerman, 1975) attempt to differentiate between a number of ways in which individuals actively seek stimulation from their environments and the extent to which they actually do so (Zuckerman, 1975). The total battery consists of 72 forced-choice items and is scored for five factors, each representing a specific dimension of sensation seeking. Since the fifth scale is assessed for males only, it was omitted from this study. The four sensation-seeking scales administered were:

1. *General Sensation Seeking:* This factor scale indicates a preference for stimulating and exciting situations, involving some risk.
2. *Thrill and Adventure Seeking:* Included in this scale are items that assess desire to engage in outdoor sports or other activities involving elements of speed or danger.
3. *Experience Seeking:* This scale assesses the seeking of new experiences through the mind and senses, and through an unconventional, nonconforming life style.
4. *Disinhibition:* This scale measures the desire to find release through social disinhibition, drinking, partying, and variety in sexual patterns.

The reliability and evidence of validity for the SSS has been confirmed (Zuckerman, 1973, 1975). Subsequent research with the SSS has shown that the scale can be considered to be a measure of a generalized construct of individual differences with respect to stimulus (or arousal) seeking (Segal, 1973b, 1977).

The Sensation-Seeking Scales pose several minor problems for the present analyses. First, several items in the total pool ask directly about the individual's experience with drugs and alcohol. *These items were not used in our scoring of the scales.* Second, there are several items keyed for more than one of the four scales. For the multivariate analyses used in our procedures, this means that there is a slight redundancy among the measures due to the method of scale construction. The redundancy has *not* been eliminated so that the results will be directly comparable with previously published data on the instrument.

Locus of Control (LC)

Rotter's (1966) Locus of Control Scale (LC) is comprised of 29 items (23 keyed, 6 fillers) presented in a forced-choice format. The scale measures the degree to which individuals believe that reinforcement for one's behavior is contingent upon personal action (low scorers) or is a function of elements "outside" oneself (high scorers). Good reliability has been demonstrated for the instrument, and validity studies have included laboratory experiments as well as correlational studies (Lefcourt, 1976; Rotter, 1966).

Alcohol–Drug-Use Survey

This questionnaire (Segal, 1973a, 1974) asks about the extent, duration, and frequency of use of a variety of drugs and alcoholic beverages, as well as the reasons for use. On the basis of the Alcohol–Drug-Use Research survey, participants were classified into one of the following four categories:

1. *Nonusers of drugs.* This group consisted of subjects who reported never using alcohol and those who indicated that they had tried drinking alcohol only once or twice with subsequent abstention. All subjects in this group also reported no use of nonprescribed drugs.

2. *Alcohol-only users.* This group was composed of subjects whose use of alcohol ranged from several times a year to several times a week or more, and who reported no use of marijuana or other drugs.

3. *Marijuana-only users.* Included in this category were subjects who reported having tried marijuana (infrequently, frequently, and for experimental use) but who had not tried or used any other types or forms of nonprescribed drugs. Almost all of the subjects in this category also used or had used alcohol.

4. *Multiple drug use.* This classification was used to designate subjects who reported having used or tried any combination (frequently, infrequently, or experimentally) of the following types of agents without a prescription: marijuana (in addition to other agents); amphetamines, metamphetamines; pain-killers (codeine, morphine, etc.); tranquilizers; barbiturates; cocaine; hallucinogenics; and opiates. Subjects in this group also reported past or present use of alcohol.

Criterion group membership (Nonuse, Alcohol-Only, Marijuana-Only, Polydrug) was derived as follows. Each participant's Alcohol–Drug-Use Survey responses was reviewed initially for completion and accuracy of responses. The total instrument was initially developed so that there were several questions pertaining to the use or nonuse of specific substances. All such questions had to be answered consistently for the survey to be considered reliable for coding. Those surveys with gross inconsistency were deleted from the study together with other data collected from the participant. The same procedure was followed for each of the two sample years. Detailed forms of the Alcohol–Drug-Use Survey were given to all 1973 subjects and 418 (82%) of the 1974 subjects. The remaining 1974 subjects received an abbreviated form of the instrument, which allowed categorization but not detailed analysis of reasons for use.

Table 4.2 shows the number of subjects belonging to each drug-use category for the four samples formed by sex and year of testing (1973 males, 1973 females, 1974 males, 1974 females). In general, there is some confounding of sample and category of drug use ($\chi^2_9 = 55.12$, $p < .001$), but the calculation of standard association measures such as λ_{ab} (.035), an index of the increased predictability of column classification from row classification and vice versa, or the contingency coefficient (.219) indicates that the level of confounding is fairly small. Collapsing across the 2-year samples, we still find

TABLE 4.2
Cross Classifiction of the Subject Pool
(Year and Sex) by Usage Category[a]

	Male 1973	Female 1973	Male 1974	Female 1974	TOTAL
Nonusers	31 (11.6)	92 (28.5)	28 (12.1)	52 (19.0)	203 (18.5)
Alcohol Only	77 (28.8)	116 (35.9)	78 (33.8)	94 (34.3)	365 (33.3)
Marijuana Only	85 (31.8)	69 (21.4)	77 (33.3)	66 (24.1)	297 (27.1)
Polydrug	74 (27.8)	46 (14.2)	48 (20.8)	62 (22.6)	230 (21.0)
TOTAL	267	323	231	274	1095

[a]Numbers given are the number of respondents; numbers in parentheses are the percentages of the sample.

that the sex distributions of drug use are different ($\chi_3^2 = 38.55$, $p < .001$) and that a series of nonindependent z-tests indicates that there are higher percentages of female nonusers ($z = -5.20$), male marijuana users ($z = 3.68$), and male polydrug users ($z = 2.59$). These sex differences in type of use seem to be consistent with previous studies.

For the analyses on reasons for using drugs reported in Chapter 7, we have used a gating procedure for the selection of subjects. Since the Chapter 7 analyses provide detailed characterizations of the reasons for using alcohol and marijuana, and the private personality constructs, we will describe the necessary gating here and use those selected respondents for our characterization of the modal pattern of substance-use reasons. These analyses eliminate a few respondents who gave responses for one drug but not another but appear to not bias sample results away from those obtained from all individuals (including those with partial data).

In the analyses of reasons for using alcohol, we selected the 854 respondents who answered the question about alcohol-use reasons. Of these 854 individuals, 425 also gave reasons for their use of marijuana. Of the 425 individuals who gave reasons for their alcohol and marijuana use, 185 also had data on the frequency of use of the more illegal drugs (hallucinogenics, tranquilizers, stimulants, narcotics–cocaine) included in more detailed analyses.

The proportions of male and female subjects in the gated analyses were roughly comparable to those in the major analyses. For the alcohol-reasons subset, 52% were female. For the marijuana-reasons analyses, 45% were female. In the polydrug analyses, 46% of the subjects were female.

THE TESTING SESSION

Since strong attitudes existed in the society at the times of data collection (Fall 1973 and Fall 1974) about drug use by college students, the testing sessions were designed to be generally relaxed and informal. At both Murray and Yale, a large classroom was used for the testing. Participants were tested in groups ranging from 35 to 50 during a morning or afternoon session. Each student was given a packet that contained an informed consent statement, the Personality Research Form, Imaginal Process Inventory, Sensation-Seeking Scales, Locus of Control, and drug-use questionnaires. The students were then directed to follow the instructions for the individual instruments and were allowed to work at their own reasonable speed.

During the testing period, participants were allowed to get up and walk around when fatigued. Furthermore, periodic breaks were scheduled at about 1-hour intervals during the testing period when various forms of relaxing material were introduced to the subjects. At Yale, 15-minute periods of cartoons were shown. At Murray, current "Top 40" and folk music was played. Moreover, participants were encouraged to stretch, talk, and generally wind-down from the responsibility of completing extensive questionnaires. Refreshments were provided at Yale in the form of soft drinks, candy bars, and other "junk" food. At Murray, students were provided with coins to feed the "junk" food machines available outside the testing room.

Since we wished to maintain contact with the participants during the subsequent months of the study, the students were asked to remember their identification numbers and to make up fictitious names with which to code their data. Much energy was invested by the respondents in this task, and it seemed to be a source of great amusement to them. Among the names chosen by the subjects were the current (at that time) president of Yale (Kingman Brewster, whose name seemed preferred by several students reporting a lot of experience with illicit drugs), Phoebe Phillantrophe, a variety of Watergate figures, Meal Ticket, Chester Drawers, and at least a dozen students who styled themselves as the current president of the United States, as well as many names based on drug experience such as "Bad Trip" and "High Times." There also was no attempt to control spontaneous comical utterances during the testing session by the participants; in fact, such declarations were implicitly encouraged and such comments as "Why am I being asked this again?", "What a stupid question!", and the like served to keep the sessions somewhat spontaneous. It is our belief that the low amount of control exercised during the sessions helped to ensure that the respondents would accurately complete the numerous items on the questionnaires. This belief is supported by the fact that only 55 questionnaires had to be discarded because of large amounts of missing data. Furthermore, there were only four subjects whose data was suspect for random responding as indicated by the PRF t Responding Scale included in the battery. That is, 95% of the participants yielded usable data.

DESCRIPTION OF DRUG USE PATTERNS
IN THE SAMPLE

Before beginning an inspection of the hypotheses of the study and formal inferential statistical tests conducted using the questionnaire data, it is helpful to put the data and the sample in their proper context by examining the frequency of use of the various substances and the reasons that the respondents gave for their own substance use. An evaluation of the overall pattern of drug and alcohol use, and the reasons for use, followed a remarkably consistent pattern in the 2 years sampled. Consequently, the following discussion presents pooled results from all samples. Relevant sex differences are given when they reached statistical significance.

Alcohol

With respect to alcohol use, it is apparent that drinking started prior to entering college life, with the majority of respondents (68%) drinking frequently for more than 1 year. As might be anticipated, due to social role expectations, among other factors, more males started drinking earlier than females; males also drink more frequently than women in the sample. Drinkers of both sexes indicated clearly that one main reason for drinking is "just to be sociable" (76%). Other reasons for drinking were "hot weather" (28%) and "feeling under pressure, tense" (26%). The pressure motive is consistent with cultural expectations that alcohol relaxes one and aids in the reduction of tension. Other reasons for using alcohol were "having nothing else to do" (28%), "feeling sad" (16%), "loneliness" (19%), "hard work" (13%), "problems" (17%), and "just feeling you have to" (20%).

When respondents were asked to be more specific about their reasons for drinking, social motives were primarily given, such as use on special occasions (42%) and "makes get-togethers more fun" (38%). Additional important reasons for drinking were: "helps you relax" (35%), "feel better" (19%), "makes you less shy" (16%), and "makes you feel happier" (18%). An apparent significant motive for drinking, therefore, is its "social lubricant" effect. Alcohol is perceived as conducive to the ease and relaxation that are part of our day-to-day living pattern, and as useful for relieving self-consciousness and raising one's level of tolerance for inadequacies perceived in oneself and others. Thus alcohol serves a purpose for social occasions as well as for the meeting of personal needs in overcoming personal inhibitions. This latter function of alcohol is particularly significant in that other reasons for drinking noted were "makes you worry less about what other people think of you" (11%), "feeling mad" (10%), and "helps you forget your problems" (9%). Using Bonferroni-type simultaneous confidence intervals, it was found that a higher percentage of male drinkers than female drinkers cited as reasons "hot weather," "hard work," "not getting ahead," "helps you relax," "helps you forget," and "makes you more satisfied with yourself."

Marijuana

Of the total sample (1095 students), 48% indicated having used marijuana once or more. In any event, almost half of the subjects reported some kind of experience with, or exposure to, marijuana. This rather high incidence of marijuana use is generally consistent with recent estimates of the use of marijuana on campuses, which have ranged from a low of 40% to a high of 60% (Blum, 1969). Our findings are also quite consistent with reports of incidence of marijuana use from other sections of the country (Brantley, 1975; Fagerberg, 1975; Ferraro & Billings, 1974a,b) where the marijuana-use rate was described as more than 50% in samples of college students. It appears, as noted by Grinspoon (1971), that few students go through college without having tried marijuana and that, as Segal and Singer (1976) have pointed out, drinking and moderate drug use in the form of marijuana may be considered a normative experience for late adolescents. Our research focuses on attempts to link this moderate experimentation with drugs to identification of personality characteristics of such users, and to explore the life styles and expectations about drinking and drug use held by such individuals.

In examining further patterns of marijuana use in the present sample, a predominant finding was that a clear majority of respondents who used marijuana had obtained it, for their first experience, almost always from a close friend. Initial marijuana use occurred most frequently in a small group of friends (57%) or with one friend (25%). The setting in which marijuana was used most frequently was in a friend's home (25%). Use in a car (17%), or in public places such as parks or beaches, was also reported. Few respondents apparently smoked marijuana in their own homes (10%), seemingly using it more in social contexts. Interestingly, the vast majority of respondents (67%) indicated that their first use was a spontaneous experience.

It is rather apparent that what is most prominent in these findings is social influence. Knowing other people, particularly close friends, who use marijuana is clearly a strong determinant related to the initiation of marijuana use. Social peers provide an opportunity for conformity to their current value systems and behavior. Those who seek to join peer groups identify with their values and are accepted by the groups (Sherif & Sherif, 1969). The group provides an opportunity for shared experiences and for reinforcing behaviors compatible with illicit drug use. Thus, while the initial experience of marijuana use seems to be clearly a social phenomenon, a finding quite consistent with that reported by the National Commission on Marijuana and Drug Abuse (1972), further important questions are: What motives does the individual give for using marijuana, and what determines the nature and pattern of continued usage? Stating the latter issue another way, what personality characteristics are related to marijuana use? Another problem is that of determining what kind of person is most susceptible to peer pressure. Additional parts of our research attempt to address these issues.

With respect to individual motives or reasons for using marijuana, an interesting paradox occurs. Although it is apparent that social influences contribute significantly to beginning experiences with marijuana, self-reports from our subjects pertaining to motives for using marijuana do not emphasize peer pressure or seeking group acceptance. Rather, the chief reasons for marijuana use were reported as satisfying curiosity about what the marijuana experience is like (88%) and to "experience something new and different" (70%). Additional motives, in rank order, were to "get kicks or get high" (39%), "expand my awareness and understanding of things" (17%), "relate better to my friends" (16%), and "get better insight into myself" (11%). In summary, the most common reasons given for use of marijuana in our survey center around: (1) curiosity and the apparent desire to use it to satisfy a need for excitement, "kicks," or pleasure; and (2) stimulation associated with a wish to seek an expansion of the capacity for self-awareness. Although marijuana use is also linked to a need to relate better to one's friends, it is not a primary motive in our sample. In general, the reasons that relate to one's social experiences for use of alcohol were found to outweigh similar reasons for the use of marijuana. Also, marijuana as a means of overcoming personal problems, such as tension or stress, was not used to the same extent as alcohol. These overall patterns of self-attributed reasons are comparable with the results of surveys cited by the National Commission on Marijuana and Drug Abuse (1972). Since our items were patterned after items used in the national surveys, the parallel response rates are an indirect validity and sample check.

The findings, taken as a whole, indicate that marijuana use is related to personality as well as to environmental or social variables. Rather than peer pressure being a major (if not the most significant) variable associated with marijuana use, it begins to appear that, based on our findings as well as those reported by the National Commission (1972), personality variables alone contribute significantly to marijuana use. The need to satisfy curiosity, desire for a "high," and desire to expand self-awareness, for example, are personality or inner experience variables more than indicators of social pressures. Consequently, it appears that peer relationships or social activities connected with marijuana use provide a socially sanctioned environment in which personal needs can be satisfied for youth. Thus, while marijuana smoking is claimed to be exciting and a pleasurable social activity to be shared and enjoyed with one's peers, the social environment created serves as a setting for satisfying more personal and perhaps deeper psychological motives for using marijuana. Additional aspects of our research address themselves to this contention.

Research surveys investigating marijuana use have indicated that many of those who tried marijuana discontinued it shortly thereafter and that others give it up after a period of use (National Commission on Marijuana and Drug Abuse, 1972). Our findings parallel those reported by the National Commission. The predominant reason for discontinuing use of marijuana was loss of interest, followed by recognition of its illegality and by fear of damage to the body and to the mind. The data from our survey continue to indicate, as was revealed by the National Commission (1972), that the basic reason for ceasing to use marijuana is loss of interest, while concern about its effects and illegality are also significant factors in the decision to refrain from or to discontinue its use.

In summary, the results of our two surveys indicate that marijuana was used, whether experimentally or regularly, by a large number of our respondents. It is quite apparent that use of marijuana no longer represents a fad—rather, there is concentrated use in the young adult, collegiate group. The present data indicate that marijuana is used not primarily as a social lubricant, as is alcohol, but as a means of gratifying a need for the effect of the drug: the "high" and to expand one's self-awareness. Thus it seems that different personal and social connotations have been attributed to alcohol and marijuana and that each is being used to satisfy different needs. Although social factors play a role in influencing marijuana use, it appears likely that personality factors may have a more important role and that social influences may shape the emerging pattern of marijuana use.

Stimulants

Of those sampled in our study, 16% indicated experience with a drug classified as a stimulant. This finding is lower than that reported by Ferraro and Billings (1974b) for thier 1970–1972 sample period, in which use of stimulants averaged 24.3%. It would appear that a decrease in use of stimulants as drugs of abuse may be occurring, perhaps due to more careful control, a change noted by Ferraro and Billings (1974b). As might be anticipated, the principal reason given for use of stimulants was to achieve more "pep or energy" (50%), followed by a desire to satisfy curiosity about the drug experience (42%), and a wish to experience something "new and exciting" (40%). As with marijuana, the use of amphetamines or stimulants is primarily for the effect of the drug, and not to overcome personal inadequacies; only 11% of the respondents said they used the drug to combat depression.

LSD and Other Hallucinogens

The use of LSD occurred in 9% of our sample, a statistic indicating a decrease in the number of college students trying LSD when our figures are compared to a 13% LSD rate reported by the National Commission (1972) in a sample of college students. This lower rate is apparently reflective of a change in attitude toward experimenting with LSD. Nevertheless, the two leading reasons cited for using LSD were to "experience something new and different" (73%) and "satisfy curiosity about what it is like (73%). Two additional reasons for using LSD were for the experience of the "high" (60%) and to expand one's awareness (58%). The drug was also used by some to achieve better self-awareness.

Depressants and Tranquilizers

Of our sample, 14% reported having tried some form of a "downer" once or more, a figure slightly less than the average rate of 16.7% reported by Ferraro and Billings (1974b) in their 3-year study. Our findings are generally consistent, however, with those cited by Fagerberg (1975) with respect to use of barbiturates. Chief among the reasons checked for using such drugs were to "experience something new and different" (33%), "satisfy curiosity" (32%), and to experience the "high" generated by the drug used (26%). Interestingly, "downers" were reported to have been used more than any other drug, except for alcohol, to "relieve anxiety or tension" (21%). Thus depressants appear to be used not only to obtain a "high" but also to provide escape or relief from anxiety or pain, a finding consistent with the medical use of these drugs.

Narcotics

Use of some form of a narcotic was experienced by 6% of our sample. Again the primary motives apparently contributing to one or more experiences with a form of a narcotics were to "experience something new and different" (68%), "satisfy curiosity" (60%), and experience the "high" (35%) the drugs produce.

SUMMARY

Overall, the results of our survey of alcohol and drug use appear to be generally representative of patterns of use of college students during the academic years 1973–1974 and 1974–1975. There seems to be a trend of slightly reduced use in our sample of all but marijuana and alcohol, but other drugs continue to be experienced. Use of alcohol is strongly related, for our sample, to social motives and to reduction of personal conflicts. Alcohol is not, it seems, generally used for the "high" it brings. Rather, its use might be associated with an "escape" motive—that is, to help to overcome or reduce the effect of personal frustration or conflict. In contrast to these uses of alcohol, marijuana and other drugs are used, it appears, for several different reasons, one of the chief ones being as a means of achieving a "high."

5 Organization of Private Personality Among Male and Female Drug and Alcohol Users

OVERVIEW

As we noted in earlier chapters, many recent groups of investigators have contrasted individuals who use drugs and alcohol with individuals who use neither class of substance on a variety of personality measures. Furthermore, we have previously pointed out that these investigations seem to converge in demonstrating consistent quantitative differences between users and non-users of drugs and alcohol. It appears that these replicated differences relate to an underlying dimension that might be called *externality* or a *generalized susceptibility* to social pressure and a corresponding need for stimulation.

Studies contrasting the scores of groups of drug and alcohol users with the scores of nonusers can only show those group tendencies that differ along the same psychological dimensions. Several writers (Allport, 1961; D. Bem & Allen, 1974) have hypothesized that intact groups of individuals might differ not only in quantitative aspects of personality but also in more qualitative ways. That is, there might be different organizations of personality variables (or differential personality structures) within groups of individuals classified in some particular manner.

To the best of our knowledge, there have been no empirical attempts to demonstrate that personality organization is qualitatively the same in users of drugs and alcohol as in nonusers of these substances. Similarly, although many writers have demonstrated sex differences in measures of personality, there have been few corresponding attempts to show that the same domains of variables are organized differently in males and females.

The notion of differential personality structure is relatively important within the area of drug-use research. First, although it has been rather typical to study differences in level of personality functioning, there has been no concomitant attempt to determine if the personalities of drug users are organized in a different manner. Since many of the psychoactive drugs do engender personal experiences that are qualitatively different from those experienced without drugs, it is possible that periodic ingestion of substances will lead to a fundamental reorganization of the private personality in either the aspects of needs or inner experience. Such reorganization could be manifested in the use group as either quite different interrelationships between specific needs or as different mixtures of quality and theme while engaging in fantasy. Indeed, we believe that if qualitative differences can be demonstrated between users and nonusers of drugs, such qualitative differences in private personality would be at least as important for understanding the phenomenology of the drug experience as simple mean differences between groups of users and nonusers. Second, since there have been so many studies contrasting individuals on *presumably* the same psychological dimensions, it seems important that we should establish that we are indeed contrasting those in our sample who use substances with their nonuser peers *on the same dimensions of private personality.*

The question of whether different organizations of psychological variables occur in different groups can be answered in a rather straightforward manner using factor analysis. In the case of drug use, we may factor a selected set of personality variables in each of several types of drug-use groups and then determine if the same dimensions (factors) underlie the relationships among the personality variables. To the extent that one can match factors found in the groups of users of drugs and alcohol with those found in the nonuser group, it may then be inferred that there is little qualitative difference in the personality structure attributable to substance use. Such a demonstration can also show that some of the factors are relatively more stable (or invariant) across the groups than other factors. The same general procedure and logic may be applied to groups differing in sex, or more generally, in any reliable classification variable.

The present chapter has two parts. In the first section, we examine the organization of the Murray needs measured by our test battery and contrast users and nonusers of substances as well as males and females on the organization of need patterns. In the second portion of the chapter, we examine the same issue in the inner experience area of the private personality measured by the Imaginal Processes Inventory. Both sets of analyses are essentially parallel, and those small differences in exact statistical treatment are pointed out at appropriate places. We should note that we chose to analyze the implied structure in the two batteries of tests separately for several reasons. First, while each of the batteries is theoretically linked to the total concept of the private personality, we believe that each battery measures conceptually, if not statistically, separable aspects of the private personality. Thus it is possible that separate analyses might reveal that the dimensions underlying one of the two domains is very stable across the groups of drug users while the other is not. Second, if the two batteries were analyzed in the same analysis, it is possible that the factor analysis of two different domains simultaneously might be biased toward greater similarity of organization across groups than a separate set of analyses would reveal. The bias would be caused by only a few dimensions linking the two domains being stable in the groups, and within-domain covariation being quite different. As we shall see, however, the notion of bias if the analyses had been done simultaneously is moot; the present results are quite clear in their implications.

We first turn our attention to the various needs that were studied in our investigation.

THE ORGANIZATION OF NEEDS

Two previous studies (Nesselroade & Baltes, 1975; Stricker, 1974) have investigated the factor pattern of the PRF scales. These two studies have both used undifferentiated high-school students of both sexes as subjects. Neither study was concerned with the stability of the factorial results over different types of individuals.

Method

Subjects.   This set of analyses uses data from all members of our college sample (see Chapter 4 for a detailed description).

Instruments.   Jackson's (1967) PRF was administered to each subject. The PRF is a psychometrically sophisticated inventory that measures a variety of Murray's (1938) needs. Individuals tested in 1973 were given the short version (Form A) of the PRF, which measures 14 needs and one response tendency, and individuals tested in 1974 were administered the long version (Form AA), which includes six additional content scales and one additional response-style scale. For the present analyses, only the 15 scales given to all subjects were used. The variables analyzed were the needs for Achievement, Affiliation, Aggression, Autonomy, Dominance, Endurance, Exhibitionism, Harmavoidance, Impulsivity, Nurturance, Order, Play, Social Recognition, and Understanding, and the scale for Infrequent Responding.

Categorization of Drug- and Alcohol-Use Patterns.   During the same testing session in which the PRF was administered, each subject also completed a questionnaire (Segal, 1973a, 1974) about his or her drug and alcohol use. On the basis of the responses to this questionnaire, individuals were classified as those who had used neither alcohol nor drugs, those who had used alcohol but not drugs, those who had used marijuana (and in most cases, alcohol) but not other drugs, and those who had used a variety of drugs including marijuana. Further details of this categorization have been given in Chapter 4.

Data Analysis. Each of the individuals in the total subject pool could be classified in three ways by sex, by year of testing, and by pattern of substance use. We decided to divide the total sample by usage pattern and by a combination of year of testing and sex to yield eight approximately equal, but overlapping, subgroups of several hundred individuals each.[1] Table 4.1 (Chapter 4) shows the number of individuals in each of the 16 possible cells. The data for each of eight groups—all nonusers of drugs and alcohol, all users of alcohol-only; all users of marijuana-only, multiple-drug users, 1973 males, 1974 males, 1973 females, 1974 females—were then factored using the method of maximum likelihood (see Lawley & Maxwell, 1971).

The statistical test developed by Lawley (1940) was used to determine the number of significant maximum likelihood factors in each of the groups. At least six significant factors were found for nonusers [$\chi^2_{32} = 40.55, p > .05$], alcohol-only users [$\chi^2_{31} = 55.66, p < .05$], marijuana-only users [$\chi^2_{30} = 33.50, p > .05$], 1973 females [$\chi^2_{30} = 41.21, p > .05$], 1973 males [$\chi^2_{30} = 37.03, p > .05$], and 1974 males [$\chi^2_{31} = 44.03, p > .05$]. Only five significant factors were found for multiple-drug users [$\chi^2_{41} = 34.31, p > .05$], and 1974 females [$\chi^2_{40} = 53.45, p > .05$]. Heywood variables were found for the Nonuser (2), Alcohol (1), Polydrug (1), and 1974 male (1) analyses and were treated in the standard manner (Jöreskog, 1967). Because it seems desirable to consider the same number of factors in each of the subgroup analyses, and

---

[1]It would have also been possible to study the factorial stability of the two instruments across the two different colleges at which the data were collected. These comparisons were not undertaken for the following reason. First, our primary intent in collecting data at two different universities was to obtain a larger and more heterogeneous sample than would have been possible at either school alone. Second, there are differences between the subjects at the two colleges on several dimensions such as general academic achievement prior to college, socioeconomic status, religious background, and race. A simple comparison between the two colleges would do little to delineate the specific difference that was responsible for inducing factor stability or instability. Third, pooling the subjects from the two colleges had the effect of providing extremely good approximations to the normal distribution of the PRF content scales.

Each of the four groups formed by categorizing the subjects by drug and alcohol use were independent of one another. Similarly, each of the four groups formed by categorizing the subjects by year of testing and sex were independent. The two sets of four groups were, however, not independent, and there is a slight confounding of the sex and alcohol/drug-use effects on factor stability. We did not factor the data in each of the 16 possible cells, because the frequencies were too small in many instances to yield stable results.

since there were six significant factors in six of the eight subgroups, six factor solutions were calculated for the two subgroups with only five significant factors.

Additionally, six maximum likelihood factors were extracted from the correlation matrix obtained from pooling all 1095 subjects. These factors were rotated to approximately oblique simple structure using the direct quartimin algorithm (Jennrich & Sampson, 1966) with Kaiser (1958) normalization. Hakstian and Abell (1974) have shown that the direct quartimin procedure produces solutions that are comparable to those produced by a skilled hand rotator, whereas Bailey and Guertin (1973) have suggested that direct quartimin may be the most invariant of several commonly used methods of oblique simple structure rotation.

Each of the eight subgroup factor matrices was rotated to a position of best least-squares fit to the total rotated factor pattern matrix using Huba's (1975) program for Browne's (1972) direct, restricted, oblique least-square alignment (Procrustean) rotation algorithm. In this procedure, the unrotated factor pattern matrix from each of the subgroup analyses was rotated so as to have as good an alignment with the total rotated factor pattern matrix as the data would allow. After each of the eight subgroup factor matrices was maximally aligned to the total matrix, factor similarity (or congruence) coefficients (Harman, 1967; Mulaik, 1972; Tucker, 1951) were calculated between all pairs of corresponding factors.

The use of Procrustean rotations to some common target matrix, while not ordinarily undertaken in the applied literature, seems preferable to rotating each of the subgroup matrices independently toward simple structure (Mulaik, 1972). Although the alignment process capitalizes on chance components of the individual factor matrices, rotations to simple structure also have this property (Humphreys, Ilgen, McGrath, & Montanelli, 1969). As Mulaik (1972) noted, independent rotations to simple structure can lead to the impression that there is less factor similarity in the subgroups than actually exists.

Results

Factor Pattern Coefficients. Table 5.1 shows the loadings[2] of each variable on the first factor in the nine aligned matrices. Simple inspection is sufficient to determine that these factors are all highly similar; the congruence coefficients between all pairs of factors range from .97 to .99. This factor has consistently high positive loadings for the needs for Affiliation and Nurturance. The factor also has consistently negative loadings for the needs for

---

[2]The usage of the term *factor loading* has been ambiguous in the psychological literature. In this book, we use the term *loading* to refer to a primary-factor pattern coefficient.

TABLE 5.1
Factor 1 Found in Each Analysis of the PRF

Need	Total	Non-users	Alcohol only	Marijuana only	Poly-drug	Male 1973	Male 1974	Female 1973	Female 1974
Achievement	.09	.09	.05	.07	.14	.14	.13	.04	.06
Affiliation	.77	.94	.79	.76	.73	.76	.62	.82	.79
Aggression	-.35	-.37	-.39	-.30	-.31	-.31	-.37	-.30	-.27
Autonomy	-.43	-.54	-.47	-.45	-.44	-.54	-.53	-.44	-.46
Dominance	.01	.01	-.02	.01	.03	.03	.09	.07	-.04
Endurance	.00	.16	.03	.03	-.01	.11	-.03	.19	.12
Exhibitionism	.09	.08	.11	.07	.06	.01	.09	.04	.15
Harmavoidance	.10	.16	.09	.10	.06	.03	-.05	.14	.07
Impulsivity	.07	.03	.11	.09	.07	.11	.05	.07	.05
Nurturance	.64	.63	.61	.65	.66	.62	.63	.74	.56
Order	.04	-.08	.09	.08	.08	.06	.02	-.02	.06
Play	.30	.28	.29	.30	.32	.35	.27	.31	.29
Social Recognition	.08	.13	.11	.04	.03	.07	.04	.08	.06
Understanding	.12	.08	.21	.13	.04	.04	.11	-.08	.08
Infrequency	-.29	-.18	-.27	-.35	-.27	-.24	-.30	-.29	-.45

TABLE 5.2

Factor 2 Found in Each Analysis of the PRF

Need	Total	Non-users	Alcohol only	Marijuana only	Poly-drug	Male		Female	
						1973	1974	1973	1974
Achievement	.20	.17	.24	.13	.18	.27	.16	.15	.16
Affiliation	.19	.23	.14	.18	.18	.18	.23	.12	.18
Aggression	.36	.34	.37	.31	.44	.52	.39	.40	.36
Autonomy	.16	.14	.25	.12	.15	.13	.20	.10	.18
Dominance	.73	.73	.66	.68	.84	.65	.67	.88	.66
Endurance	-.02	.13	.03	.09	-.03	.28	.02	.12	.04
Exhibitionism	.73	.85	.79	.76	.62	.73	.71	.72	.77
Harmavoidance	-.18	-.19	-.12	-.13	-.24	-.28	-.14	-.21	-.09
Impulsivity	-.01	.12	.13	.09	.08	.12	.02	.12	.03
Nurturance	-.01	-.10	.06	-.03	.05	-.04	.00	.04	.03
Order	.08	.12	.10	.09	.17	.18	.08	.11	.09
Play	.24	.23	.23	.20	.23	.30	.26	.21	.25
Social Recognition	.29	.29	.36	.29	.32	.32	.32	.31	.29
Understanding	.20	.16	.15	.17	.24	.00	.21	.12	.23
Infrequency	.01	.08	-.05	.03	.05	.02	.00	.07	.09

Aggression and Autonomy. The need for Play loads moderately, in a positive direction, on the factor. Neither need for Social Recognition nor need for Dominance load on the factor, indicating that this *Generalized Need for Group Membership* is relatively independent of one's motive for belonging to the group.

The loadings of the variables on the second factor in each analysis are shown in Table 5.2. This second factor is again quite stable, with the factor similarity coefficients between the pairs of factors ranging from .94 to .99. The needs for Dominance and Exhibitionism consistently load at a very high positive level, and the needs for Aggression, Play, and Social Recognition load consistently in a positive direction at a moderate level. This factor would appear to be the *Extraversion* factor commonly found in most personality inventories.

The third factor in each analysis seems to be conceptually stable, although the loadings do fluctuate somewhat from one subgroup to another. Table 5.3 shows the loadings of the variables on the third factor found in each subgroup analysis. Of primary interest is the fact that each of the subgroup factors has a high positive loading for the need for Impulsivity and a high negative loading for the need for Order. There are also consistent positive, albeit small, loadings for the needs for Exhibitionism and Play and a consistent negative loading for Harmavoidance. Consequently, this factor appears to be a *Generalized Tendency to Impulsive Action,* or alternatively, an ego-strength dimension. The factor similarity coefficients between the pairs of factors range from .82 to .99, with the vast majority of the coefficients exceeding .94. The appearance of minor amounts of instability may be due to the generally high communality of the Impulsivity scale.

Table 5.4 shows the loadings of the variables on the fourth factor found in each analysis. These loadings are relatively unstable across the analyses. The factor similarity coefficients between the pairs of factors range from .67 to .99. In general, this factor is loaded in a high positive manner by the needs for Endurance and Achievement. Thus it might be concluded that this factor represents the *Generalized Achievement Motivation Dimension* that has been frequently studied by personality researchers. The other variables load somewhat inconsistently on the factor. For instance, the needs for Nurturance and Order load on the factor in the nonuser group, suggesting that achievement motivation is linked to social competency in a fairly traditional manner for these individuals. These variables are not consistently related to the factor in the other groups. The need for Understanding loads on the factor in the 1973 male, 1973 female, and nonuser groups but is not consistently related to the factor in the other groups. Thus, even though an achievement motivation factor can be found in each of the eight subgroups, this factor changes somewhat in its expression for different groups of individuals.

The fifth factor found in each of the analyses is fairly stable across subgroups. The congruence coefficients between pairs of factors range from

TABLE 5.3

Factor 3 Found in Each Analysis of the PRF

Need	Total	Non-users	Alcohol only	Mari-juana only	Poly-drug	Male 1973	Male 1974	Female 1973	Female 1974
Achievement	-.03	-.28	-.11	.07	.02	-.01	-.03	-.03	.00
Affiliation	.07	-.09	.13	.13	.09	.09	.10	.17	.02
Aggression	.16	.12	.06	.26	.13	.11	.19	.21	.14
Autonomy	-.01	-.10	-.13	.07	-.03	-.01	-.01	.08	-.05
Dominance	-.11	.08	.00	-.17	-.15	-.09	-.14	-.13	-.11
Endurance	-.07	-.12	-.04	-.15	-.09	-.25	-.08	-.12	-.11
Exhibitionism	.12	.16	.21	.09	.25	.26	.15	.17	.13
Harmavoidance	-.22	-.41	-.40	-.21	-.30	-.23	-.26	-.21	-.37
Impulsivity	1.03	.63	.64	.77	.96	.84	1.03	.82	.89
Nurturance	.09	.16	-.02	.11	.02	.07	.09	-.04	.05
Order	-.45	-.73	-.67	-.60	-.50	-.62	-.43	-.63	-.46
Play	.14	.33	.31	.27	.16	.22	.14	.28	.21
Social Recognition	-.09	-.14	-.18	-.09	-.13	-.10	-.16	-.09	-.07
Understanding	.03	-.03	-.07	.07	-.06	.06	-.03	.07	-.01
Infrequency	.05	-.14	.10	.08	.00	.07	.05	-.04	-.03

TABLE 5.4
Factor 4 Found in Each Analysis of the PRF

Need	Total	Non-users	Alcohol only	Mari-juana only	Poly-drug	Male 1973	Male 1974	Female 1973	Female 1974
Achievement	.46	.48	.54	.68	.45	.60	.47	.69	.53
Affiliation	.04	-.06	.09	.02	.06	.09	.04	.20	.01
Aggression	-.05	-.09	-.03	-.11	.01	-.42	-.14	-.17	-.07
Autonomy	-.01	.05	-.03	.01	-.01	.14	.03	.09	.06
Dominance	.12	.24	.21	.17	.03	.26	.16	.07	.18
Endurance	.94	.61	.88	.67	.99	.48	.95	.58	.69
Exhibitionism	-.01	-.03	-.05	-.05	.06	.41	.03	.01	-.11
Harmavoidance	-.16	-.33	-.20	-.28	-.14	.07	-.08	-.23	-.28
Impulsivity	-.01	-.15	-.02	-.09	-.06	-.18	.00	-.13	.01
Nurturance	.14	.41	.14	.18	.16	.19	.11	.08	.37
Order	.13	.27	.16	.13	.08	.10	.07	.14	.24
Play	-.12	-.20	-.17	-.12	-.14	-.30	-.15	-.10	-.16
Social Recognition	-.11	-.18	-.21	-.12	-.07	-.20	-.12	-.06	-.12
Understanding	.06	.35	.07	.04	.18	.51	.02	.40	.12
Infrequency	.06	-.14	.10	.06	.08	.13	.01	.01	.12

.88 to .99. The loadings on this set of factors are shown in Table 5.5. There are consistent negative loadings for the needs for Harmavoidance and Social Recognition, and a consistent positive loading for need Autonomy. This factor can be conceived of as a generalized need for what might be called a *"Bohemian" Life Style,* or what Suchman (1968) has termed a "hang-loose" ethic. Alternately, this factor may be thought of as a generalized need toward independent action and attitudes. Individuals scoring high on this factor crave autonomy, describe themselves as relatively fearless in taking risks to achieve autonomy, and have little desire to achieve recognition from their peers.

Table 5.6 shows the loadings of the variables on the sixth factor found in each of the analyses. This factor, like the fourth factor, is somewhat unstable, with the factor similarity coefficients between the pairs of factors ranging from .73 to .98. Indeed, the pattern of instability for this factor parallels that of the fourth factor; the factor found in the nonuser group is most unlike those found in the other groups. Over all subgroupings, the factor has consistent positive loadings for the need for Play and consistent negative loadings for the needs for Achievement and Understanding. Inspection of the items comprising the PRF Play scale has led us to believe that this measure primarily taps a desire for organized social play. In light of this observation, it is not difficult to reconcile the negative loadings of the needs for Achievement and Understanding on this factor.

Factor Correlations.   Since the same factors have been identified in each of the subgroup analyses, it is appropriate to inquire if the correlations among these factors are about the same in each subgroup. Table 5.7 shows the correlations between each pair of factors within each aligned factor pattern matrix. It should be noted that the Procrustean procedure itself does not guarantee that the correlations among the oblique factors will be the same in the aligned matrices, and indeed, in a "forced" solution the correlations will be quite dissimilar. In spite of this freedom, the correlations are stable. Such invariance of the factor correlations is yet another indication that motivational organization in each of the groups is approximately the same.

Validation of the Procrustean Rotations.   A variety of authors (see Horn & Knapp, 1973, for a review) have argued that Procrustean rotations capitalize on chance to an inordinately large degree and can create factorially stable results even when such results are illusory. There is no statistical procedure for validating Procrustean rotations (Browne, 1972; Mulaik, 1972), and therefore a Monte Carlo procedure was used to demonstrate the validity of the Procrustean transformations undertaken in this study.

Expanding upon the procedures of Horn and Knapp (1973) and Jackson and Morf (1974), Huba et al. (1977a,b) have suggested that researchers should

TABLE 5.5
Factor 5 Found in Each Analysis of the PRF

Need	Total	Non-users	Alcohol only	Mari-juana only	Poly-drug	Male 1973	Male 1974	Female 1973	Female 1974
Achievement	-.07	.09	-.01	-.16	-.10	-.10	-.04	-.12	-.12
Affiliation	.00	.14	.01	-.10	-.04	-.10	.01	-.08	.03
Aggression	-.25	-.06	-.23	-.32	-.20	-.27	-.21	-.19	-.16
Autonomy	.58	.57	.77	.52	.65	.56	.70	.49	.60
Dominance	.06	.08	.02	.08	.06	.04	.02	.09	.06
Endurance	.04	.16	.05	.13	.04	.23	.04	.18	.15
Exhibitionism	-.03	-.17	-.14	.07	-.09	-.13	-.13	-.06	-.04
Harmavoidance	-.42	-.36	-.28	-.38	-.36	-.55	-.41	-.55	-.26
Impulsivity	-.12	.09	.13	.03	-.06	.03	-.09	.01	-.04
Nurturance	-.07	-.14	.06	-.03	.06	.04	-.02	.08	-.13
Order	-.27	-.34	-.29	-.24	-.24	-.16	-.22	-.24	-.22
Play	.16	.03	.02	.04	.15	.11	.24	.00	.13
Social Recognition	-.58	-.57	-.43	-.63	-.57	-.56	-.53	-.62	-.63
Understanding	.30	.19	.31	.25	.34	.15	.37	.19	.31
Infrequency	.04	.23	.07	-.02	.05	.13	.00	.21	-.01

TABLE 5.6
Factor 6 Found in Each Analysis of the PRF

Need	Total	Non-users	Alcohol only	Mari-juana only	Poly-drug	Male 1973	Male 1974	Female 1973	Female 1974
Achievement	-.42	-.45	-.41	-.36	-.50	-.62	-.37	-.44	-.48
Affiliation	.20	.29	.29	.11	.17	.23	.16	.23	.32
Aggression	.11	.21	.23	.03	.18	-.13	.06	.01	.11
Autonomy	-.12	-.06	-.06	-.19	-.03	.02	-.21	-.12	-.06
Dominance	-.08	-.04	-.13	.05	-.12	.00	-.09	-.19	.04
Endurance	.04	-.30	-.04	-.09	.05	-.35	.05	-.25	-.12
Exhibitionism	.02	-.07	-.06	.02	.01	.31	.02	.07	-.07
Harmavoidance	-.15	-.16	-.16	-.19	-.02	.02	-.20	-.31	-.07
Impulsivity	-.02	.31	.24	.01	.03	-.06	-.03	.07	.08
Nurturance	-.04	.06	.05	.00	.06	-.02	-.17	.05	.07
Order	.00	.33	.15	-.01	-.02	.10	-.05	.19	.05
Play	.57	.41	.41	.56	.56	.53	.69	.51	.39
Social Recognition	.12	.03	.20	.08	.21	.08	.17	.24	.09
Understanding	-.47	-.27	-.49	-.64	-.37	-.30	-.49	-.25	-.43
Infrequency	.03	.02	.20	-.02	-.03	-.02	.03	.03	.16

TABLE 5.7
Correlations Among the Factors in Each Group

Factor pair	Total	Non-users	Alcohol only	Marijuana only	Poly-drug	Male 1973	Male 1974	Female 1973	Female 1974
1 and 2	.03	.06	.00	.16	.06	.20	.25	.10	.01
1 and 3	-.08	-.05	-.02	.06	-.04	-.05	-.09	-.16	-.07
1 and 4	.09	-.04	-.04	.05	.02	-.09	.15	-.07	.04
1 and 5	-.17	-.03	-.14	-.06	-.07	-.04	.11	-.08	-.15
1 and 6	.02	-.18	.02	.04	.10	-.14	-.16	.06	-.15
2 and 3	.26	.08	.12	.24	.14	.05	.28	.19	.24
2 and 4	.22	-.04	.20	.18	.19	-.10	.10	.01	.23
2 and 5	-.01	.13	.05	-.06	-.10	-.03	-.04	.14	-.02
2 and 6	.11	.07	.13	.04	.07	-.23	-.19	-.10	.10
3 and 4	-.18	-.19	-.12	-.19	-.25	.03	-.14	-.08	-.24
3 and 5	.27	.06	-.07	.09	.09	.00	.25	.32	.30
3 and 6	.32	-.08	.14	.06	.30	.38	.29	.24	.20
4 and 5	.18	-.06	.25	.26	.05	-.04	.07	.13	.06
4 and 6	-.29	-.07	-.28	-.20	-.32	-.13	-.21	-.13	-.36
5 and 6	-.19	-.04	-.05	-.23	-.20	-.26	-.17	-.19	-.28

demonstrate that their factor matrices can be rotated to their target matrix with less stress than is generated by rotating the factor matrices to some random permutation of the actual target matrix. Furthermore, it has been suggested that several random target matrices be used so that approximate confidence intervals for the random results can be derived. The overall stress (sum of squared error) was the greatest in attempting to rotate the 1973 male-factor matrix to the total group-factor matrix. Thus this matrix was chosen to demonstrate that the total group-factor matrix provides a better target for all of our factor matrices than some randomly generated target-factor matrix.

The value of the stress measure in rotating the 1973 male matrix to the total sample-target matrix was 1.90. The values of the stress measure when rotating the 1973 male matrix to five random targets formed by randomly ordering the columns in each row of the real target matrix were 5.83, 5.90, 6.13, 6.34, and 6.57. Thus it is possible to conclude that for the most stressful rotation, the total group rotated factor pattern matrix provides a much better target (by a factor of 3.1:1) than some random target matrix. This demonstration, then, shows that our factor matrices have been aligned to a position that is quite consistent with the data.

Discussion

In this first series of analyses, we have demonstrated a large amount of factorial stability for the Murray needs measured by the short form of the PRF across groups differing in substance-use pattern. Indeed, in general, it may be concluded that the dimensions of personality measured by this instrument are qualitatively the same in groups formed by either drug and alcohol use or sex. Such a finding is also consistent with the demonstration of Huba and Hamilton (1976) that Murray's needs have a stable factor pattern even when they are measured using different testing formats.

Although the overall conclusion can be drawn that the factors of Murray's needs are relatively stable, it is interesting to note that four of the factors are more stable than the remaining two. In particular, it appears that the generalized Achievement Motivation and Playfulness dimensions are possibly qualitatively different for individuals who use neither drugs nor alcohol. Achievement Motivation in the nonusers is intimately related to the needs for Order, Nurturance, and Understanding and may represent the expression of achievement needs through socially desirable means. Individuals who use drugs or alcohol are apparently not as likely to express their needs for achievement through socially desirable activities. The expression of Playfulness in the nonusers is positively related to the needs for Impulsivity and Order and negatively to the need for Endurance. It appears that the expression of playfulness for nonusers of drugs and alcohol is at once brash and simultaneously concerned with the following of rules. It is entirely possible that this playfulness dimension in nonusers is representative of the "jock" pattern of the impulsive athlete in a college group.

With the minor exceptions noted previously, the factor structure of the PRF *is stable* across different types of substance users and across the sexes. This finding strongly supports the conceptual basis of those studies that have sought to demonstrate the quantitative differences between groups of users and nonusers of drugs and alcohol and between males and females. Furthermore, the finding of a stable factor pattern in our subjects permits a comparison of our results with those obtained by Stricker (1974) and Nesselroade and Baltes (1975).

Two factors mitigate against a direct comparison of the results of the previous factorings and the results of this study. First, both of the previous studies were conducted using all 20 of the PRF scales, whereas our study used a subset of 14 PRF content scales. Second, both of the previous sets of investigators present their results as correlations between reference axes and the original variables, whereas we have followed Gorsuch's (1974) suggestion and presented the primary factor pattern coefficients (or the weights to be applied to the oblique factors to generate the observed variables). In spite of some methodological incompatibility, however, convergence between the three studies can be seen.

Our first factor seems to be weakly comparable to the seventh factor found by Nesselroade and Baltes but has no counterpart among the factors of Stricker. Our second factor is very similar to the second factor found by Nesselroade and Baltes and the third factor found by Stricker, whereas our third factor seems to be comparable to the first factor found by Stricker and the first factor found by Nesselroade and Baltes. Our fourth factor seems to be about the same as the sixth factor found by Nesselroade and Baltes but has no counterpart among the factors found by Stricker. The fifth factor found in our analyses is very similar to the third factor found by Nesselroade and Baltes and the fourth factor found by Stricker. Our sixth factor has no counterpart among the Nesselroade and Baltes factors but does correspond to the sixth Stricker factor.

The general instability of the factors across studies, as opposed to the stability within our study, is partially attributable to the differences in subjects and methods across the studies. Our subjects were several years older, on the average, than the subjects in either of the other two studies, and the Stricker sample was rather small. Stricker used an analytical procedure for his simple structure rotations (promax), which is roughly comparable to the direct quartimin procedure used in our study (Hakstian & Abell, 1974). Nesselroade and Baltes, on the other hand, rotated their matrix to approximate simple structure by hand. It is possible, then, that greater similarity between the present results and those of Nesselroade and Baltes would have been obtained if both investigators had used the same analytical procedure for simple structure rotation.

Since we believe that our results indicate that there are stable dimensions underlying the set of Murray needs measured by the PRF, it seems justifiable to speculate on the possible relationships of these factors to other theoretical constructs. First, these data give factorial support for the large amount of literature that has accumulated on several individual needs such as Achievement and Affiliation. Second, it is likely that our results converge with S. Bem's (1974) recent work on psychological androgeny. The first factor found in our analyses (need for Group Membership) would appear to be a stereotypic pattern commonly assigned to the traditional feminine role. The third (extraversion) factor found, with its high loadings for Dominance, Exhibitionism, and Aggression, reflects the stereotypic male machismo pattern. These factors are only minimally correlated into a negative direction (−.08) in the analysis based upon the total sample. Third, the Bohemian or generalized autonomy motivation factor consists of a pattern of needs that might underlie much of the "march to the tune of a different drummer" or "tune out and turn on" behavior that characterized a visible minority of the college population during the 1960s and early 1970s; it has also been implicated as a strong concomitant of recreational drug use for individuals of college age (Suchman, 1968). The results we present later (Chapter 6, this volume) also find strong relationships between drug use and the indicators of this factor.

Finally, it should be emphasized that our results on the stability of the organization of motivational states are derived from samples of young adults. There is very little difference in the way in which motivations are organized in youthful users and nonusers of drugs and alcohol. Similarly, the motivational patterns of young men and young women are essentially the same. We do not know, however, the extent to which our results are generalizable to either the differences that might be obtained by comparing older men and women or by comparing nonusers of drugs and alcohol with chronic users of either substance. This study does demonstrate that moderate and relatively short-term use of a variety of drugs and alcohol is not associated with the reorganization of motivational patterns in a large and reasonably heterogeneous sample of college students.

THE CONSISTENCY OF DAYDREAMING STYLES

Ongoing thought or waking consciousness has much of the changing, fluctuating variability that led William James to characterize it as the stream of consciousness. Experimental studies have called attention to this variability in sequence as a function of general information-processing requirements (Singer, 1975a, b) or specific situational factors such as posture or social context (Pope, 1978). There is, however, an increasing body of research derived from questionnaire surveys of self-reports of daydreaming and related aspects of waking mentation that suggests that private experience shows certain structural consistencies and a limited number of basic styles of ongoing thought (Giambra, 1974, 1977; Isaacs, 1975; Singer & Antrobus, 1963, 1972; Starker, 1974). The analyses presented here examine more intensively the question of whether one can classify self-reports of daydreaming and related mentation by means of a limited number of dimensions that show consistency across samples of males and females and across samples of youthful alcohol users and multiple-drug users or teetotalers.

Singer and Antrobus (1963, 1972) developed a battery of 28 self-report scales, which they have called the Imaginal Processes Inventory (IPI). The IPI scales sample broadly from the interlocking domains of style of thinking (e.g., tendency to become bored, distractibility, rate of thinking, visual and auditory imagery), attitudes toward daydreaming (e.g., absorption in daydreaming, acceptance of daydreaming as a "normal" adult activity), and the content of spontaneous thought (e.g., guilt daydreams, hostile daydreams, curiosity about the lives of other people, curiosity about nature or mechanical devices). The IPI scales have respectable levels of internal consistency (Singer & Antrobus, 1972) and minimal correlations with social desirability (Oakland, 1968).

Several previous studies (Giambra, 1974; Isaacs, 1975; Singer & Antrobus, 1963, 1972; Starker, 1974; Starker & Singer, 1975a) have identified at least three orthogonal factors underlying the 28 IPI scales. Following the terminology suggested by Singer and Antrobus (1972), these factors have been called *Positive-Vivid Daydreaming, Anxious-Distractible Daydreaming or Mindwandering,* and *Guilty-Dysphoric Daydreaming.* In each of the studies cited, the three factors have emerged in substantially the same form. Some support for the meaning of these factors has come from different measures developed from studies of imagery, reflective thought, night dream patterns, and thought-sampling laboratory studies (Singer, 1974b).

Method

Subjects. The subject pool used for these analyses was identical to that used for the previous analyses on Murray needs.

Instrument. The Imaginal Processes Inventory (IPI) of Singer and Antrobus (1970, 1972) was administered to all subjects. All but one of the 28 IPI scales consist of 12 items answered in a Likert format; the Absorption in Daydreaming scale has 20 items. Within each scale, approximately half of the items are keyed in one direction. Oakland (1968) has shown that the item pool from which the IPI was developed is relatively free of social desirability responding. Detailed descriptions of the 28 IPI scales and item statistics are given by Singer and Antrobus (1972).

Categorization of Drug- and Alcohol-Use Patterns. The participants were divided as in the previous analyses into drug-use groups of nonusers, alcohol-only users, marijuana-only users, and polydrug users. The simultaneous categorization by drug-use pattern, sex, and year of testing was maintained for the present anlayses. Thus eight overlapping groups of several hundred individuals—all nonusers of drugs and alcohol; all users of alcohol only; all users of marijuana only; multiple-drug users; 1973 males; 1974 males; 1973 females; 1974 females—were used for the factor analyses of the IPI.

Data Analysis. The data for each of the eight groups were factored separately using the method of maximum likelihood (see Lawley & Maxwell, 1971). Since the distributions of some of the IPI variables, both within subgroups and in the total sample, were decidedly non-normal (and defied transformation to normality), it was not possible to accurately apply the statistical test developed by Lawley (1940) to determine the number of factors as we did previously. Nonetheless, the maximum likelihood method might be used for its property of minimizing residual partial correlations (see Morrison, 1976). Therefore, first the scale correlations for the total sample of 1095 subjects were factored using the method of principal components (i.e., unities were used as communality estimates) and all 28 latent roots (6.2, 3.8, 2.2, 1.6, 1.5, 1.1, 1.0, .92, .84, .83, .76, .73, .69, .62, .58, .54, .46, .44, .43, .41, .37, .35, .32, .27, .26, .22, .19, .18) were examined. A scree plot (Cattell, 1966) of the 28 eigenvalues appears to indicate that there are *eight* common factors underlying the 28 IPI scales. Consequently, eight-factor maximum likelihood solutions were calculated from the full sample correlation matrix and from each of the eight subgroup correlation matrices, as it seemed desirable to consider the same number of factors in each of the subgroups. Heywood variables were found for the 1973 male (1), 1973 female (1), 1974 female (1), Nonuser (2), Alcohol (1), and Polydrug (1) groups and were treated in the manner suggested by Jöreskog (1967).

The goodness of fit for the eight-factor solutions can be assessed in alternate ways that do not involve formal statistical tests. Coefficients for the reliability of a maximum-likelihood factor solution have been suggested by Tucker and Lewis (1973) as well as by Bentler and Bonett (1981). The Bentler–Bonett coefficient measures the amount of the covariance among the measures explained: The index is a multivariate analog of multiple correlation measures of percentage of variance. The value of the Bentler–Bonett coefficient for the total sample eight-factor solution is .94. Adequate values were found for the 1973 males (.92), 1974 males (.89). 1973 females (.90), 1974 females (.93), nonuser (.89), alcohol-only (.92), marijuana only (.91), and polydrug (.90) solutions. We conclude that the reliability coefficients indicate that eight factors capture most of the reliable major sources of covariation among the IPI scales for all groups studied.

The eight-factor solution from the total sample was rotated to approximate oblique simple structure using the direct quartimin algorithm (Jennrich & Sampson, 1966) with Kaiser (1958) normalization. As we noted earlier, direct quartimin produces rotated solutions that are typically comparable to those obtained by a skilled hand rotator (Hakstian & Abell, 1974), which are relatively invariant over the sampling of variables (Bailey & Guertin, 1973) and are nonsingular (Jennrich & Sampson, 1966).

Again, each of the subgroup factor matrices was rotated to a position of best least-squares fit to the total (simple structure) *rotated* factor pattern matrix using Huba's (1975) program for Browne's (1972) method of direct, restricted, oblique Procrustean rotation. That is, the unrotated factor pattern matrix from each of the subgroup analyses was rotated so as to have as good an alignment with the total rotated factor pattern matrix as the data would allow. After each of the eight subgroup factor matrices was maximally aligned to the total matrix, factor similarity (or congruence) coefficients (see Mulaik, 1972) were calculated between all pairs of corresponding factors.

The hierarchical factor pattern of the IPI was next examined using the eight primary-factor solutions obtained from the total group of subjects. The correlations among the primary factors were factored using the method of iterated principal factors (see Mulaik, 1972) with iteration until the estimated communalities stabilized with less than a .0001 discrepancy from one cycle to another. Three second-order factors were extracted after an inspection of the scree plot. The second-order factors were rotated to approximate orthogonal simple structure using the normalized varimax procedure (Kaiser, 1958). Finally, the original variables were projected on the second-order factors, and the primary factors were orthogonalized in relationship to the second-order factors using the procedure of Schmid and Leiman (1957). The second-order factor analysis was performed because the primary-factor analyses yielded so many highly correlated factors.

Results

The loadings on the first factor found in each analysis are shown in Table 5.8. The factor was extremely stable across the different groups; factor similarity coefficients between the pairs of factors ranged from .95 to .99. The pattern of loadings on the factor indicates that the dimension can be interpreted as *Guilty–Dysphoric Daydreams*. In each of the groups, there is a very high positive loading for the frequency and intensity of Guilt and Fear-of-Failure

TABLE 5.8

Rotated Loadings for Factor 1 in Each Analysis of the IPI

	Total	Non-users	Alcohol only	Mari-juana only	Poly-drug	Male 1973	Male 1974	Female 1973	Female 1974
Daydreaming frequency	-0.07	-0.08	-0.14	-0.04	-0.03	-0.09	-0.17	-0.03	-0.06
Night dreaming frequency	0.02	-0.10	-0.10	-0.02	0.10	0.12	0.11	-0.08	-0.07
Absorption in daydreaming	0.00	0.02	0.03	0.06	-0.01	0.08	0.00	-0.03	0.06
Acceptance of daydreaming	-0.32	-0.35	-0.30	-0.33	-0.40	-0.40	-0.39	-0.34	-0.33
Positive reactions to daydreaming	-0.17	-0.12	-0.13	-0.23	-0.18	-0.26	-0.14	-0.21	-0.12
Frightened reactions to daydreams	0.44	0.39	0.43	0.44	0.56	0.46	0.46	0.43	0.46
Visual imagery in day-dreams	-0.11	-0.11	-0.09	-0.11	-0.14	-0.08	-0.10	-0.10	-0.10
Auditory images in day-dreams	0.03	0.10	0.04	0.05	0.03	0.05	0.04	0.03	0.04
Problem-solving daydreams	0.17	0.25	0.31	0.06	0.16	0.18	0.21	0.19	0.14
Present-oriented daydreams	0.07	0.17	0.11	0.13	0.11	0.13	0.11	0.12	0.07
Future in daydreams	-0.15	-0.17	-0.16	-0.16	-0.19	-0.18	-0.14	-0.20	-0.12
Past in daydreams	0.22	0.19	0.34	0.23	0.13	0.22	0.29	0.15	0.14
Bizarre-improbable day-dreams	0.04	0.19	0.00	0.08	0.06	0.08	0.03	0.06	0.07
Mindwandering	-0.06	-0.03	-0.08	-0.14	-0.02	-0.10	-0.09	-0.10	0.01
Achievement-oriented day-dreams	0.08	0.12	0.18	0.21	0.06	0.25	0.17	0.15	0.06
Hallucinatory-vividness of daydreams	0.35	0.39	0.38	9.38	0.41	0.45	0.35	0.34	0.35
Fear-of-failure daydreams	0.83	0.86	0.85	0.82	0.80	0.80	0.76	0.81	0.92
Hostile daydreams	0.57	0.48	0.58	0.61	0.62	0.54	0.59	0.71	0.58
Sexual daydreams	-0.06	-0.10	-0.10	0.00	-0.10	-0.19	-0.08	0.11	-0.06
Heroic daydreams	0.41	0.39	0.47	0.38	0.52	0.43	0.47	0.48	0.39
Guilt daydreams	0.89	0.86	0.86	0.89	0.88	0.83	0.94	0.87	0.85
Interpersonal curiosity	0.05	0.01	-0.01	0.05	0.04	0.12	0.13	-0.10	-0.03
Impersonal-mechanical curiosity	0.16	0.38	0.18	0.05	0.23	0.17	0.08	0.16	0.26
Boredom susceptibility	0.14	0.20	0.27	0.13	0.11	0.22	0.21	0.15	0.17
Mentation rate	-0.15	-0.14	-0.21	-0.15	-0.07	-0.23	-0.28	-0.08	-0.10
Distractibility	0.11	0.13	0.04	0.10	0.14	0.11	0.13	0.11	0.08
Need for external stimu-lation	-0.10	-0.06	-0.17	-0.15	-0.17	-0.14	-0.17	-0.13	-0.01
Self-revelation	0.03	-0.01	-0.04	0.02	-0.16	0.03	-0.07	0.03	-0.06

daydreams. Moderately high positive loadings for the Frightened Reactions, Hallucinatory Vividness, Hostile, and Heroic Daydreaming scales on the factor suggests the speculation that an individual who has many fantasies of guilt and potential failure will experience these daydreams as both frightening and real and will seek to resolve the guilt feelings by daydreaming of either revenge or some heroic exploit.

The second factor found in each of the analyses also appears to be rather stable. The factor similarity coefficients between the pairs of second factors shown in Table 5.9 range from .91 to .99. There are consistently high positive loadings for the reported intensity of both visual and auditory imagery in

TABLE 5.9

Rotated Loadings for Factor 2 in Each Analysis of the IPI

	Total	Non-users	Alcohol only	Mari-juana only	Poly-drug	Male 1973	Male 1974	Female 1973	Female 1974
Daydreaming frequency	0.00	0.17	0.02	-0.01	0.16	0.02	0.05	0.04	0.07
Night dreaming frequency	0.08	0.27	0.20	0.03	0.20	0.18	-0.04	0.21	0.14
Absorption in daydreaming	0.14	0.15	0.17	0.25	0.31	0.25	0.32	0.18	0.17
Acceptance of daydreaming	0.12	0.23	0.17	0.13	0.05	0.02	0.15	0.19	0.12
Positive reactions in daydreaming	0.14	0.07	0.15	0.24	0.20	0.32	0.18	0.10	0.09
Frightened reactions to daydreaming	0.25	0.24	0.28	0.35	0.26	0.40	0.15	0.27	0.30
Visual imagery in day-dreams	0.83	0.89	0.82	0.76	1.01	0.77	0.76	0.81	0.79
Auditory images in day-dreams	0.95	0.85	0.95	0.94	0.79	0.80	0.97	0.94	0.96
Problem-solving daydreams	0.10	0.19	0.09	0.16	0.03	0.00	0.06	0.13	0.24
Present-oriented daydreams	0.00	-0.04	-0.01	-0.12	-0.06	-0.07	0.03	0.09	-0.04
Future in daydreams	0.10	0.03	0.13	0.11	0.07	0.08	0.07	0.08	0.03
Past in daydreams	0.11	0.11	0.09	0.20	0.16	0.04	0.16	0.06	0.17
Bizarre-improbable day-dreams	0.03	-0.06	0.06	0.06	-0.02	0.04	0.07	0.11	-0.03
Mindwandering	0.07	0.08	0.03	0.11	0.03	0.08	-0.06	0.09	0.07
Achievement-oriented daydreams	0.06	0.09	0.04	0.04	0.02	-0.08	0.11	0.09	0.12
Hallucinatory-vividness of daydreams	0.52	0.53	0.50	0.51	0.46	0.58	0.41	0.54	0.55
Fear-of-failure daydreams	0.00	0.02	0.02	-0.01	0.04	0.05	0.03	-0.02	-0.04
Hostile daydreams	0.06	0.14	0.12	0.13	0.02	0.00	0.17	0.11	0.11
Sexual daydreams	0.14	0.15	0.17	0.11	0.21	0.33	0.17	0.13	0.14
Heroic daydreams	0.00	0.04	-0.01	0.05	0.04	0.01	0.10	-0.04	0.03
Guilt daydreams	0.04	0.06	0.11	-0.02	0.11	0.10	0.07	0.06	0.00
Interpersonal curiosity	-0.01	-0.04	-0.08	0.11	0.13	-0.01	0.00	0.05	-0.03
Impersonal-mechanical curiosity	0.03	0.02	0.03	0.05	0.04	0.13	-0.13	0.07	-0.04
Boredom susceptibility	0.05	0.02	0.05	-0.03	-0.02	-0.08	0.01	0.04	0.07
Mentation rate	0.11	0.06	0.15	0.16	0.12	0.14	0.17	0.14	0.15
Distractibility	-0.02	-0.06	0.00	-0.04	-0.11	-0.02	-0.07	-0.03	-0.07
Need for external stimu-lation	0.11	0.16	0.23	-0.01	0.08	0.23	-0.02	0.21	0.15
Self-revelation	-0.01	0.10	0.07	0.03	-0.01	0.12	0.13	0.04	-0.03

daydreams and for the extent to which daydreams are experienced so vividly that they sometimes appear to be "real." This factor is clearly one of *Vividness of Self-Reported Imagery* and corresponds to a general factor reported by several other investigators (see Paivio, 1971, chap. 14).

The loadings on the third factor found in each of the subgroup analyses are shown in Table 5.10. This factor rather clearly represents a generalized *Mindwandering–Distractible* mental style. The IPI scales for Mindwandering, Boredom Susceptibility, and Distractibility load in a consistently high, positive manner on all of the factors shown in Table 5.10. The Daydreaming Frequency scale consistently loads at a moderately high, positive level on the

TABLE 5.10

Rotated Loadings for Factor 3 in Each Analysis of the IPI

	Total	Non-users	Alcohol only	Mari-juana only	Poly-drug	Male 1973	Male 1974	Female 1973	Female 1974
Daydreaming frequency	0.34	0.42	0.34	0.44	0.42	0.39	0.29	0.32	0.43
Night dreaming frequency	-0.01	0.05	-0.01	0.10	-0.06	-0.03	-0.05	0.02	0.06
Absorption in daydreaming	0.13	0.21	0.15	0.21	0.21	0.22	0.24	0.19	0.16
Acceptance of daydreams	-0.02	-0.06	0.07	-0.11	-0.05	-0.02	-0.01	-0.01	-0.07
Positive reactions to daydreaming	-0.01	0.03	-0.01	-0.02	0.09	0.06	0.02	-0.02	0.01
Frightened reactions to daydreaming	0.04	0.06	0.05	0.05	0.04	0.01	0.13	0.12	0.03
Visual imagery in daydreams	0.04	0.06	0.02	-0.01	0.10	-0.07	-0.04	0.07	0.08
Auditory images in daydreams	0.01	0.00	-0.02	-0.01	-0.06	-0.06	0.00	0.00	-0.05
Problem-solving daydreams	-0.10	-0.09	-0.06	-0.10	-0.15	-0.13	-0.14	-0.09	-0.10
Present-oriented daydreams	0.10	0.09	0.02	0.05	0.03	0.08	0.07	0.04	0.07
Future in daydreams	0.14	0.23	0.17	0.09	0.04	-0.05	0.15	0.16	0.11
Past in daydreams	0.09	0.03	0.07	0.10	0.07	0.17	0.00	0.05	0.12
Bizarre-improbable daydreams	0.06	0.06	0.05	0.02	0.08	0.06	0.11	0.13	0.01
Mindwandering	0.81	0.77	0.81	0.82	0.82	0.85	0.70	0.83	0.73
Achievement-oriented daydreams	0.06	0.04	0.02	0.02	0.04	0.06	0.01	0.02	0.07
Hallucinatory-vividness of daydreams	-0.05	-0.10	-0.03	0.05	-0.12	0.04	-0.06	-0.11	-0.03
Fear-of-failure daydreams	0.08	0.18	0.05	0.02	0.14	0.04	0.09	0.10	0.09
Hostile daydreams	0.09	0.13	0.09	0.10	0.10	0.12	0.22	0.06	0.12
Sexual daydreams	0.18	0.15	0.19	0.26	0.21	0.29	0.30	0.18	0.15
Heroic daydreams	0.00	-0.04	-0.05	0.03	-0.01	0.09	-0.06	-0.02	-0.02
Guilt daydreams	0.03	0.00	0.07	-0.02	0.09	0.01	0.04	0.06	0.06
Interpersonal curiosity	0.04	-0.05	0.03	0.14	-0.02	0.04	0.00	0.06	-0.02
Impersonal-mechanical curiosity	-0.22	-0.22	-0.23	-0.24	-0.24	-0.28	-0.19	-0.18	-0.34
Boredom susceptibility	0.66	0.61	0.71	0.62	0.68	0.67	0.54	0.67	0.62
Mentation rate	-0.05	0.04	-0.11	-0.14	0.02	-0.15	-0.03	-0.12	-0.09
Distractibility	0.70	0.65	0.68	0.67	0.71	0.62	0.75	0.70	0.73
Need for external stimulation	-0.12	-0.11	-0.15	-0.19	-0.10	0.02	-0.19	-0.17	-0.18
Self-revelation	0.02	-0.10	0.08	0.00	0.06	0.05	0.01	0.06	0.01

factor. This factor was extremely stable over the classifications of subjects; the congruence coefficients between the pairs of factors shown in Table 5.10 range from .94 to .99.

The fourth factor found in the analyses was less stable than the first three factors with the similarity coefficients between pairs of factors ranging from .78 to .94. The loadings on the fourth factor found in each of the analyses are shown in Table 5.11. The highest loading on each of the fourth factors is for the IPI scale of Future in Dreaming. The Interpersonal Curiosity and Problem Solving in Daydreams scales also load on the factor in a consistent,

positive manner, suggesting that this factor represents *Pl*
about interpersonal events. There is also a positive loadin
of Daydreaming scale, suggesting that daydreams are a
adult activity to the extent that one is able to use
anticipate social events. Individuals who are high on the r ...
also tend to reveal personal information about themselves. This factor
corresponds with one found in earlier studies (Singer & Antrobus, 1963, 1972)
to relate to Guilford's Thoughtfulness scale.

TABLE 5.11

Rotated Loadings for Factor 4 in Each Analysis of the IPI

	Total	Non-users	Alcohol only	Mari-juana only	Poly-drug	Male 1973	Male 1974	Female 1973	Female 1974
Daydreaming frequency	-0.06	0.09	-0.17	0.18	0.12	0.00	-0.03	0.02	0.07
Night dreaming frequency	-0.09	0.03	-0.02	0.15	0.07	0.00	-0.02	0.02	-0.08
Absorption in daydreaming	0.02	0.08	0.06	-0.02	-0.07	0.06	0.01	0.00	0.05
Acceptance of daydreaming	0.34	0.30	0.37	0.29	0.40	0.43	0.36	0.25	0.41
Positive reactions to daydreaming	0.24	0.35	0.17	0.18	0.36	0.14	0.20	0.35	0.24
Frightened reactions to daydreaming	-0.04	-0.18	-0.02	-0.22	-0.14	-0.04	-0.01	-0.12	-0.17
Visual imagery in day-dreaming	-0.04	-0.03	-0.03	0.01	0.03	-0.09	-0.09	-0.02	0.04
Auditory images in day-dreaming	0.00	0.02	-0.03	0.10	-0.07	-0.07	0.10	-0.04	-0.03
Problem-solving day-dreams	0.33	0.30	0.24	0.29	0.52	0.40	0.41	0.38	0.34
Present-oriented day-dreams	-0.16	0.06	0.07	0.14	0.10	-0.10	-0.14	0.21	-0.15
Future in daydreams	0.62	0.54	0.61	0.57	0.54	0.48	0.66	0.59	0.62
Past in daydreams	0.13	0.26	0.32	0.10	-0.06	0.07	0.24	-0.24	0.10
Bizarre-improbable day-dreams	-0.26	-0.20	-0.29	-0.31	-0.22	-0.05	-0.21	-0.38	-0.31
Mindwandering	0.09	0.07	0.08	0.03	0.14	0.06	0.03	0.08	0.08
Achievement-oriented daydreams	0.21	0.33	0.32	0.31	0.13	0.32	0.25	0.32	0.22
Hallucinatory-vividness of daydreams	-0.12	-0.16	-0.12	-0.15	-0.21	0.05	-0.28	-0.20	-0.13
Fear-of-failure day-dreams	0.00	0.01	-0.12	0.01	-0.05	-0.11	0.00	-0.11	0.08
Hostile daydreams	-0.13	-0.08	-0.06	-0.03	-0.05	-0.15	-0.18	0.01	-0.05
Sexual daydreams	0.00	-0.18	0.07	0.23	0.17	0.01	0.03	0.34	0.05
Heroic daydreams	0.05	0.07	0.13	0.02	0.16	0.13	0.05	0.23	0.02
Guilt daydreams	0.02	-0.01	-0.08	-0.01	0.01	-0.09	-0.02	-0.02	0.01
Interpersonal curiosity	0.47	0.47	0.54	0.51	0.29	0.51	0.46	0.49	0.34
Impersonal-mechanical curiosity	0.05	0.04	0.11	0.13	0.26	0.21	0.18	-0.07	0.06
Boredom susceptibility	-0.31	-0.45	-0.31	-0.42	-0.28	-0.18	-0.29	-0.38	-0.35
Mentation rate	0.24	0.34	0.33	0.27	0.44	0.33	0.34	0.28	0.21
Distractibility	0.22	0.26	0.26	0.14	0.07	0.09.	0.25	0.19	0.16
Need for external stimu-lation	0.23	0.29	0.20	0.34	0.25	0.45	0.19	0.31	0.22
Self-revelation	0.28	0.33	0.28	0.28	0.28	0.28	0.30	0.33	0.26

The fifth factor found in each of the analyses is rather stable with the factor similarity coefficients between the pairs of factors ranging from .87 to .97. The factor has consistently high, positive loadings for the Absorption in Daydreaming, Positive Reactions to Daydreaming, and Problem-Solving Daydreaming scales with a small positive loading for the Hallucinatory–Vividness scale. The pattern of loadings suggest that this is a factor of *Intense Mental Involvement*. The loadings of each of the variables on the factor are given in Table 5.12.

TABLE 5.12
Rotated Loadings for Factor 5 in Each Analysis of the IPI

	Total	Non-users	Alcohol only	Mari-juana only	Poly-drug	Male 1973	Male 1974	Female 1973	Female 1974
Daydreaming frequency	0.22	0.21	0.25	0.29	0.21	0.27	0.28	0.34	0.18
Night dreaming frequency	0.02	0.01	0.16	0.15	-0.01	-0.05	0.06	0.00	0.02
Absorption in daydreaming	0.77	0.70	0.78	0.62	0.68	0.65	0.60	0.74	0.71
Acceptance of daydreaming	0.14	0.21	0.13	0.26	0.29	0.24	0.27	0.20	0.24
Positive reactions to daydreaming	0.43	0.45	0.47	0.55	0.34	0.45	0.42	0.48	0.44
Frightened reactions to daydreams	0.41	0.52	0.43	0.32	0.38	0.40	0.46	0.36	0.40
Visual imagery in daydreams	0.01	-0.10	0.03	0.16	-0.08	0.07	0.13	-0.01	0.08
Auditory images in day-dreams	-0.06	-0.01	-0.10	-0.09	0.13	0.11	-0.09	-0.08	-0.03
Problem-solving day-dreams	0.35	0.35	0.30	0.47	0.42	0.56	0.51	0.35	0.24
Present-oriented day-dreams	0.06	0.02	0.05	0.21	0.11	0.06	0.12	-0.03	0.11
Future in daydreams	0.02	0.04	-0.01	-0.05	0.12	0.09	-0.07	0.13	0.03
Past in daydreams	0.09	0.12	0.03	0.07	0.19	0.05	0.18	0.13	0.05
Bizarre-improbable day-dreams	0.12	0.08	0.17	0.06	0.10	0.08	0.08	0.05	0.17
Mindwandering	0.03	0.07	0.05	0.08	0.08	0.08	0.16	0.07	0.05
Achievement-oriented daydreams	0.14	0.11	0.07	0.17	0.21	0.15	0.16	0.10	0.08
Hallucinatory-vividness of daydreams	0.26	0.32	0.25	0.24	0.34	0.17	0.30	0.31	0.28
Fear-of-failure day-dreams	0.03	-0.09	0.09	0.02	0.05	0.08	0.04	0.09	-0.04
Hostile daydreams	0.03	0.07	0.05	0.08	0.14	0.14	-0.03	0.04	0.07
Sexual daydreams	0.16	0.20	0.22	0.30	0.21	0.14	0.10	0.19	0.32
Heroic daydreams	0.02	0.04	0.01	0.15	-0.02	0.02	0.13	-0.01	0.02
Guilt daydreams	-0.01	0.02	0.07	0.09	-0.06	0.01	-0.07	0.03	0.11
Interpersonal curiosity	0.11	0.17	0.15	-0.16	0.02	0.12	0.05	-0.03	0.16
Impersonal-mechanical curiosity	-0.12	-0.10	-0.07	-0.11	-0.11	-0.18	0.05	0.00	-0.06
Boredom susceptibility	-0.03	0.05	-0.17	0.05	0.02	0.10	0.07	-0.05	-0.05
Mentation rate	0.01	0.10	0.04	0.04	0.05	0.09	-0.07	0.10	-0.09
Distractibility	-0.02	-0.04	0.09	-0.01	-0.01	-0.07	-0.03	0.04	0.04
Need for external stimu-lation	-0.14	-0.10	-0.14	0.05	-0.12	-0.31	-0.16	0.01	-0.18
Self-revelation	0.06	0.10	0.14	0.10	0.05	0.00	0.12	-0.01	0.15

TABLE 5.13

Rotated Loadings for Factor 6 in Each Analysis of the IPI

	Total	Non-users	Alcohol only	Mari-juana only	Poly-drug	Male 1973	Male 1974	Female 1973	Female 1974
Daydreaming frequency	-0.04	-0.09	0.04	-0.20	-0.11	-0.03	0.02	-0.32	-0.06
Night dreaming frequency	-0.02	-0.15	-0.01	-0.23	-0.15	-0.05	0.00	-0.26	-0.04
Absorption in daydreaming	-0.03	-0.08	-0.04	0.11	0.07	-0.02	0.03	-0.07	-0.04
Acceptance of daydreaming	-0.02	-0.06	0.06	0.04	-0.11	0.08	-0.07	0.11	0.02
Positive reactions in daydreaming	-0.04	0.03	-0.03	-0.04	-0.04	-0.06	-0.03	0.01	-0.04
Frightened reactions to daydreams	0.00	0.00	0.05	0.17	0.18	0.01	0.00	0.10	0.00
Visual imagery in daydreams	-0.03	-0.05	-0.04	-0.19	-0.06	-0.07	0.00	0.00	-0.11
Auditory images in day-dreams	0.00	0.00	-0.04	-0.06	-0.04	-0.06	-0.02	0.10	0.02
Problem-solving day-dreams	0.15	0.24	0.28	0.34	0.17	0.09	0.17	0.24	0.23
Present-oriented day-dreams	1.03	0.61	0.57	0.53	0.49	1.01	0.90	0.48	1.02
Future in daydreams	-0.05	0.00	0.08	0.03	0.09	-0.07	-0.08	0.08	-0.08
Past in daydreams	-0.11	-0.14	-0.27	-0.07	-0.29	-0.13	-0.16	-0.33	-0.05
Bizarre-improbable day-dreams	-0.41	-0.69	-0.58	-0.63	-0.65	-0.44	-0.44	-0.60	-0.43
Mindwandering	-0.01	0.02	0.00	0.05	-0.07	0.02	-0.07	0.03	0.05
Achievement-oriented daydreams	-0.10	-0.19	-0.27	-0.11	-0.25	-0.13	-0.09	-0.28	-0.10
Hallucinatory-vividness of daydreams	0.03	0.04	0.04	0.10	0.02	0.04	-0.05	-0.02	0.08
Fear-of-failure day-dreams	0.03	0.13	0.12	0.07	0.07	0.08	0.05	0.12	-0.02
Hostile daydreams	-0.02	-0.09	-0.09	-0.17	-0.04	-0.02	0.05	-0.10	-0.06
Sexual daydreams	0.01	0.12	-0.10	-0.24	0.02	0.09	0.00	-0.23	-0.06
Heroic daydreams	-0.10	-0.06	-0.21	-0.20	-0.23	-0.09	-0.22	-0.30	-0.05
Guilt daydreams	-0.01	0.08	0.09	-0.01	0.11	-0.01	-0.01	0.11	-0.04
Interpersonal curiosity	0.02	-0.07	0.03	0.20	0.19	-0.01	0.05	0.11	-0.02
Impersonal-mechanical curiosity	-0.02	-0.08	-0.08	-0.18	-0.27	0.04	-0.07	0.01	0.08
Boredom susceptibility	-0.08	-0.07	-0.06	-0.05	-0.13	-0.09	-0.07	-0.14	-0.12
Mentation rate	0.10	0.07	0.11	-0.15	-0.02	0.05	0.11	0.01	0.12
Distractibility	0.07	0.11	0.00	0.06	0.13	-0.03	0.06	0.25	0.13
Need for external stimu-lation	0.03	-0.02	0.03	-0.05	0.11	0.04	0.03	-0.01	-0.06
Self-revelation	0.01	0.01	0.04	0.11	0.12	0.11	0.04	0.03	-0.08

The loadings of the variables on the eighth factor found in each analysis are total sample, is a doublet factor. Factor similarity coefficients between the factors shown in Table 5.13 range from .63 to .97. In all of the analyses, the factor has high loadings for the Present Orientation in Daydreaming (positive) and Bizarre Daydreams (negative) scales, but the pattern of loadings for the other variables changes as a function of the sample. At the present time, it seems that this factor is uninterpretable, and we are not sure if it is found in the same form in each of the subgroups we have studied.

TABLE 5.14

Rotated Loadings for Factor 7 in Each Analysis of the IPI

	Total	Non-users	Alcohol only	Mari-juana only	Poly-drug	Male 1973	Male 1974	Female 1973	Female 1974
Daydreaming frequency	0.11	0.02	0.23	0.04	-0.06	-0.03	0.21	-0.11	0.13
Night dreaming frequency	-0.04	-0.06	0.02	-0.17	-0.13	-0.10	0.00	-0.08	0.06
Absorption in daydreaming	0.01	-0.01	-0.04	0.13	0.03	0.06	0.05	0.03	-0.02
Acceptance of daydreaming	-0.14	-0.09	-0.11	-0.13	-0.22	-0.08	-0.26	-0.08	-0.21
Positive reactions in day-dreaming	0.11	0.06	0.12	0.12	0.15	0.24	0.12	0.04	0.14
Frightened reactions to daydreaming	-0.09	-0.01	-0.10	0.01	0.00	-0.04	-0.10	0.01	-0.05
Visual imagery in day-dreams	0.01	-0.02	-0.01	-0.13	0.06	0.01	0.11	-0.05	0.01
Auditory images in day-dreams	-0.03	-0.03	-0.01	-0.06	-0.09	-0.02	-0.08	0.00	-0.01
Problem-solving day-dreams	0.09	-0.01	0.14	0.22	0.13	-0.04	0.14	0.10	0.02
Present-oriented day-dreams	0.06	-0.07	-0.23	-0.21	-0.20	0.01	0.02	-0.32	0.06
Future in daydreams	0.25	0.24	0.34	0.42	0.35	0.35	0.40	0.37	0.25
Past in daydreams	-0.19	-0.10	-0.53	-0.21	-0.15	0.01	-0.35	0.23	-0.21
Bizarre-improbable day-dreams	0.24	0.12	0.20	0.37	0.23	0.06	0.27	0.38	0.22
Mindwandering	-0.04	-0.05	-0.02	0.03	-0.12	-0.06	0.00	0.03	-0.10
Achievement-oriented daydreams	0.69	0.80	0.60	0.62	0.77	0.58	0.58	0.77	0.70
Hallucinatory-vividness of daydreams	0.04	0.00	0.05	0.13	0.04	-0.05	0.08	0.09	0.09
Fear-of-failure daydreams	0.06	0.10	0.13	0.16	0.06	0.10	0.13	0.12	0.07
Hostile daydreams	0.28	0.32	0.31	0.10	0.23	0.36	0.28	0.14	0.22
Sexual daydreams	0.28	0.49	0.27	0.15	0.26	0.41	0.25	-0.09	0.23
Heroic daydreams	0.53	0.54	0.61	0.47	0.52	0.54	0.40	0.52	0.58
Guilt daydreams	0.03	0.08	0.14	0.05	0.13	0.10	0.11	0.10	0.05
Interpersonal curiosity	0.04	-0.01	0.11	0.21	0.18	0.15	0.11	0.24	0.19
Impersonal-mechanical curiosity	0.26	0.21	0.26	0.32	0.08	0.20	0.39	0.24	0.22
Boredom susceptibility	0.05	0.03	0.02	0.13	0.08	-0.11	0.12	-0.05	0.01
Mentation rate	0.08	0.06	0.04	-0.02	0.01	-0.04	0.10	0.02	0.14
Distractibility	0.01	0.04	-0.05	-0.06	0.11	0.15	-0.10	0.12	0.05
Need for external stimu-lation	0.04	0.03	0.03	0.08	0.13	-0.06	0.13	0.06	-0.05
Self-revelation	-0.10	0.04	0.04	-0.19	-0.03	-0.15	-0.01	-0.05	-0.07

The loadings of the variables on the seventh factor found in each analysis are shown in Table 5.14. The factor is somewhat unstable over the subject classifications; factor similarity coefficients between pairs of factors range from .77 to .97. There are consistently high, positive loadings for Achievement-Oriented and Heroic Daydreams on the factor, with moderately high, positive loadings for Hostile and Sexual Daydreams as well as Impersonal–Mechanical Curiosity and the Future in Daydreaming. Thus the overall pattern of loadings on the factor suggests that this factor is one of *Success Orientation in Daydreaming*. A person who scores highly on the scales comprising this factor might be seen as an individual who fantasized a great deal about challenging situations with successful outcomes.

TABLE 5.15

Rotated Loadings for Factor 8 in Each Analysis of the IPI

	Total	Non-users	Alcohol only	Mari-juana only	Poly-drug	Male 1973	Male 1974	Female 1973	Female 1974
Daydreaming frequency	0.42	0.16	0.60	0.23	0.20	0.46	0.20	0.33	0.38
Night dreaming frequency	0.50	0.28	0.28	0.37	0.25	0.56	0.45	0.39	0.55
Absorption in daydreaming	0.13	0.11	0.17	0.34	0.11	0.13	0.14	0.14	0.16
Acceptance of daydreaming	0.19	0.24	0.18	0.25	0.19	0.22	0.14	0.24	0.19
Positive reactions in daydreaming	0.12	0.33	0.23	0.11	-0.01	0.01	0.24	0.18	0.16
Frightened reactions to daydreams	-0.04	-0.09	-0.14	0.24	0.18	-0.10	0.01	-0.03	-0.01
Visual imagery in daydreams	0.07	0.13	0.16	0.00	-0.08	0.20	0.05	0.16	0.02
Auditory images in daydreams	-0.04	0.09	0.05	-0.15	0.19	0.12	-0.10	0.01	0.02
Problem-solving daydreams	-0.01	-0.02	0.22	-0.04	-0.03	0.08	-0.04	-0.11	0.07
Present-oriented daydreams	0.07	-0.09	-0.01	-0.29	-0.15	0.09	0.10	-0.15	0.06
Future in daydreams	-0.11	0.11	-0.10	0.04	0.06	0.04	-0.10	-0.11	-0.10
Past in daydreams	0.18	0.09	0.37	0.32	0.21	0.34	0.24	0.61	0.13
Bizarre-improbable daydreams	0.12	0.23	-0.04	0.30	0.28	-0.03	0.11	0.09	0.25
Mindwandering	0.12	0.10	0.13	0.14	0.12	0.11	0.13	0.13	0.25
Achievement-oriented daydreams	-0.12	-0.33	0.00	-0.10	-0.16	0.02	-0.04	-0.16	-0.12
Hallucinatory-vividness of daydreams	-0.12	-0.10	-0.09	-0.11	0.02	-0.18	-0.01	-0.19	-0.07
Fear-of-failure daydreams	-0.07	0.00	-0.09	-0.01	-0.08	-0.12	-0.26	0.02	-0.01
Hostile daydreams	0.13	-0.01	0.01	-0.15	-0.04	0.14	0.13	0.14	-0.03
Sexual daydreams	0.31	0.60	0.12	0.06	0.15	0.15	0.43	0.34	0.18
Heroic daydreams	0.02	0.00	0.05	-0.07	-0.09	-0.05	0.06	0.02	0.00
Guilt daydreams	-0.03	0.06	-0.16	0.01	-0.06	-0.05	-0.01	-0.05	-0.11
Interpersonal curiosity	0.05	0.15	0.13	0.29	0.28	-0.02	0.08	0.27	0.10
Impersonal-mechanical curiosity	0.07	0.14	0.08	-0.18	0.00	0.03	-0.06	-0.02	0.27
Boredom susceptibility	-0.07	-0.10	0.02	-0.18	-0.03	-0.12	-0.06	-0.12	0.00
Mentation rate	0.25	0.16	0.10	0.23	0.34	0.25	0.23	0.21	0.22
Distractibility	-0.02	0.12	-0.15	0.11	0.21	0.15	0.04	-0.08	0.01
Need for external stimulation	0.20	0.05	0.04	0.15	0.35	0.02	0.42	0.06	0.25
Self-revelation	0.27	0.17	0.05	0.33	0.42	0.22	0.28	0.26	0.29

The loadings of the variables on the eight factor found in each analysis are shown in Table 5.15. This factor is the most unstable over the subgroupings of subjects; the congruence coefficients between pairs of factors range from .41 to .92 with the vast majority of the coefficients being smaller than .70. This factor, then, appears to be residual from each analysis.

Primary-Factor Correlations. Since six of the eight factors identified in each of the subgroup analyses appear to be congruent, it is appropriate to inquire if the correlations among these primary factors are the same in each subgroup. Table 5.16 shows the correlations between each pair of factors within each aligned factor pattern matrix. It should again be noted that the

TABLE 5.16

Correlations Among the Primary Factors

of the IPI in Each Group

Factor pair	Total	Non-users	Alcohol only	Mari-juana only	Poly-drug	Male 1973	Male 1974	Female 1973	Female 1974
I & II	.20	.17	.14	.16	.11	.10	.22	.13	.23
I & III	.14	.05	.03	.23	.11	.12	.08	.08	.12
I & IV	-.20	-.02	-.02	-.13	-.19	-.09	-.19	.01	-.07
I & V	.22	.04	.11	.07	.15	.16	.26	.12	.14
I & VI	-.10	-.16	-.26	-.08	-.09	-.12	-.13	-.24	-.03
I & VII	.28	.22	.01	.12	.18	.07	.08	.03	.26
I & VIII	-.12	-.04	.06	-.02	-.20	-.12	-.16	-.12	.06
II & III	.12	.22	.03	.20	.16	.01	.09	.11	.27
II & IV	.24	.19	.15	.20	.14	.25	.20	.14	.26
II & V	.52	.46	.45	.38	.37	.23	.33	.47	.55
II & VI	-.11	.03	-.10	.00	-.04	-.15	-.12	-.10	-.09
II & VII	.17	.18	.16	.23	.12	.24	.16	.03	.17
II & VIII	.42	.19	.12	.37	.15	.17	.16	.22	.35
III & IV	-.04	.05	.01	-.06	-.06	-.10	.03	-.09	.05
III & V	.41	.33	.36	.28	.28	.25	.19	.36	.32
III & VI	-.11	-.03	-.09	-.03	-.15	-.14	-.09	-.10	-.08
III & VII	.00	.03	-.04	.01	.09	.13	.13	.03	-.01
III & VIII	.15	.04	.01	.13	.09	-.02	.14	.04	.06
IV & V	.22	.19	.09	.31	.28	.10	.15	.14	.12
IV & VI	.10	.00	-.06	-.19	-.08	.01	-.01	-.24	.16
IV & VII	.12	.05	-.18	-.11	-.04	-.05	.18	-.26	.02
IV & VIII	.29	-.03	.18	-.10	-.04	.13	.21	-.15	.19
V & VI	-.05	-.03	-.01	-.25	-.16	-.11	-.11	.01	-.10
V & VII	.10	.11	.14	-.13	.05	.19	.07	.06	.16
V & VIII	.33	.15	.09	-.17	.15	.20	.08	.12	.28
VI & VII	-.15	-.03	.04	.12	.16	-.08	-.12	.30	-.08
VI & VIII	-.06	.13	-.08	.26	.22	-.07	.01	.29	-.13
VII & VIII	.05	.19	.14	.27	.16	.01	.02	.32	.02

Procrustean procedure itself does not guarantee that the correlations among the oblique factors will be the same in the aligned matrices. In spite of this freedom, the correlations are generally stable. Such invariance over subject sampling of the factor correlations is yet another indication that the organization of private cognitive states is approximately the same in the subgroups.

Validation of the Procrustean Rotations. Similarly to the PRF analyses, the Monte Carlo procedure was used to ascertain that the Procrustean transformations had not inordinately capitalized on chance. For the IPI analyses, the most stressful (2.97) analysis was in rotating the 1973 female factor matrix to the total sample factor matrix. Three random target matrices were formed by randomly ordering the columns in each row of the target matrices. The values of the stress measure when rotating the 1973 female matrix to these random hypotheses were 11.55, 11.65, and 12.88, allowing us to conclude that for the most stressful rotation, the total group factor pattern matrix provides a much better target (by a factor of 3.9:1) than some random set of hypotheses. This demonstration, then, shows that our subgroup-factor matrices have been aligned to a position that is quite consistent with the data and, presumably, the underlying causal structure.

Second-Order Factor Analysis.   Since it has been shown that, for the most part, the primary factors of the IPI are stable over different ways of classifying subjects, it seems reasonable to investigate the second-order factor pattern of the inventory. For the hierarchical analysis, we used the correlation matrix among the primary factors obtained from the total sample, because these correlations should be the best estimate of the correlation of the factors in an undifferentiated sample of college students. These correlations have been previously given as a second column of Table 5.16.

Iterated principal-factor analysis was used to extract three factors from the primary-factor correlation matrix. These three second-order factors were rotated to approximate simple structure using the varimax procedure. The loadings of the primary factors on the three, orthogonal second-order factors are shown in Table 5.17. Before interpreting the second-order factors, however, it seemed most reasonable to project the original variables onto the second-order factors and then to orthogonalize the primary factors using the theorem of Schmid and Leiman (1957). The projections of the original variables on the second-order factors and the orthogonalized primary factors are shown in Table 5.18. Our interpretations of the second-order factors are based on the first three columns of loadings in Table 5.18.

TABLE 5.17

Rotated Loadings of the IPI Primary Factors
on the Second-Order Factors

	Second-Order Factor		
Primary Factor	I	II	III
I	-.15	.69	.16
II	.65	.37	.18
III	.01	.05	.65
IV	.54	-.13	-.07
V	.45	.24	.58
VI	.01	-.22	-.10
VII	.12	.40	-.08
VIII	.59	-.02	.12

TABLE 5.18
Second-Order and Orthogonalized Primary-Factor Loadings in the IPI for Total Sample

	S_I	S_{II}	S_{III}	$P_I{}^*$	$P_{II}{}^*$	$P_{III}{}^*$	$P_{IV}{}^*$	$P_V{}^*$	$P_{VI}{}^*$	$P_{VII}{}^*$	$P_{VIII}{}^*$
Daydreaming frequency	.35	.07	.39	-.05	.00	.26	-.05	.14	-.03	.10	.34
Nightdreaming frequency	.31	.04	.10	.02	.05	-.01	-.06	.01	-.02	-.04	.40
Absorption in daydreaming	.53	.25	.57	.00	.09	.09	.01	.49	-.03	.01	.11
Acceptance of daydreaming	.47	-.24	.05	-.22	.08	-.02	.28	.09	-.02	-.12	.15
Positive reactions in daydreaming	.52	.06	.23	-.12	.09	-.01	.20	.27	-.04	.10	.10
Frightened reactions to daydreaming	.23	.47	.39	.31	.16	.03	-.03	.26	.00	-.08	-.03
Visual imagery in daydreams	.57	.25	.17	-.08	.53	.03	-.04	.00	-.03	.01	.06
Auditory images in daydreams	.55	.34	.14	.02	.61	.00	.00	-.04	.00	-.03	-.03
Problem-solving daydreams	.38	.20	.13	.12	.07	-.08	.28	.22	.15	.08	-.01
Present-oriented daydreams	-.01	-.11	.02	.05	.00	.07	-.14	.04	.98	.06	.05
Future in daydreams	.40	-.02	.03	-.11	.06	.11	.52	.01	-.05	.22	-.08
Past in daydreams	.23	.14	.21	.15	.07	.07	.11	.06	-.11	-.17	.14
Bizarre-improbable daydreams	.02	.28	.17	.03	.02	.04	-.21	.07	-.40	.21	.10
Mindwandering	.19	.00	.56	-.04	.04	.62	.07	.02	.00	-.03	.10
Achievement-oriented daydreams	.22	.39	.06	.05	.04	.04	.17	.09	-.09	.63	-.10
Hallucinatory-vividness of daydreams	.27	.52	.26	.24	.34	-.04	-.10	.16	.03	.03	-.09
Fear-of-failure daydreams	-.14	.60	.18	.57	.00	.06	.00	.02	.03	.05	-.05
Hostile daydreams	.01	.56	.18	.39	.04	.07	-.11	.02	-.02	.26	.10
Sexual daydreams	.39	.16	.24	-.04	.09	.14	.00	.10	.01	.25	.25
Heroic daydreams	.05	.51	.04	.28	.00	.00	.04	.01	-.10	.48	.02
Guilt daydreams	-.11	.64	.16	.62	.03	.02	.01	-.01	.00	.03	-.02
Interpersonal curiosity	.32	.01	.07	.03	-.01	.03	.39	.07	.02	.03	.04
Impersonal-mechanical curiosity	.04	.19	-.20	.11	.02	-.17	.04	-.08	-.02	.24	.06
Boredom susceptibility	-.20	.22	.46	.10	.03	.50	-.26	-.02	-.07	.05	-.06
Mentation rate	.38	-.09	-.03	-.10	.07	-.04	.20	.01	.10	.07	.20
Distractibility	.08	.06	.44	.08	-.01	.53	.18	-.01	.06	.01	-.01
Need for external stimulation	.26	-.09	-.15	-.07	.07	-.09	.19	-.09	.03	.03	.16
Self-revelation	.32	-.05	.07	.02	-.01	.01	.24	.04	.01	-.09	.22

S_I - S_{III} refers to second-order factors.

$P_I{}^*$ - $P_{VIII}{}^*$ refers to orthogonalized primary factors.

The first second-order factor appears to be a broadly based dimension of *Positive–Constructive Daydreaming.* Individuals scoring high on this factor report a high level of mental activity, characterized by tendencies to have many diurnal and nocturnal dreams, and a high level of both visual and auditory imagery. This mental activity is channeled into curiosity about others, problem-solving activities of an inner nature, and daydreams of sexual exploits. These individuals accept their daydreaming as a constructive adult mode of thought and report that they often have positive emotional reactions to their daydreams. People scoring highly on this dimension also feel free to discuss their private thoughts with others. Overall, then, this factor represents a generalized tendency toward a purposeful mental style with generally positive inner experiences.

The second second-order factor appears to represent a generalized *Guilt and Fear-of-Failure Orientation* in daydreaming. Individuals with high scores on the factor have many daydreams with the themes of failure and guilt and yet also daydream of great achievement and individual heroism. Large amounts of hostile affect are expressed in the daydreams of these individuals, and the daydreams are themselves often perceived as frightening. The daydreams, however, are not centered in the past and do not relate to any mental style variables that might indicate free-floating anxiety. Thus this factor may be a manifestation of a kind of punitive superego coupled with a strong approach–avoidance conflict about success.

The third second-order factor deals with an individual's reported control of his thought patterns. The high scorer on this dimension experiences frequent bouts of mindwandering and reports being easily bored. High scorers are easily distracted by external influences and yet also become highly absorbed in their daydreams. These daydreams are not of any particular thematic content but nonetheless often have a frightening quality. This dimension, then, represents one of *Attentional Control* with the high scorer experiencing a sense of powerlessness about concentration.

The pattern of orthogonalized primary factors presented in the last eight columns of Table 5.12 indicates that although much of the variance in the IPI can be explained by the three second-order factors, the full array of primary and second-order factors must be considered in order to account fully for the common variance in the instrument.

As a point of clarification, we should note that the method of hierarchical factoring employed here can be quite nicely approximated by simply extracting three maximum-likelihood factors from the original correlation matrix between the scales and rotating those dimensions. The three second-order factors can also be approximated by extracting three principal components or principal axes factors. Therefore, while the current method of hierarchical factor analysis is perhaps technically more correct than other procedures used in the past, the commonly presented small number of rotated principal components solutions provide reasonable approximations for this set of data.

Discussion

Several major findings have been presented in this second set of factor analyses. First, it has been shown that at least six out of eight primary factors in the IPI are relatively stable over sampling effects caused by categorizing subjects by their sex and what type of substances they use. Second, it has been shown that the factors have about the same correlations in each of the subgroups. Third, the hierarchical factor pattern of the IPI has been explored, and it appears that there are three second-order factors underlying the domain of private cognitive experiences sampled by the IPI.

The present results converge with previous empirical findings and theoretical statements. First, the second-order factors found in the present analysis correspond rather well to factors previously found in the IPI by a variety of workers (Giambra, 1974, 1977; Isaacs, 1975; Singer & Antrobus, 1963, 1972; Starker, 1974; Starker & Singer, 1975a). Our three second-order factors seem to be equivalent (conceptually, if not strictly numerically) to the factors the previous workers have called *Positive-Vivid Daydreaming, Guilty-Dysphoric Daydreaming,* and *Anxious-Distractible Daydreaming.* Because of our hierarchical analysis of the IPI, however, it has been possible to fix these factors at the second-order level and to further delineate the primary factors of private cognitive experience.

Second, the present results converge with the theoretical writings of Singer (1975a,b), who has noted that there are patterns of daydreaming that have a positive effect for the individual. Evidence has been found in the present data for both adaptive and maladaptive patterns of mental activity at two different levels of factoring. Furthermore, as Singer and Singer (1972) note, evidence for persistent and consistent patterns of private mental activity makes it clear that in order to construct a more adequate theory for personality, it will be necessary to consider individual differences in spontaneous private processes as well as individual differences in social behaviors, motivations, and abilities.

Third, in the previous analyses in this chapter using data collected on the same subjects, it was shown that factors of Murray needs found in Jackson's (1967) Personality Research Form are relatively stable over samples differentiated by sex and pattern of substance use. Our present results indicate that the factors of private cognitive experiences are at least as stable over sex and pattern of substance use as factors representing personality traits or motivational orientation. Thus it appears that drug or alcohol use in college students does not cause reorganization of either motivations or patterns of daydreaming and mental style.

GENERAL CONCLUSIONS

As we noted in the introduction to this chapter, the analyses presented are the first that have raised the issue of whether the *organization* of personality and private experience is the same in groups of drug users and nonusers. Within the context of the generally confirmatory methodology[3] used, it seems that there is strong, demonstrable stability of the organization of needs and daydreaming when contrasting groups of college student nonusers with their peers who do experiment with and use licit and illicit substances. Of course, the finding of general stability must be confined to the context of student drug use; most individuals in the polydrug group were certainly not drug "abusers" in the sense that they require treatment for a drug-related problem, and at the youthful age studied, drug-use history was of relatively short duration. Thus generalizability of the current results to a comparison of older nonusers and chronic users of substances is an open issue and will require more study using appropriate groups of individuals.

Throughout this chapter, we have treated the hypotheses regarding the stability of organization as causal in nature, although the critical reader will recognize that this research is strictly correlational. That is, given the results obtained from this concurrent data that there are no differences between the most extreme groups in organization, it is equally possible that: (1) there were no presubstance-use differences between the groups before some of the individuals started using substances, and the substances had no effect on organization; or (2) there were differences in organization before any of the individuals started using drugs, and substance use by the "different" individuals had the effect of making them more like their nonuser peers. Strictly adhering to the rules of scientific psychology, we cannot prefer one of these explanations from the current data; consideration of other sources of data and convergent results do, we believe, favor the first explanation that there were no pre-existing differences and that the substance use had no effect of significance on personality organization.

A first support for the hypothesis of no drug effect comes from the simultaneous finding of no differences between male and female subjects when drug use was ignored. In the case of sex, there is a definite causal order

---

[3]Since the time that these analyses were originally conducted, we have become aware of the procedure for the simultaneous maximum likelihood factor analysis in several groups developed by Jöreskog (1971) and refined by Sörbom (1974; Sörbom & Jöreskog, 1976). The IPI dataset is not appropriate for the simultaneous factor analysis procedure because of the poor distribution of the variables; some preliminary work with the Jöreskog–Sörbom procedure in the PRF dataset leads to the same conclusion reached here, and future work will focus on the more full reanalysis of this dataset using that method.

(it would be absurd to argue that differences in personality organization cause gender!), and the gender influence is, we believe, a more pervasive, general, and certainly long-term influence on personality organization than short-term experimentation with substances.

A second source of support comes from the large literature that we have previously reviewed (Chapter 2) on mean differences between groups in *level* of personality functioning. In general, this literature seems quite consistent in implicating certain variables (such as independence, rebelliousness, and the like) as strong correlates or causes of adolescent drug use. If the same dimensions of personality did not underlie the responses of both nonusers and polydrug users, such comparison on the same scales would be virtually meaningless, and we would expect that it would not be possible to consistently demonstrate differences between groups.

Third, the model in which there are no presubstance-use differences among the subjects who continue to remain nonusers and those who begin drug experimentation is more parsimonious than that of the compensatory nature of substance use in counteracting differences in private personality organization. Furthermore, if the effect of adolescent drug use was to *relieve* problems in personality organization, we would then expect that drug use would in fact make certain individuals more healthy and less susceptible to developing problem behaviors, a finding which seems directly contradicted by a large amount of data (see Jessor & Jessor, 1977, for a review).

Consequently, we believe that until longitudinal studies directly test the model by presenting time-lagged results, it is quite reasonable to operate under the assumption that there are no significant effects of short-term use of substances on the organizational structure of private personality. Such a conclusion makes it possible to contrast the mean level of private personality functioning of individuals who use drugs and alcohol with their peers who do not. This conclusion provides for a more simple model for the effect of personality differences on susceptibility to drug use and possible abuse.

6

Private Personality Differences Among Substance Use Groups

As discussed in Chapter 5, our data indicate that those aspects of private personality assessed by the Imaginal Processes Inventory and the Personality Research Form have a fairly invariant structure over different forms of youthful substance use. That is, our data show that the same personality dimensions apply equally well to nonusers of substances and their peers who use different types of psychoactive drugs. Given the applicability of the basic personality system to these contrasted groups, we may now inquire about the extent to which the groups differ in mean levels of functioning on the various facets of private personality.

In the process of reviewing the literature on adolescent drug use and personality in Chapter 1, we concluded, as have many other scholars (see Gorsuch & Butler, 1976; Sadava, 1975), that the various studies formed a confusing net of results encompassing both confirmations and disconfirmations of different theoretical systems. Also noted in Chapter 1 was the fact that part of the current confusion concerning the personality correlates and determinants of youthful substance use is a direct result of the reactive nature of much research in the area.

Methodologically, it seems quite possible to argue that the confusing nature of this research stems from a general disregard for some basic technical issues implicit in the assessment of personality (see Bentler & Eichberg, 1975). Some of the potential problem areas not receiving adequate attention are the derivation of measurement instruments from within accepted theoretical frameworks, the use of instruments with demonstrated reliability and construct validity, and the replication or cross-validation of specific findings. Even in cases where sound instruments are used, there is frequently no explicit theoretical rationale for the choice of personality variables.

One means of overcoming these problems caused by ignoring technical issues is to attempt to predict drug use (or any other criterion variable) from theoretically derived personality constructs with demonstrated validity and reliability, and then demonstrate that the basic findings can be replicated in independent samples (see Wiggins, 1973). An alternate procedure is developing adequate, theoretically based personality assessment constructs within the context of a theory of drug use. This latter approach has been ably demonstrated by Jessor and his associates (Jessor, 1975; Jessor & Jessor, 1977). This second alternative, unfortunately, is an extremely involved and costly venture. The proliferation of project-specific personality scales, moreover, may not indicate how the phenomenon can be explained by pre-existing theoretical constructs with rich networks of correlates and consequences. It is our belief that psychological variables with demonstrated significance within some macrolevel theoretical framework will thus provide greater understanding of the role of psychological processes with respect to the use or nonuse of substances than will project-specific constructs.

The present analyses are directed at examining the personality–drug-use relationship. In Chapter 2, we noted that our conception of private personality subsumes the stream of consciousness with its typical fantasies and daydreams at the core level. More accessible areas of private personality are generalized motives and generalized attitudes about sources of reinforcement. The most exposed facet of the private personality is the cluster of wishes for experience and behavioral indicators of experiencing the full range of possibilities.

In Chapter 4, we presented a detailed summary of various assessment instruments selected to measure aspects of the private personality. A short discussion of those considerations is appropriate here as we have argued that it is necessary to use instruments with exemplary psychometric characteristics in the search to conclusively determine how the private personality is linked to youthful drug and alcohol use.

First, let us consider the inner core of private personality. Singer and Antrobus (1970, 1972) have undertaken an extensive scaling effort resulting in the development of the Imaginal Processes Inventory (IPI), which assesses many different types of spontaneous thought content and style. The 28 scales of the IPI have acceptable levels of internal consistency (Singer & Antrobus, 1972). Furthermore, the IPI scales seem fairly free of social-desirability responding, and evidence to date (Huba, 1980; Isaacs, 1975) indicates that the individual scales have higher levels of validity than might be expected in this "soft" area of scaling.

Motivational tendencies have been extensively categorized and described in the metatheory of Murray (1938). Of the many efforts to scale Murray's basic motives, the Personality Research Form of Jackson (1967) is the most definitive. First, the PRF has quite high levels of internal consistency and reliability (Bentler, 1964; Jackson, 1967; Stricker, 1974), and the method of scale construction virtually guarantees that the PRF scales are free of response-style variance (Jackson, 1967). Second, a number of investigations have established convergent and discriminant validity (Jackson & Guthrie, 1968) as well as a consistent nomological network (see Chapter 4) for the inventory. Of all current personality inventories, Jackson's PRF is perhaps the most technically sound. Furthermore, the set of PRF scales is extremely exhaustive of the domain.

The concept of sensation seeking was assessed using the battery developed by Zuckerman (1975). Although Zuckerman's scaling effort does include several possible technical problems such as overlapping keying and under-factoring, there was a conscious effort in the development of forced-choice items to control for social-desirability responding. The scales for sensation seeking were developed after principal components analysis and have high levels of reliability (Zuckerman, 1975). From a theoretical point of view, moreover, the large network of consistent and replicable correlates for the scales argues strongly for validity for both test and the system (Zuckerman, 1975).

The final scale used in our battery—Rotter's Locus of Control measure—was developed to measure the extent of an individual's tendency to perceive reinforcements from the environment as a consequence of behavior. The 23-item forced-choice instrument (Rotter, 1966) has come under attack for its psychometric properties but has had major theoretical impact (Lefcourt, 1976). Of the various measures used in our final battery, this scale probably has the weakest psychometric properties.

In speculating about the role of private personality in drug-taking behavior, we feel it is likely that sensation-seeking tendencies are the most crucial private personality determinant of beginning drug experimentation. Several previous investigators (Kilpatrick, Sutker, & Smith, 1976; Segal & Merenda, 1975) have presented evidence that drug and alcohol experiences can be regarded as novel for youth. We believe that there are several salient characteristics of drug taking that cause the beginning experience to be regarded as a "new" one to be actively sought by the potential user. First, drug experiences are commonly depicted in both popular and scientific literatures as a means of achieving quite extraordinary cognitive and affective experiences. Second, within the college youth culture, drug and alcohol consumption are components of a wide variety of social situations. Third, the disinhibitory function of alcohol and other drugs (e.g., barbiturates) may allow the individual to participate in dangerous, thrilling behaviors because typical ego controls are loosened. Fourth, certain drugs such as cocaine, amphetamines, and marijuana purportedly produce a "rush" or feelings of uncontrolled euphoria and thrill. Fifth, certain drugs such as marijuana are reported to transform experiences such as sex or movie viewing and make them more exciting and unique. Consequently, the most direct link between substance use and our concept of private personality is to be found at the sensation-seeking node.

After initial drug experiences, it is likely that drug and alcohol use are initially maintained (during a nonaddictive interval) by the individual's learned experience that drug ingestion will satisfy more central motivations or, alternatively, allow motivational tendencies to be expressed. Concomitantly, the individual learns that substances make it easier to cope with undesirable forms of inner experience and enhance positive inner experiences. Thus the constellation of generalized motives and characteristic inner experiences are probably most important for maintaining substance use after the early experimental stage.

In predicting which measures in our battery of private personality indicators should be the most related to differentiating the groups of substance users, we most carefully consider the nature of the samples. As noted earlier (Chapter 4), most individuals in the substance-user groups were relatively new initiates to the drug with fairly low usage rates. Therefore it is likely that the sensation-seeking facet should be most highly related to the categories. Since some individuals within the groups had relatively long-term histories of experience with the substance, it also seems likely that the motivational tendencies will differ between groups, although not in as strong a manner. Furthermore, we can argue that to the extent to which increasingly illicit drugs are seen as producing more novel and mystical experiences by youth, there should be a linear relationship between the sensation-seeking measures and the categories of drug use ordered (nonusers through alcohol users, marijuana users, and polydrug users) in terms of the legal and social penalties for use. It also seems likely that those generalized motives related to the seeking of sensations will be linearly related to the four substance-user categories.

We do not know how inner-experience variables will be related to the current substance-use categories. From our perspective, perceived effects on inner experience would only be realized after moderate experiences with a drug, and it is unlikely that these processes will maintain early experimentation. Consequently, we believe that it is more possible that the core inner-experience variables will be related to the number of times a drug has been used or to perceived motives for use rather than simple experimentation. This secondary question is further addressed by additional analyses in the next chapter.

METHOD

Subjects

The subjects for this set of analyses were the total sample of 1095 college students described in Chapter 4. Drug classifications were the same as those described in Chapter 4 and used in the analyses for Chapter 5.

Data Analysis

Following derivation of the four criterion groups, separate stepwise discriminant analyses were computed for males and females in each of the 2 sample years. That is, four discriminant analyses were calculated in which there were four criterion groups: *nonusers, alcohol-only* users, *marijuana-only* users, and *polydrug* users. The independent variables in the analyses were the total set of personality variables scored from the PRF, IPI, SSS, and LC items, resulting in the attempted discrimination of the four groups from 48 individual difference measures.

The present discriminant analyses can be seen as the multivariate analog of a normal oneway analysis of variance (ANOVA). In ANOVA, we attempt to determine if the groups are significantly different on some measure. When there are multiple measures expected to differ between the groups, however, one must assess group differences in the context of covariation between individual measures. In the current analyses, group dispersion (or difference) is assessed in combination with the covariance structure of the private personality measures. Rather than testing group differences on each of the scale scores independently, the procedure seeks linear combinations of the original measures that will best discriminate the groups. A statistical test, analogous to the *F* ratio in ANOVA, determines if the discrimination is significantly greater than that expected by chance.

In the current discriminant analyses, variables were entered in a stepwise manner similar to stepwise multiple linear regression. That is, the analysis was recomputed for between 1 and 48 variables entered in order of importance for providing additional discrimination between the criterion groups. The stepwise (and full) discriminant analyses were computed using the program BMDP7M, April 1975 release (Dixon, 1975), with the entry of variables determined by the *F*-to-enter criterion given by Jennrich (1977). The entry criterion was set so as to include all variables, and the removal criterion was set to 0.0 so that no variables would be excluded from the equations once entered.

After the discriminant functions were calculated, they were used to predict drug-use classification from the personality variables using the log likelihood method with all a priori probabilities of group membership set *equal* to one another (i.e., to .25). The actual classification rates should, therefore, be viewed as conservative, since it seems unlikely that the population membership percentages in the four groups are equal.

A difficulty with discriminant analysis is that the linear combination generated to maximally differentiate the groups is frequently difficult to interpret psychologically (Morrison, 1976; Tatsuoka, 1971). Several supplementary analyses were undertaken to render the results more interpretable. First, we calculated the loadings of the original variables on the discriminant variable. As opposed to the weights normally generated by a canned computer program, the loadings are not regression coefficients (from the measures to the combination) with attendant ambiguities of interpretation (Darlington, 1968) but are bivariate correlations between the linear combination and the original measures. Loadings have proven to be more interpretable in canonical correlation analysis (Bentler & Huba, in press; Cooley & Lohnes, 1971) of which discriminant analysis is a special case (Cooley & Lohnes, 1971; Morrison, 1976; Tatsuoka, 1971). A second strategy to facilitate interpretation was a set of univariate omnibus tests and planned contrasts on the means of the original measures. The omnibus F tests were normal *univariate* tests, whereas the planned contrast for each set of means was a linear trend test ranking the groups nonusers, alcohol-only, marijuana-only, and polydrug users. Our use of the univariate F ratios given for the omnibus hypothesis and linear trend has been primarily descriptive as opposed to inferential because of criticisms of post hoc univariate testing articulated by Wilkinson (1975). Nonetheless, since multiple samples have been used, it is possible to moderate the use of univariate F ratios with an examination of whether the difference exists in more than one of the independent samples.

A further comment should be made on our use of multiple samples in the current analyses and those of Chapter 8. Since significance testing after most multivariate procedures requires the assumption of multivariate normality (a condition that may not be justifiable for any set of psychological data), and the procedures do not have known robustness properties over violation of this assumption, it seems most reasonable to calculate analyses in several fairly large samples to determine if the same conclusions can be repeatedly reached. Assuming that violations of multivariate normality will not occur in the same manner for each sample, this replication strategy partially ensures that the conclusions will be accurate.

Finally, a series of best predictor replication analyses was calculated to determine the accuracy of the best set of predictor variables obtained in stepwise analyses limited to most differentiating measures. For each sample, the best set of predictor variables (6 or 7) was used to predict classifications in the other sample of the same sex. Thus we have used the best set of predictors from a first sample (e.g., 1973 males) and determined if the same variables would discriminate equally well in a second sample (1974 males). In the replication analyses, optimal weights were estimated in the replication sample rather than attempting to directly cross-validate the discriminant function weights from the first sample. Recent research has shown that optimally derived weights are not easy to generalize, and the intent here is to determine which theoretical aspects of private personality should be considered in a parsimonious conception of substance use.

RESULTS

Discriminant analyses, allowing all 48 variables to enter the function, should first be considered. There was significant separation between the four criterion groups in each of the four samples: For the 1973 males, Wilks' λ was .38 (χ^2_{144} = 232.4, $p < .001$); for the 1974 males λ was .33 (χ^2_{144} = 222.6, $p < .001$); for the 1973 females λ was .37 (χ^2_{144} = 281.3, $p \leq .001$); and for the 1974 females, λ was .32 (χ^2_{144} = 281.3, $p < .001$). Decomposition of the total Bartlett's χ^2 indicated that only one dimension was necessary to explain the between-groups dispersion for two of the samples (1974 males and 1973 females), whereas two dimensions were necessary to explain all of the between-groups dispersion for the remaining samples (1973 males and 1974 females). Since it is desirable to consider the same number of dimensions in each of the groups, we have limited our consideration to the first discriminant function in each of the samples.

Table 6.1 shows the standardized discriminant coefficients and discriminant function loadings derived separately for each of the four samples. The absolute size of these coefficients represent the relative contribution of the associated variable to the discriminant function. The interpretation of standardized discriminant function weights is analogous to the interpretation of standardized regression coefficients and must be treated with the same cautions suggested by Darlington (1968). The discriminant-function loadings are the correlations between the original variables and the discriminant variables. As with the standardized weights, a positive coefficient indicates that a high score on the variable tends to be associated with the nonuse of substances, whereas a negative coefficient indicates that a high score on the variable tends to be associated with the use of substances. The loading coefficients presented in the last four columns of Table 6.1 may be interpreted much as one interprets a set of orthogonal factor loadings if it is remembered that the underlying "latent" variable has been generated in order to maximally differentiate the criterion groups and not because of some inner cohesiveness of the data.

Examining first the standardized discriminant-function coefficients, it can be seen that individual weights bounce, both in magnitude and sign, from

TABLE 6.1
Standardized Discriminant Coefficients and
Loading of Original Variables on Discriminant Variables

Variable	Discriminant Function Coefficients				Discriminant Function Loadings			
	1973 Male	1974 Male	1973 Female	1974 Female	1973 Male	1974 Male	1973 Female	1974 Female
1. Frequency	.174	-.172	-.075	.028	-.10	-.29	-.19	-.15
2. Night dreaming	-.233	-.013	.036	.055	-.25	-.25	-.18	-.16
3. Absorption in daydreaming	.052	-.249	.084	-.059	-.01	-.03	-.12	-.30
4. Acceptance of daydreaming	-.047	-.024	.063	-.087	-.04	-.13	-.18	-.24
5. Positive reactions to daydreaming	.001	-.105	.073	.088	.15	-.03	.07	.02
6. Frightened reactions to daydreaming	.095	-.030	-.066	.015	.05	.21	-.14	-.21
7. Visual imagery in daydreams	-.079	-.020	.101	.218	.07	.06	-.14	-.11
8. Auditory imagery in daydreams	-.101	-.023	-.123	-.172	-.01	.10	-.23	-.27
9. Problem solving in daydreams	-.070	.289	-.145	-.119	-.07	.18	-.08	-.11
10. Present-oriented daydreams	-.282	-.133	.040	.091	.17	-.09	.13	.16
11. Future-oriented daydreams	-.129	.085	.058	.175	.07	.10	.07	.11
12. Past-oriented daydreams	.051	.090	-.093	-.021	-.10	.16	-.05	-.15
13. Bizarre-improbable daydreams	-.165	.018	.080	.009	-.09	.03	-.19	-.20
14. Mindwandering	-.207	-.123	.145	-.058	-.16	-.05	-.07	-.16
15. Achievement-oriented daydreams	.029	-.129	-.289	-.174	.20	.17	-.10	.03
16. Hallucinatory-vivid daydreams	.037	.189	-.007	.102	-.01	.24	-.14	-.16
17. Fear-of-failure daydreams	-.040	.432	.172	-.028	-.09	.36	-.02	-.01
18. Hostile daydreams	.074	-.127	-.150	-.034	.05	.12	-.21	-.11
19. Sexual daydreams	.202	.220	-.090	-.109	.15	.02	-.19	-.31
20. Heroic daydreams	.250	.130	.158	.157	.20	.25	-.10	.13
21. Guilt daydreams	-.067	-.238	.003	-.158	-.04	.27	-.08	-.11
22. Interpersonal curiosity	-.068	-.121	.013	-.080	-.04	-.11	-.01	-.07
23. Impersonal curiosity	-.088	.018	.068	.320	-.05	.16	-.09	.19
24. Boredom susceptibility	-.343	-.009	-.092	-.117	-.29	.01	-.07	-.16

25. Mentation rate	-.063	.071	.107	-.081	-.04	-.03	.04	-.06
26. Distractibility	.234	.003	-.071	.022	.00	-.03	.02	.01
27. Need for external stimulation	.117	-.085	-.028	-.055	-.13	-.21	-.20	-.29
28. Self-revelation	-.156	.012	-.111	-.137	-.25	-.15	-.25	-.32
29. Achievement	.078	.146	.121	.078	.24	.14	.00	.11
30. Affiliation	.106	.003	-.031	-.022	.15	-.09	-.08	.13
31. Aggression	-.062	.139	.118	-.055	-.09	.02	-.09	-.23
32. Autonomy	.057	-.102	-.160	-.102	-.36	-.37	-.58	-.47
33. Dominance	.012	.312	.132	.044	.06	.17	-.04	-.04
34. Endurance	-.011	-.032	-.043	.069	.14	.13	-.09	.05
35. Exhibitionism	.065	-.325	.007	.060	-.03	-.25	-.16	-.12
36. Harmavoidance	-.297	-.103	.261	.038	.49	.39	.65	.45
37. Impulsivity	.021	-.004	-.044	.044	-.35	-.39	-.42	-.35
38. Nurturance	.150	-.105	.027	.047	.21	.08	.21	.26
39. Order	-.031	-.007	-.158	-.198	.29	.31	.37	.18
40. Play	-.134	.084	.050	-.082	-.13	-.26	-.15	-.27
41. Social recognition	.024	.186	.273	.262	.25	.33	.46	.34
42. Understanding	-.208	-.079	-.108	-.143	-.17	-.24	-.31	-.23
43. Infrequency	-.025	.063	.066	-.131	-.11	.06	-.21	-.20
44. Locus of control	-.054	-.063	-.030	-.028	-.23	-.16	-.24	-.21
45. General sensation seeking	.118	.102	.081	-.112	-.43	-.52	-.64	-.57
46. Thrill and adventure seeking	.172	-.271	.020	-.084	-.26	-.44	-.47	-.36
47. Experience seeking	-.506	-.295	-.498	-.324	-.69	-.63	-.86	-.80
48. Disinhibition	-.322	-.427	-.293	-.259	-.37	-.52	-.57	-.56

sample to sample. The apparent nonreplicability is perhaps to be expected; the weights, of course, are coefficients to be applied to the *independent portions* of the private personality variables in order to predict type of substance use. Some relationships do hold across samples, however. The most stable weights are those applied to the experience sensation seeking and disinhibition scales. Furthermore, substantial weights for three samples indicate that the need for social recognition should be heavily weighted. Overall, though, the cross-sample replication is disappointing when we consider only prediction weights.

When the discriminant-function loadings are examined, however, quite a different picture emerges. As can be seen in Table 6.1, the loadings in the four samples are quite similar. Congruence coefficients were calculated between the dimensions generated for the four samples and are shown in Table 6.2. Product-moment correlations calculated on either the loadings or the columns of discriminant-function weights give almost identical values and thus are not presented here. The coefficients indicate that there is a high degree of similarity in the pattern of loadings. The first principal component of the similarities in Table 6.2 was calculated. The loadings for 1973 males (.87), 1974 males (.76), 1973 females (.90), and 1974 females (.89) shows that a fairly stable, robust dimension of individual variation has been derived to differentiate users from nonuser peers.

Before an interpretation of the discriminant dimensions can be given, it is necessary to examine the centroids (or mean scores) of the criterion groups on the dimension. The sample centroids for the criterion groups are shown in Table 6.3. The ordering of the centroids gives information essential to interpreting the meaning of the discriminant dimensions. In each sample, the centroids are linearly related to increasing experience with substances; nonusers score at one extreme with polydrug users and alcohol and marijuana

TABLE 6.2
Congruence Coefficients for Discriminant Loadings

	1973 Males	1974 Males	1973 Females	1974 Females
1973 Males	--			
1974 Males	.79	--		
1973 Females	.82	.74	--	
1974 Females	.83	.71	.93	--

TABLE 6.3
Average Discriminant Function Scores
for Drug-Use Groups

Group	1973 Males	1974 Males	1973 Females	1974 Females
Nonusers	1.40	1.82	0.82	1.25
Alcohol only	0.67	0.73	0.47	.57
Marijuana only	-0.11	-0.62	-0.97	-0.44
Polydrug	-1.16	-1.24	-1.36	-1.45

users in the middle. Our discriminant function differentiates the groups in a manner relating to increasing involvement with psychoactive substances.

Remembering that a positive discriminant-function loading indicates that a high score on the original measure is associated with nonuse of substances and that a negative coefficient means that a high score on the measure is associated with the use of substances, we can interpret the discriminant loadings. There are extremely high negative loadings on the dimension for all four of the sensation-seeking measures. The simple, unweighted untransformed average loading for Experience Seeking is –.74, and this result, in conjunction with the average loadings for General Sensation Seeking (–.54), Disinhibition (–.51), and Thrill and Adventure Seeking (–.38), suffice to argue that *the sensation-seeking constructs are largely synonymous with the best possible way to differentiate the four groups of substance users* from the private personality variables assessed in our battery. Within the motivational domain, we find that the needs for Autonomy and Impulsivity are related strongly and consistently to substance use while high levels of the needs to Avoid Harm and gain Social Recognition are related to the nonuse of substances. An increased need for Order is also somewhat related to the nonuse of substances. Within the inner-experience domain, only the needs for External Stimulation and Self-Revelation and the Day- and Night-dreaming Frequency scales are related to substance use; other indicators of mental style and content are not consistently related to the most differentiating linear combination. The set of loadings generally confirms our expectations about the strength of linkages to the different facets of private personality.

In conjunction with the discriminant-function loadings, examining the means for the different groups on major variables related to discrimination helps to clarify an interpretation of multivariate differences. Table 6.4 presents the mean score for each criterion group on a selected set of the

TABLE 6.4
Means and Univariate *F* Ratios of Variables Significantly Different Between Drug-Use Groups

	Nonusers	Alcohol Only	Marijuana Only	Multi-Drug	F	F Linear	η
Auditory Imagery In Daydreams							
Male 1973	36.55	36.12	35.81	36.49	.06	.00	.03
Male 1974	37.28	33.85	34.60	33.56	1.05	2.19	.12
Female 1973	35.80	33.58	37.71	39.13	3.70*	5.24*	.18
Female 1974	31.73	36.67	36.00	39.47	5.00**	12.85**	.23
Need for External Stimulation							
Male 1973	38.16	39.66	41.66	40.14	2.65*	3.46	.17
Male 1974	38.35	39.55	40.73	41.21	1.74	4.68*	.15
Female 1973	39.18	40.51	41.70	41.43	2.26	4.51*	.15
Female 1974	37.40	38.99	40.68	41.32	4.02**	11.60**	.21
Self-Revelation							
Male 1973	35.55	35.21	38.13	38.47	3.13*	5.07*	.19
Male 1974	37.68	36.78	37.43	40.33	2.02	2.10	.16
Female 1973	39.06	38.60	42.59	40.24	4.55**	3.20	.20
Female 1974	36.90	38.03	41.71	41.18	5.91**	13.40**	.25
Need for Affiliation							
Male 1973	15.06	14.32	14.33	13.73	.98	2.58	.11
Male 1974	14.07	15.21	15.27	15.08	.94	1.56	.11
Female 1973	15.43	16.01	16.25	14.28	3.78*	2.80	.18
Female 1974	15.62	16.67	16.39	15.16	3.60*	.84	.20
Need for Autonomy							
Male 1973	7.65	8.17	9.47	9.99	5.65**	13.43**	.25
Male 1974	7.46	8.30	9.23	10.16	5.80**	15.58**	.26
Female 1973	6.17	6.53	8.45	9.93	18.55**	51.40**	.39
Female 1974	6.58	6.47	7.91	9.66	12.28**	27.59**	.35

Need for Exhibitionism							
Male 1973	9.81	9.87	10.54	9.99	.53	0.22	.08
Male 1974	9.71	10.50	11.45	11.95	2.56	6.74**	.18
Female 1973	9.50	9.52	11.33	9.45	3.85*	0.57	.19
Female 1974	9.17	9.29	11.00	9.61	3.11*	1.76	.18
Need for Harmavoidance							
Male 1973	10.39	9.06	7.31	6.51	10.50**	27.67***	.33
Male 1974	10.21	8.72	7.62	6.15	6.84***	19.19***	.29
Female 1973	11.74	11.20	8.23	7.08	22.98***	59.63***	.42
Female 1974	10.98	11.37	9.62	7.69	11.29***	23.48***	.33
Need for Impulsivity							
Male 1973	8.84	9.38	9.65	11.23	5.50***	10.90***	.24
Male 1974	8.25	10.18	10.94	11.94	6.85***	20.43***	.29
Female 1973	9.88	9.87	12.65	11.41	11.32***	13.64***	.31
Female 1974	10.11	10.48	12.00	12.20	6.49***	15.98***	.27
Need for Order							
Male 1973	10.94	10.68	10.02	8.64	3.32*	6.56*	.19
Male 1974	12.11	10.32	9.00	9.04	4.39***	11.04**	.23
Female 1973	11.40	11.23	8.58	9.65	7.96***	11.11**	.26
Female 1974	10.33	10.88	9.14	9.44	2.53	2.93	.17
Need for Play							
Male 1973	11.48	11.56	12.26	12.27	.84	1.59	.10
Male 1974	10.93	12.45	13.09	13.08	3.47*	8.95***	.21
Female 1973	11.68	12.64	12.91	12.65	2.31	2.91	.15
Female 1974	11.58	12.95	13.56	13.60	4.58***	12.00***	.22
Need for Social Recognition							
Male 1973	11.32	10.97	10.18	9.32	2.52	5.74*	.17
Male 1974	12.46	11.26	10.16	9.36	4.46**	12.35***	.24
Female 1973	11.71	11.81	9.75	8.50	11.42***	28.86***	.31
Female 1974	11.73	12.50	11.89	9.34	8.59***	11.45***	.30

(continued)

TABLE 6.4 (continued)

	Nonusers	Alcohol Only	Marijuana Only	Multi-Drug	F	F Linear	η
Need for Understanding							
Male 1973	12.48	12.58	12.86	13.54	1.23	2.32	.12
Male 1974	12.32	12.21	12.84	14.13	3.34*	5.79*	.21
Female 1973	12.06	12.62	14.07	13.28	5.97***	8.46***	.23
Female 1974	12.11	11.95	13.06	13.27	2.92*	5.76*	.18
General Sensation Seeking							
Male 1973	9.48	11.43	13.05	12.96	10.60***	28.00	.33
Male 1974	9.57	11.78	12.90	14.52	13.06***	38.25***	.38
Female 1973	8.95	10.17	13.17	13.48	22.66***	55.09***	.42
Female 1974	9.31	10.01	12.94	13.40	18.98***	47.08***	.42
Thrill and Adventure Seeking							
Male 1973	8.29	9.68	10.95	10.30	6.24***	12.73***	.26
Male 1974	7.90	9.95	10.60	11.50	9.42***	28.18***	.33
Female 1973	8.11	8.52	10.32	10.78	10.99***	27.71***	.30
Female 1974	8.04	8.41	9.67	10.18	6.29***	16.50***	.26
Experience Sensation Seeking							
Male 1973	5.48	7.21	9.09	10.01	24.04***	65.24***	.46
Male 1974	6.29	7.37	9.09	11.10	21.50***	53.70***	.47
Female 1973	5.09	6.24	9.72	10.37	49.87***	124.54***	.56
Female 1974	5.15	6.44	9.18	10.13	42.11***	115.01***	.56
Disinhibition							
Male 1973	4.19	5.58	6.26	6.46	7.03***	20.43***	.27
Male 1974	4.00	5.45	6.80	7.19	12.53***	33.40***	.38
Female 1973	2.98	4.18	5.20	5.45	20.40***	49.67***	.40
Female 1974	3.19	4.67	5.56	6.18	18.18***	53.74***	.41

* $p < .05$
** $p < .01$
*** $p < .001$

original measures. Scale means are presented in Table 6.4 if the measure significantly discriminated between criterion groups in at least two of the samples using univariate F ratios as the index of separation.

The variables that discriminate among the four groups *univariately* include Auditory Imagery in Daydreams (for females only), the need for External Stimulation, and Self-revelation from the inner experience domain; and the needs for Affiliation (females only), Autonomy, Exhibitionism (females only), Harmavoidance, Impulsivity, Order, Play (1974 subjects only), Social Recognition, and Understanding. The sensation-seeking scales are significantly different between the four groups in all samples. For most of these variables, the linear contrast indicates that the groups are different on the personality variables in a manner that parallels illicit drug involvement.

The final column of Table 6.4 shows the estimated coefficient η or correlation ratio for the drug classification variable and the personality measure. The square of this coefficient is the percentage of the variance in the personality measure accounted for by the drug classification. As may be seen, the coefficients range from values of .023 to .565. The coefficients for the sensation-seeking variables all exceed .25, indicating that, at minimum, the drug-use classification accounts for almost 7% of the sensation-seeking variance. Across all samples, the classification variables account for about 25% of the total variance in experience sensation-seeking tendencies. These coefficients, then, are another indication of the strength of the relationship between drug-use involvement and individual personality variables.

From the discriminant functions, it is possible to attempt to classify individuals using their function scores in standard log-likelihood methods (see Morrison, 1976; Tatsuoka, 1971). Although classification for the sake of classification was not our primary goal in this investigation, the percentage of correct classification (or the "hit" rate) serves as a utility index for discriminant functions. That is, to the extent that perfect classification of drug-use patterns exists given knowledge about the personality variables, we can argue that the personality differences are quite important. Table 6.5 presents the results of classification based on the first discriminant variable in each sample. The predicted classifications were derived from an optimally weighted combination of all 48 original variables, and it was assumed that all a priori probabilities of any subject belonging to any one of the four criterion groups were equal. The overall correct classification (or "hit" rate) for male 1973 subjects was 60.7% and is closely approximated by the overall hit rate for 1974 male subjects of 62.3%. Comparable results were obtained for the female samples with overall hit rates of 61.3% and 65.3% obtained in the 1973 and 1974 groups, respectively. These correct classification rates, it should be noted, reflect a level of correct classification obtained by including all potentially spurious sources of variance in the analysis and thus are somewhat larger than would be expected in a cross-validation study.

TABLE 6.5
Classification Results

	Group	Percent Correct	Predicted			
			Nonuse	Alcohol	Marijuana	Polydrug
(a)	1973 Males					
	Nonuse	67.7	21	4	5	1
	Alcohol	54.5	15	42	13	7
	Marijuana	56.5	6	13	48	18
	Polydrug	68.9	1	10	12	51
	Total	60.7	43	69	78	77
(b)	1974 Males					
	Nonuse	71.4	20	6	2	0
	Alcohol	62.8	11	49	11	7
	Marijuana	51.9	5	14	40	18
	Polydrug	72.9	1	1	11	35
	Total	62.3	37	70	64	60
(c)	1973 Females					
	Nonuse	66.3	61	15	9	7
	Alcohol	51.7	29	60	18	9
	Marijuana	63.8	8	8	44	9
	Polydrug	71.7	3	7	3	33
	Total	61.3	101	90	74	58
(d)	1974 Females					
	Nonuse	67.3	35	12	3	2
	Alcohol	57.4	18	54	14	8
	Marijuana	63.6	6	10	42	8
	Polydrug	77.4	1	5	8	48
	Total	65.3	60	81	67	66

Although the discriminant functions have been presented as if the full function was of primary interest (as indeed it is), the variables were entered into the analysis in a stepwise fashion. That is, the variables with the greatest discriminating power were added to the analysis one at a time in the order of their independent contributions to the total discrimination using the partial F ratio procedure provided in the program BMDP7M (Dixon, 1975). Table 6.6 presents the optimal order to entering variables for each of the four samples. Interestingly, the Experience Sensation Scale was consistently the single best predictor in the four separate analyses. The remaining variables in each of the

TABLE 6.6
Steps in Which Variables Entered the Analysis
in Each of the Four Groups

	Variable	1973 Males	1974 Males	1973 Females	1974 Females
1.	Frequency of daydreaming	32	15	44	46
2.	Night dreaming frequency	6	45	45	41
3.	Absorption in daydreaming	24	19	39	47
4.	Acceptance of daydreaming	22	44	41	39
5.	Positive reactions to daydreaming	48	37	42	28
6.	Frightened reactions to daydreaming	39	17	47	44
7.	Visual imagery in daydreams	41	48	10	16
8.	Auditory imagery in daydreams	40	20	9	15
9.	Problem-solving daydreams	21	18	30	19
10.	Present-oriented daydreams	3	23	46	26
11.	Future-oriented daydreams	19	8	7	22
12.	Past-oriented daydreams	43	27	38	8
13.	Bizarre-improbable daydreams	20	47	27	20
14.	Mindwandering	31	9	33	14
15.	Achievement-oriented daydreams	38	22	18	27
16.	Hallucinatory-vivid daydreams	46	28	40	25
17.	Fear-of-failure daydreams	47	4	32	12
18.	Hostile daydreams	37	13	14	48
19.	Sexual daydreams	13	10	12	13
20.	Heroic daydreams	5	2	20	5
21.	Guilt daydreams	45	16	13	36
22.	Interpersonal curiosity	10	7	43	18
23.	Impersonal curiosity	9	30	28	4
24.	Boredom susceptibility	2	43	34	17
25.	Mentation rate	29	38	31	32
26.	Distractibility	7	46	22	38
27.	Need for external stimulation	28	39	29	45
28.	Self-revelation	17	26	8	23
29.	Achievement	25	32	5	31
30.	Affiliation	36	14	24	11
31.	Aggression	11	21	11	37
32.	Autonomy	35	35	6	35
33.	Dominance	18	5	23	43
34.	Endurance	8	24	48	29
35.	Exhibitionism	34	11	26	21
36.	Harmavoidance	15	34	15	6
37.	Impulsivity	26	41	4	42
38.	Nurturance	16	36	37	10
39.	Order	42	25	21	9
40.	Play	27	40	36	40
41.	Social recognition	44	12	19	3
42.	Understanding	12	31	25	30
43.	Infrequency	23	33	3	24
44.	Locus of control	33	42	35	33
45.	General sensation seeking	30	29	16	7
46.	Thrill and adventure seeking	14	6	17	34
47.	Experience seeking	1	1	1	1
48.	Disinhibition	4	3	2	2

four analyses do not yield a generally similar array of discriminant variables. The stepwise discriminant procedure, of course, capitalizes heavily on the peculiarities of a given sample, and it is not likely that all variables that best predict in one sample will do so in a supposedly comparable sample, but similarities are present. In addition to experience sensation seeking, the most consistently discriminating variable is disinhibition sensation seeking. More detailed analysis of the steps in which the different variables entered the discriminant function reveals that little theoretically interesting information is provided by the stepwise procedure. From the order of entry shown in Table 6.6, we calculated Kendall's concordance coefficient (W). The obtained value of .36, while statistically greater than zero ($\chi^2_{47} = 67.68$, $p < .05$), is insufficient to argue that the results indicate a set of consistent patterns of entry into the prediction equation. Converting the concordance coefficient shows that the average value of Spearman's rank order correlation coefficient (ρ) is .14. Nor is there generality within the sexes; the order of entry for both the two male samples ($\rho = .03$) and the two female samples ($\rho = .24$) is quite different. Further analysis of the order of entry in relationship to the facet of private personality was undertaken using the Kruskal–Wallis oneway analysis of variance on ranks, with the daydreaming variables forming one category, the Murray need and locus-of-control variables forming the second category, and the sensation-seeking variables forming the third set. In the rank ANOVA, only the χ^2 value of 8.28 for the 1973 female sample was sufficiently large enough to allow us to conclude that the variables form the domains entered in different orders; the χ^2 values for the 1973 males (3.35), 1974 males (5.10), and 1974 females (4.09) could not be rejected at even the marginal .05 level of significance. Consequently, it is our impression that while there were replicable individual differences among the groups on a series of variables that can be combined into a robust, replicable individual-differences dimension, it is rather difficult to definitively choose either individual variables, other than Experience and Disinhibition Sensation Seeking, or a particular facet of private personality from the current battery as the best predictors of type of substance use.

In order to determine how much of the classification rates would shrink when only the best set of predictors in each sample were used, log-likelihood classifications were computed using only those predictors that entered the discriminant functions at a nominal level of significance (critical ratios significant at the .05 level in the stepwise procedure[1]). Table 6.7 shows the

---

[1]Since stepwise procedures of all kinds require complicated sequential tests that are not fully developed if a nominal level of significance is to be maintained, an approximate procedure was used. We set the computer program at an F-to-enter value determined so as to fix the confidence interval at .95 for the appropriate number of degrees of freedom in the sample. Once entered into the equation, all variables were retained. This approximate procedure, while seemingly

TABLE 6.7
Summary of Stepwise Discriminant Analyses

Derivation Group	Classification Rate	Variables	Replication Group	Classification Rate
1973 Males	48.7%	Experience seeking Boredom susceptibility Present-oriented daydreams Disinhibition Heroic daydreams Night dreaming Distractibility	1974 Males	41.1%
1974 Males	42.9%	Experience seeking Heroic daydreams Disinhibition Fear-of-failure daydreams Dominance Thrill and adventure seeking	1973 Males	42.3%
1973 Females	50.5%	Experience seeking Disinhibition Infrequency Impulsivity Achievement Autonomy Future-oriented daydreams	1974 Females	49.3%
1974 Females	54.0%	Experience seeking Disinhibition Social recognition Impersonal curiosity Heroic daydreams Harmavoidance General sensation seeking	1973 Females	46.4%

predictors used in these truncated analyses, the correct rate of classification in the derivation sample, and the correct rate of classification obtained using only those variables (with sample specific optimal weights) in the matched replication sample of the same sex. Examining the rates for males, using the best seven predictors for the 1973 males, a correct classification rate of .49 can be obtained from these measures in the 1973 male sample and a rate of .42 using the same variables with the data from the 1974 male sample. For the 1974 males, a correct classification rate of .43 is obtained using the best six predictors, and a rate of .43 is found using the same variables in the data from

"standard" in the literature, probably errs in the current case by admitting one or two too many discriminant predictor variables. A detailed consideration of the prediction results did show, however, that the omission of one or two variables from any of the sets does not serve to lower the level of prediction more than a few percent, so it seems that the approximate procedure is adequate in this case.

the 1973 males. Turning to the female samples, for the 1973 females, the best seven predictors allow a correct classification rate of .51, and the same seven predictor variables in the data from the 1974 female sample allow a classification rate of .49. Finally, the best seven predictors for the 1974 females allow a hit rate of .54 in classification in the derivation data, and a hit rate of .46 in the data for the 1973 females.

Finally, we should note that the discriminant analysis was repeated for the combined sample with results approximating the rough average of those presented here. In this chapter we have chosen to present the separate results from the four different samples because it seems to us that the relatively consistent findings across samples argue for the robustness of the analyses in spite of any difficulties that might have arisen from the inevitable violation of multivariate procedure assumptions. We can briefly summarize the results obtained for the total sample as follows.

The overall multivariate test for the difference between the four drug-use groups was highly significant (Wilks' λ = .54, χ^2_{144} = 664.56). Two discriminant functions were necessary to explain all the between-groups dispersion with the pattern of loadings on the first dimension similar to the first dimension found for each of the individual samples (see Table 6.2). The overall pattern of individual tests of the means of the observed measures was also about the same as that found for the four samples, although a difference was found between the groups for more of the variables due to the increased statistical power of the univariate analyses of variance.

The obtained differences on the 26 variables for which there is a significant univariate effect can be summarized most succinctly using the correlation ratio (coefficient η) for the drug-use classification variable and the personality measure. The scales that had a significant univariate F ratio and the corresponding correlation ratio (which is an algebraic transformation of F) are: (1) Daydreaming Frequency (.11); (2) Night Dreaming Frequency (.12); (3) Acceptance of Daydreaming (.11); (4) Future Orientation in Daydreaming (.09); (5) Bizarre-Improbable Daydreams (.12); (6) Sexual Daydreams (.10); (7) Boredom Susceptibility (.12); (8) Need for External Stimulation (.15); (9) Self-Revelation (.15); (10) Need for Achievement (.09); (11) Need for Affiliation (.12); (12) Need for Autonomy (.34); (13) Need for Exhibitionism (.15); (14) Need for Harmavoidance (.36); (15) Need for Impulsivity (.23); (16) Need for Nurturance (.18); (17) Need for Order (.20); (18) Need for Play (.15); (19) Need for Social Recognition (.24); (20) Need for Understanding (.16); (21) Infrequent Responding (.10); (22) Locus of Control (.14); (23) General Sensation Seeking (.40); (24) Thrill and Adventure Seeking (.29); (25) Experience Sensation Seeking (.53); and (26) Disinhibition (.40).

Because the two sexes were mixed and the replicability from year to year was not perfect, it should not be expected that the log-likelihood classifications for the total combined sample should be quite as high as was obtained for the four individual samples. A slight decreased accuracy in prediction was found for the total sample with the accuracy of correct prediction being 50.2%.

DISCUSSION

The intent of these analyses was to determine the extent to which drug users could be differentiated from nonuser peers on the basis of theoretically meaningful personality and individual-difference constructs. It has been shown, using constructs for four quite different but related facets of the private personality that youthful drug takers are different fron nonusers on several theoretically grounded dimensions. In addition, individuals may be correctly classified into one of four drug- and alcohol-use categories on the basis of their private personality scores with a maximum of between 60% and 65% accuracy. While such prediction rates may appear appallingly low, they are much higher than chance level (25%) and typical values obtained in the prediction of drug and alcohol use from personality (see Segal & Merenda, 1975). At least part of the predictive efficacy can be attributed to the use of highly reliable, robust personality measures; it is well known that relationships are psychometrically attenuated by low reliability measurements. The fact that relatively little predictive covariance has been lost to measurement error leads us to conclude that our predictive accuracy estimate of around 60% is indicative of the amount of true overlap between the phenomenon of youthful drug and alcohol use and general personality functioning as defined within the measurement domain of the private personality framework.

The fact that we were able to successfully differentiate the four substance-use groups in the samples deserves comment, particularly in light of general arguments abounding in the literature of psychology (see Mischel, 1968) about the futility of applying a trait approach to the explanation of any fairly discrete behavior. Although it is abundantly clear from our analyses that presence, absence, or type of substance-use behavior is not synonymous with personality, the two domains are related in a statistically significant manner with some level of robustness and predictive utility. Many variables in our analyses did not discriminate between the groups, but this result should not be construed as indicative that personality is only minimally related to substance use. Some of the individual variables *within our attempted total domain sample* are highly related to the phenomenon. For instance, reexamining Table 6.1, it is possible to observe that there are average differences between groups of 10–20% of the total range of the personality scale. Also, some of the correlation ratios are quite high given the relatively crude criterion grouping. On the four measures of sensation seeking, the groups differ in monotonically increasing order quite dramatically. There is certainly no reason to believe that all variables which might be measured in the private personality domain are related to substance use; our wide and hopefully comprehensive inclusion of variables virtually guaranteed that all scales would not be related to substance use. In spite of the wide domain sampling and the consequent loss in power for the multivariate tests, we were able to show that these were differences between the groups using methods that penalized us for the number of "irrelevant" measures included.

The actual constellation of individual variables that are different between drug-use groups have strong interpretive meaning. First, all four sensation-seeking measures—General Sensation Seeking, Experience Sensation Seeking, Disinhibition, and Thrill and Adventure Seeking—are highest for the marijuana and polydrug users. Consequently, it appears that the individual who seeks experience through drugs also seeks to have an enriched life through the seeking of new, varied, and thrilling activities. Such an individual prefers activities like visiting museums, traveling, riding rollercoasters, canoeing through whitewater, and hedonistically sampling new foods. Such individuals have an external orientation; they wish to capture all that the world has to offer and need to find stimulation through a variety of activities. Drugs are certainly purported to help the individual experience new thoughts and emotions, make mundane events adventurous, provide the thrill of "getting caught," and lower inhibitions about socially disapproved activities. Individuals high in the needs for external experience turn to drugs directly, then, to have these needs met.

Other characteristics that separate nonusers of drugs from their peers who have experimented widely with substances include the needs for autonomy, harmavoidance, impulsivity, order, and understanding. Involvement in drug use seems related to a need to be autonomous in an extremely monotonic way. Individuals seeking to be free of the influence of others while expressing themselves tend to try many different types of substances. Although it can certainly be argued that autonomous individuals will seek to perform behaviors that are counternormative, it must also be remembered that in current society, drug use is a means for the individual to demonstrate individuality and express dissatisfaction with the dominant culture. Consequently, if one is to attempt to argue from this finding that individuals rejecting the society will turn to drugs, one must also realize that it is that very same dominant society that has defined drug use as a deviant behavior. Involvement with drugs also seems to be monotonically related to the need to avoid harm in a very definitive manner. It is, of course, not particularly suprising that individuals who fear harm to themselves in general will be wary of ingesting substances that could have deleterious effects on physical and mental health when taken in sufficient quantity.

Impulsivity and order are also strongly related to the drug-use classification system. Users of substances tend to be more impulsive and less orderly than those individuals who do not use drugs. The moderate levels of impulsivity manifested by the polydrug-use subjects do appear, however, to represent a sort of playfulness and openness rather than weak ego control or recklessness.

Finally, individuals who use drugs tend to have lowered levels of the need to achieve social recognition and heightened levels of the need to understand. Within our society, drug use has frequently been stigmatized (Chapter 1) and, in any case, certainly is not generally associated with deeds worthy of social recognition. In fact, the reverse has been the case, and in the dominant culture the drug user is frequently considered a drug abuser or, more bluntly, a junkie. Again, it is not surprising that within this social framework, the individual with great need to achieve social recognition would be a nonuser of drugs and alcohol. The Need for Understanding Scale, within the PRF, measures a tendency for the individual to actively seek knowledge about how different large-scale phenomena work. It is quite possible that the relationship between this personality scale and increasing involvement in substance use is indication that people with heightened tendencies to tackle abstract philosophical problems and complex sets of amorphous information will turn on to drugs to provide them with altered perceptions and potentially greater understanding.

Additionally, the need for exhibitionism is only related to substance-use involvement among women. From our perspective, such a relationship reflects that involvement with drugs may be much more distinctive for college women than for men; public drug use then serves to make the female user more a focus of attention by peers than the same behavior does for men. This contention is strongly supported by the trend of the means in both female samples; nonusers, alcohol-only users, *and* polydrug users have about the same mean level on this need, whereas the average scores of marijuana users are several points higher. The use of highly illegal substances is functionally not a way for women to express themselves in a manner that will draw attention (a fact not surprising in light of the severe legal penalties for possessing these drugs without a prescription), whereas marijuana use, illegal but with minor penalties not as frequently enforced, is a means of attracting attention from peers and others. For the male subjects, social norms presumably do not make this behavior as distinctive, and consequently, it is not an effective means of satisfying exhibitionistic tendencies.

In general, then, within the needs facet of the private personality domain, the variables related to drug involvement seem to be those that: (1) deter drug use; (2) can be more readily expressed while under the influence of drugs; and (3) can be satisfied by ingesting drugs. Heightened levels of the needs to achieve social recognition and avoid harm seem to serve as deterrents to involvement in drug use. Autonomy needs, playful needs, and mystical needs can be expressed within the current culture by taking drugs.

Turning now to the inner experience facet of private personality, we find that substance users differ from nonusers in their tendency to reveal private thoughts to others. Individuals who use marijuana and other drugs are more willing to share their insights and desires with others. Taken in conjunction with the parallel trend for the need to understand, this pattern indicates that the drug-user's search for meaning is augmented by sharing her or his thoughts with others.

Also among the inner-experience variables we find that there are group differences on the Need for External Stimulation Scale. Drug users have a slight preference for external, as opposed to internal, sources of stimulation, but this trend is not strong. This result then clarifies the finding of the strong relationship between all aspects of sensation seeking and drug use; while drug users seek all types of experiences of both external and internal natures, there is some slight preference for external experiences. The external preference may be an attempt to provide new information in the search for understanding.

Finally, there is a tendency for females who use marijuana and other drugs to have elevated levels of auditory imagery in their daydreams and fantasies. This element of sound in consciousness for the women drug users is of a general sort.

Mean levels of locus of control were not significantly different between the drug-use groups in at least two of the samples when the difference was assessed using an omnibus F ratio. When the total F is partitioned into a specific a priori linear term, the four groups are different in three samples ($F = 4.39$, 6.92, and 6.59 for 1973 males, 1973 females, and 1974 females, respectively). Collapsing across all four samples, the mean score for nonusers (10.76) was lowest, followed by the means for alcohol (11.09), marijuana (11.73), and polydrug (12.42). Although we have not emphasized this finding because of its somewhat ephemeral nature aided and abetted by post hoc comparisons, the finding of a relationship is consistent with previous literature. We should point out, however, that the weakness of the differentiation does indicate why studies frequently fail to find a locus-of-control and drug-use linkage; the relationship is, at best, fairly small.

In summary, there was the expected amount of minimal overlap between inner experience and drug involvement at this early experimentation stage. Sensation-seeking tendencies were found to be highly related to substance use, and many different types of motivation were correlated. Our overall picture of the group differences is that youthful drug-use experimentation can be conceived of as a way of obtaining new experiences, as a means within the current society of expressing certain characterological motivations, and as a way of disinhibiting one's behavior in order to satisfy needs. It does not seem that the pattern of results suggests that youthful drug users are particularly deviant or pathological in comparison to their peers who have not experimented with psychoactive substances.

The personification of the contrasting private personality styles between drug users and nonusers has consistently been reported in psychological research. Hogan et al. (1970), for instance, described their nonuser subjects as tending to be rather conventional and lacking in spontaneity and verve. Such terms as "responsible," "dutiful," "authoritarian compliance," "deferentiation to external authority," and "extreme self control" were used by the authors to describe the individuals who had not tried drugs. In contrast, the same authors characterized those individuals who used drugs in moderate amounts as having "hostility toward conventions and rules," "impulsiveness," "nonconforming," "overconcern with personal pleasure," "social skillfulness," "broad interests," and "intellectual curiosity." Other research provides similar findings. Holroyd and Kahn (1974) found marijuana users to be impulsive and curious, whereas nonusers were reported to be oriented toward achievement and social approval (as in our study, this description was based on PRF variables). Victor, Grossman, and Eisenman (1973) cited the primary difference between users and nonusers of marijuana as "openness to experience."

Attributes that have been found to differ between the four substance-use groups cannot be clumped together under the heading of a "trait," which presumably causes or explains drug use. Our analyses (presented in Chapter 5) have made it quite clear that the major correlates of drug use are not interchangeable measures of some general trait. Consequently, it seems more fruitful to think of the present results as supportive of a generalized life style, a concept originally suggested by Suchman (1968).

The life style that we find represented among the drug users in our various samples is one that incorporates many common themes of late adolescence. As we noted earlier, this period of life encompasses the breaking of close family ties and the development of an individual life style outside of the goals and norms of the nuclear family. During this period, youth typically seek to sample the full range of possibilities, and it seems that the most adventurous of these seekers sample drugs as a way of inducing different experiences and emotions. The college years are also a period for the individual to seek an identity beyond that provided by the family unit in earlier years. This seeking of autonomy constitutes the individual's attempt to define who he or she is within adult society. Again, we find that the most autonomous of the students turn to drugs. We must remember, however, that the majority defines youthful drug use as "defiant" and even "deviant" and that partaking in this behavior is a way for the precocious youth to openly express autonomy.

The adolescent years are also a time for trying to grapple with the place of the individual within society and the determining of long term plans and goals. Our data indicate that the drug user has a higher need for understanding her or his personal universe than does the peer who does not experiment with drugs. Given all the mystical writings and counterculture lore that have surrounded the use of drugs, it is not surprising that drug experimentation should be associated in the mind of the adolescent with a search for meaning among all the new information confronting her or him. Simultaneously, we find that the individual experimenting with drugs has a lower need for social recognition in traditional ways. This strongly implies that the search for experience and understanding is realized to be counterproductive to traditional success as defined by the majority culture. Nonetheless, the individual uses drugs in order to try to define the themes behind the conventions.

It should be clear from the foregoing that we do not think that our data indicate that the typical college student experimenting with psychoactive substance use is particularly pathological or in special danger of harming himself or society. Indeed, we feel that the pattern of group differences found indicates that college student drug use can best be conceptualized as a pattern of exploratory behavior.

An important direct implication of our data is that approaching drug use among adolescents using a multidimensional deviance theory viewpoint is insufficient to capture the complexity of the phenomenon. Although we do not mean to imply that chronic use of certain substances does not pose the potential for personal and social adjustment problems, the regular use of certain drugs (such as alcohol and marijuana) by a large percentage of adolescent and adult Americans (see Abelson et al., 1972, 1973; Chambers, Inciardi, & Siegal, 1975) does show that the infusion of large supplies of marijuana and other psychoactive drugs into college campuses has not led to major social upheaval or massive psychic imbalance among young adults. Within our samples, experience with a variety of psychoactive substances *is the norm,* and the pattern of personality correlates that we have found suggests that substance-use experimentation has become an integral part of youthful development and exploration. Furthermore, it seems possible—in light of the heterogeneous set of personality attributes associated with the behavior that drug use may be incorporated into the lifestyle of a large number of college graduates—that experimentation may be revived when certain needs must be met.

Although the present analyses have been directed toward predicting and attempting to explain part of youthful substance *experimentation* and *initiation* from the private personality variables, we are cognizant that the present analyses really do not address the issue of whether or not the individual's private personality characteristics are related to the circumstances and perceived consequences of use. For instance, it is quite likely that while the inner-experience variables have not served to differentiate individuals who have experimented only a few times with marijuana from those who have never tried the drug, the inner-experience variables may be intimately related to the maintenance of marijuana use. The next chapter addresses the issue of how the private personality concept is related to perceived reasons for and consequences of adolescent drug use.

A further issue we would be remiss to neglect is that our predictions of who uses drugs have quite simply been based on "main effects" of personality variables. It has recently been argued (Dunnette, 1975) that interactions of different personality measures may be the true causal mechanisms for substance use in youth, but studies in related areas of psychology (see Wiggins, 1973) have generally concluded that interactions between personality dimensions are not robust across samples. Since the links between adolescent drug use and personality are still only being systematically explored, we have focused on personality variables singly and in some *additive* combinations determined through various mathematical procedures. While we have also based our interpretation of the results on our perceptions of the functional significance of various results within social situations, as well as the general social milieu, we would certainly agree with various interactionist-perspective writers (see Endler & Magnusson, 1976) that interactions between certain personality aspects and the characteristics of the environment are critical. The current study, however, has chosen to focus on those explanations that may be derived from studying the personality system. The next set of analyses partially examines the issue of the social context and perceived rewards of drug use as related to personality.

7

Interrelations of Private Personality and Reasons for Substance Use

INTRODUCTION

The chapter reports the findings from a series of studies undertaken to explore: (1) the relationships between reasons or motives for use of alcohol and other drugs; and (2) the domains of private personality, measured by the scales in our assessment battery. This set of analyses also attempted to determine more precisely the extent to which situational or social variables are related to substance use.

An important issue in understanding the use of various chemical substances (including alcohol) by young people is the extent to which "the user" differentiates among various chemicals with respect to the attainment of a specific desired effect. The choice of a desired effect may, to no small degree, be related to specific personality characteristics. That statistically significant, but only moderately, powerful success has been achieved in predicting drug and alcohol use from personality variables, as noted in Chapter 6, may be related to a high level of complexity in the relationship between personality and substance use. While it is customary in personality research to conceive of personality as a multidimensional phenomenon, most drug use research has generally conceptualized drug use as a continuum, ranging from total nonuse to the use of "heavier" street drugs such as heroin (cf. Jessor & Jessor, 1977; Kandel, 1975; Kandel & Faust, 1975). This "continuum approach," as Khavari, Mabry, and Humes (1977) have pointed out, may not be methodologically sound because it does not use statistical techniques "optimally suited for assessing the multidimensional nature of behavior." In order to obtain a more complete understanding of the multiple or complex relationship between drug use and personality, the drug criterion measure should be subjected, when appropriate data exists, to multivariate analysis. Appropriate multivariate procedures help to determine the extent to which personality variables are associated with different components of variance in the criterion variables. For example, Burkhart, Schwarz, and Green (1978), in their extension of the work on sensation seeking previously done by Segal (1973b), show a compelling need to develop multidimensional measures of drug use to test for relationships with personality constructs.

Even in those studies such as our prediction results (Chapter 6) or those of Smith and Fogg (1977, 1978), where there is an attempt to predict categories (rather than a continuum) of drug use, the categories typically combine all users of a similar substance. Notable exceptions to this trend are the work of Tomkins (1966a,b; Ikard & Tomkins, 1973), who emphasized the multidimensional structure of cigarette smoking, the alcoholism research of Horn and Wanberg (1969, 1970, 1973,), and the polydrug-use research of Carlin and Stauss (1977). Although many of the indicators from the private personality domain did not directly differentiate between classes of substance users, it is quite possible that these variables may be directly related to either the frequency of substance use or to specific motives for use. That is, although certain aspects of private personality do not serve to predict who will or will not use a drug, they may nevertheless be strong indicators of frequent or continued use of a substance associated with a particular set of reasons. Similarly, those variables that do differentiate significantly between users and nonusers may not be related to why a substance is used or how much of the substance is typically consumed. The present analyses address these issues.

It is particularly important that the multidimensional structure of motives and perceived gains from using a drug be extensively examined. There has been repeated speculation in most treatises on the psychology, phenomenology, and sociology of substance use that certain drugs are used predominately to achieve altered emotional reactions to conscious experience (see Tart, 1975, Chap. 10). We may differentiate between the adolescent who uses alcohol in an automobile on Friday nights with three of his or her same-sex friends and the adolescent who sits alone drinking in his or her room the night before an examination, but it is also important that we try to link the functional differences of such use patterns with more fundamental personality processes. Furthermore, it seems crucial, particularly within the realm of private personality, to consider how substance use is tied, in a compensatory manner, with certain typical experiences of consciousness (such as those that our daydreaming scales assess) and more generalized needs and wishes toward action (as manifested in the sensation-seeking and Murray needs scales). That is, by studying the self-attributed reasons for the use of various substances, we may begin to perceive the significance of substance use within the context of a particular personality style that may be predisposed toward self-medication as a means of coping, particularly when situational contingencies foreclose other options.

Another area of necessary study is the way in which individuals who use many different substances choose different substances to achieve desired effects, if indeed this is the case. For example, consider the youth who uses both marijuana and alcohol. A highly stylized pattern of differential use may have evolved in which marijuana is used when the individual is at a party with other youths or when the person is in a fairly positive emotional state. Alcohol use, in contrast, may be confined to those times when the individual feels generally dysphoric or anxious. Such stylized use, itself, would argue toward the notion of a youthful drug "connoisseur," who, rightly or wrongly, has decided that certain feelings and states should be medicated, diminished, or enhanced through the use of chemicals. Significant recent work by Carlin and Stauss (1977) indicates that polydrug users can be reliably categorized along such dimensions as streetwise and recreational use, and that such a functional classification is uniquely suited toward understanding personality and neuropsychological differences between individuals with histories of drug abuse.

In this chapter, we examine different patterns and reasons for using substances and try to determine if motivational clusters of reasons for using particular substances are manifestations of more general personality styles. Furthermore, we determine if the reasons that different substances are taken by polydrug users are compensatory, and if there is direct evidence for the concept of a youthful drug "expert" who has developed a stylized pattern of mood alteration. The individual indicators, subsamples, and methods of analysis are discussed as the data and results are introduced.

In all candor, it must be pointed out that the analyses presented in this chapter are the most post hoc and exploratory in the book, and that statistical assumptions are sometimes violated in order to try to make sense of the data available to use. We do, however, feel that the exploration of these data are justified, since the area of perceived gains and losses from drug use and personality structure have not been explored extensively by previous workers. Furthermore, the analyses to be given do seem consistent with each other and with the major conclusions of other chapters. Consequently, although we do not argue that these results are as "conclusive" or "definitive" as others presented, we do believe that they suggest further avenues for study.

METHOD

Subjects

In order to carry out the analyses with a sufficiently sizable number of subjects, we are limited to reporting only on reasons given for alcohol and for marijuana use. The number of subjects who reported polydrug use ($N = 185$) was too small to allow for inclusion in this set of detailed statistical analyses.

Since the particular focus of these analyses is upon reasons for the use of alcohol and marijuana, those participants who reported never having used any of these substances were deleted. There were approximately an equal number of males and females in this subsample but with somewhat different proportions representative of the two colleges (i.e., more females than males at Murray State and more males than females at Yale). Since the effect of the different colleges and the effect of sex were examined separately in earlier analyses (Segal & Singer, 1976), and since sex differences are taken into account in the analyses to be cited later, the somewhat different proportions of males to females did not appear to have to be specifically treated. The age of the participants was extremely homogenous across the schools and subsamples for the students included in the present analyses.

Instruments

The summary scores from the Personality Research Form (PRF), Imaginal Processes Inventory (IPI), Sensation-Seeking Scales, and Locus of Control batteries were included in some of the present analyses; descriptions of these inventories are given in Chapter 4.

Participants who used alcohol were asked to indicate (dichotomously) which of the following reasons made them feel like having a drink: (1) just to be sociable; (2) hot weather; (3) feeling under pressure, tense; (4) pain; (5) hard work; (6) having problems; (7) feeling lonely; (8) having nothing else to do; (9) feeling mad; (10) just feeling that you had to have a drink sometimes; (11) feeling sad; (12) not getting ahead; and (13) feeling tired. Participants also indicated (dichotomously) which of the following aspects of drinking was most important[1]: (1) is something people do on special occasions; (2) sometimes helps you feel better; (3) makes you feel less shy; (4) makes you feel more satisfied with yourself; (5) helps you relax; (6) helps you get along better

---

[1]The second set of reasons for alcohol use was presented to the subjects under the instructions that they should choose the one reason that was most important to them. Of the 854 subjects who provided data on reasons for alcohol use, 284 (33.26%) checked more than one response in this second set of 12 reasons as opposed to 511 (59.84%) who checked more than one item in the first set. Consequently, through various internal data checks, we concluded that the subjects, in general, used the same psychological set as implied by the previous 13 reasons where they were asked to check all reasons that apply. Analyses including all 25 reasons, or only the first 13, are consistent in a way predictable from the content of the items. We have, however, taken a conservative approach here and used only the 13 dichotomous items with the "proper" instructions. Since the additional reasons provide other interesting contextual information, we have calculated the loadings of the 12 additional indicators on the factors and canonical dimensions generated using only the first 13 variables. These "pseudo-loadings" were calculated after the analyses were completed and do not influence either significance tests or rotations in any way. Therefore, the loadings provided for the second set of reasons may be ignored entirely if our projection of the variables onto the dimensions seems inelegant to the reader. We do, however, speak throughout the succeeding sections as if all 25 variables were "real."

with people; (7) helps you forget your problems; (8) makes get-togethers more fun; (9) gives you more confidence in yourself; (10) makes you feel happier; (11) helps you forget you're not the kind of person you'd like to be; and (12) makes you worry less about what other people think of you.

Those individuals who also used marijuana were asked to indicate (again in a dichotomous manner) which of the following reasons applied to their motive for using the drug: (1) to experience something new and different; (2) to get better insight into myself; (3) to get "kicks" or to get "high"; (4) to satisfy my curiosity about what it was like; (5) to overcome feelings of boredom or depression; (6) to give me more pep or energy; (7) to relieve anxiety or tension; (8) to be more creative; (9) to relate better to my friends; (10) to expand my awareness and understanding of things; and (11) friends or acquaintances pressured me into it.

Data Analysis

Individual factor analyses of reasons for using alcohol and reasons for using marijuana were calculated using principal-components analysis. Patterns of "hard"-drug use were calculated using the maximum likelihood procedure (Jöreskog, 1967). Factor rotation was accomplished in the oblique case using the direct quartimin algorithm (Jennrich & Sampson, 1966), which has been highly recommended because of its ability to recover simple structure (Hakstian & Abell, 1974) and invariance over variable sampling (Bailey & Guertin, 1973). Principal components analysis was chosen because it presumably would not capitalize as much on the marginal frequencies of the dichotomous indicators as an iterated solution might.

Canonical correlation analysis was used to test the interrelationship of several domains of variables. For each application of canonical correlation analysis, the variables were intercorrelated and the resulting product-moment coefficients were input for canonical correlation tests. Canonical correlation analysis was chosen as a principal statistical method because it summarizes the cross-domain covariation in as few statistically reliable dimensions as possible. Because of the well-known lack of interpretability inherent in canonical correlation solutions when there is more than one dimension (Bentler & Huba, in press; Cliff & Krus, 1976; Huba et al., 1979; Wilkinson, 1977; Wingard et al., 1979), the canonical loadings (see Cooley & Lohnes, 1971) obtained for the two domains were rotated to approximate simple structure. The rotation procedure is a generalization of Bentler's (1977) orthosim method and seeks the best simultaneous simple-structure position for two matrices (Bentler & Huba, in press). Finally, the canonical correlations were adjusted for the transformations. As Cliff and Krus (1976) point out, an orthogonal transformation of the solution retains the explanatory power of the dimensions found to span two domains and conserves variance. Furthermore, it should be noted that the rotated canonical correlation loadings may be interpreted much as one interprets rotated principal component loadings, if it is remembered that the canonical dimensions have been generated so as to maximize the multivariate correlation of the two domains.

Canonical correlation analysis, then, determines a set of dimensions for each of two groups of measures simultaneously under the constraints of one of the dimensions from the first set, is maximally correlated with one of the dimensions from the second set, and is uncorrelated with all other dimensions in either group of measures. A formal statistical test, with the usual assumptions for maximum likelihood estimation, is applied to detemine the number of robust dimensions. The dimensions in each set, if there are more than one, are then rotated to a simultaneous, weighted position of best simple structure using an orthogonal transformation. The final result of the analysis and rotation is two sets of within-set orthogonal dimensions, one set for each domain, which explain all statistically reliable covariation between the domains present in the correlations across sets.

As a final assessment of the overall redundancy between the two domains in the canonical correlation analyses, the Stewart and Love (1968) redundancy coefficient was calculated (see Cooley & Lohnes, 1971, pp. 170–171). Although the redundancy index has been attacked in the past for faulty derivation, Gleason (1976) reviews the criticisms and shows that the coefficient is firmly grounded through an alternate derivation. The redundancy coefficients provide information analogous to squaring the correlation coefficient in the bivariate case: An index of the extent to which variance and covariance in one domain can be predicted for the other domain is provided.

It should also be noted that we have used original variables in the canonical correlation analyses even though the private personality variables (Chapter 5) and the motives for using substances (Chapter 7, first three analyses) were simplified using factor analysis. Although related to factor analysis conceptually (see Van de Geer, 1971), canonical correlation analysis seeks to simplify a rectangular (domain by domain) submatrix of the total set of bivariate correlation coefficients. Consequently, only the cross-domain covariation is studied. Had we only used factor analytically derived scores in our canonical analyses, it is quite likely that we would have thrown away reliable variance in a measure because such portions of the variance could not be attributed to *within-domain* factors.

RESULTS

Factor Analysis of Reasons for Using Alcohol

The 13 response categories to the question "What makes you feel like having a drink?" were factor analyzed using principal components analysis for the 854 participants who responded to the question. Four components met the

TABLE 7.1
Rotated Factor Loadings for Alcohol-Use Variables

Variables	I	II	III	IV
To be social	.19	.91	.20	-.04
Hot weather	-.16	.09	.86	-.07
Pressure	.65	-.02	.07	.11
Pain	.12	-.02	.03	.71
Hard work	.04	-.04	.69	.27
Problems	.78	.02	-.09	.09
Feeling lonely	.79	-.01	-.07	.04
Nothing to do	.34	-.14	.28	-.48
Feeling mad	.60	.09	-.02	-.12
Have to have	.19	-.48	.17	-.06
Feeling sad	.78	.00	-.09	.04
Not getting ahead	.36	-.09	.11	.03
Feeling tired	.14	-.06	.23	.58
Special occasions*	-.13	.18	-.12	-.04
Feel better*	.31	-.11	.21	.07
Feel less shy*	.16	-.02	.09	-.02
Feel satisfied*	.19	-.07	.09	.07
Helps to relax*	.22	-.16	.20	.09
Get along better*	.19	-.05	.09	-.04
Forget*	.39	-.11	.12	-.02
Fun*	.04	.02	.17	-.08
More confidence*	.26	-.10	.22	.05
Happier*	.25	-.14	.12	.05
Not person want to be*	.30	-.08	.08	.09
Worry less*	.28	-.09	.08	-.01

*
pseudo-loading

Kaiser–Guttman rule of roots greater than one and were rotated using the direct quartimin method. The variables from the second set of 12 reasons were regressed on the rotated components scores to obtain pseudo-loadings for these items. The loadings and pseudo-loadings for the four factors are shown in Table 7.1.

Inspection of the first factor shows high loadings for the use of alcohol to relieve sadness, loneliness, anger, and pressure, as well as to help deal with problems. Alcohol is also used to feel better, forget, combat low self-esteem, because of feelings of not getting ahead, and to worry less. This factor appears to closely resemble the "personal-effects" motives described by Jessor, Graves, Hanson, and Jessor (1968). Such drinking is motivated by an attempt to use alcohol to transcend problems, perhaps either to change the situation enough so that the problems are no longer bothersome or to drink just to "block out" troubles. Stated another way, drinking may serve to *reduce* negative affective experiences. Cahalan, Cisin, and Crossley (1969) also found that drinking played a significant role in helping people who were depressed or anxious. Alcohol, for our sample, thus apparently has a perceived role in coping with personal needs and problems.

The second factor has its largest loadings for the use of alcohol to be sociable and on special occasions. High scorers on this factor deny they have to have a drink. although it might be argued that this factor is primarily specific to one of our variables, we believe that it is a real common factor: Had we included variables for *specific* occasions (weddings, holiday dinners, etc.), it is likely they would have defined the same common factor. This factor, then, appears to represent a tendency to drink in those social situations that institutionalize alcohol consumption.

The third factor has loadings for the use of alcohol because of hot weather, hard work, having nothing else to do, when feeling tired, and to help relax, feel better, and build confidence. This third factor might reflect the oft-portrayed use of alcohol, particularly in bars, as reward for hard work or as a means of cooling off.

Finally, the fourth factor has to do with the use of alcohol to relieve physical problems: There are high loadings for drinking when in pain and when feeling tired. High scorers on this dimension do not attribute their drinking to having nothing else to do; on the contrary, they feel they have other options, and this factor then would appear to represent self-medication tendencies for feelings of physical fatigue.

The estimated intercorrelations among the primary factors are relatively small. The highest correlation is between factors I and III (.26).

Factor Analysis of Reasons for Using Marijuana

Of the 854 subjects who used alcohol, 425 also used marijuana. The 11 responses to the question "Why do you use marijuana?" were factored using principal components analysis. Four factors were found to adequately reproduce the correlation matrix among the 11 reasons using the Kaiser–Guttman rule of roots greater than unity. The factors were rotated to approximate oblique simple structure using the direct quartimin algorithm. Table 7.2 shows the loadings of the variables on the four rotated factors.

The highest loadings on the first factor are for the use of marijuana to reduce anxiety, to overcome boredom and depression, to increase one's "pep," and, to a much lesser extent, to enhance creativity. Although this factor appears to represent the use of marijuana to deal with or possibly overcome negative affective states, it also suggests that marijuana may be used for a specific effect, apart from social motives. The second factor shows appreciable loadings for using marijuana for new experiences to satisfy curiosity and to "get high." This second factor appears to be marijuana experimentation. The third factor has its highest loadings for the use of marijuana to expand awareness and increase insight. There is also a modest loading for the use of the drug to increase creativity and a negative loading for curiosity. These loadings suggest that this factor is representative of what may be called a desired self-growth through the use of drugs. It appears that the

TABLE 7.2
Rotated Factor Loadings for Marijuana-Use Variables

Variables	I	II	III	IV
1. To experience something new and different	-.06	.83	-.02	.03
2. To get better insight into myself	.18	.02	.74	-.06
3. To get "kicks" or to get "high"	-.01	.66	.21	.16
4. To satisfy my curiosity about what it was like	.19	.44	-.48	-.25
5. To overcome feelings of boredom and depression	.78	-.08	-.06	.00
6. To give me more pep or energy	.71	-.03	.03	.12
7. To relieve anxiety or tension	.76	.08	.08	-.02
8. To be more creative	.44	.05	.48	.01
9. To relate better to my friends	.06	.17	.05	.74
10. To expand my awareness and understanding of things	-.02	.16	.78	-.12
11. Friends or acquaintances pressured me into it	.05	-.03	-.16	.77

sensation of the drug is important, and that the attainment of these effects may be a specific reason for continued use of marijuana by some individuals. The fourth factor has appreciable loadings for the use of marijuana to increase relatedness to others, and when under pressure from friends. This factor appears to reflect marijuana consumption because of enhanced personal relationships, particularly in those situations in which marijuana smoking is the norm.

The marijuana-use factors were only slightly correlated. The highest correlation between the factors was .22 (Factors I and III), indicating that these generalized motives for marijuana use can generally be considered independent of one another.

Factor Analysis of "Hard" Drug-Use Patterns

Of the 425 subjects who used marijuana and alcohol, 185 used additional drugs without prescription. Since small numbers of subjects used each of the specific types of "hard" drugs, it was not possible to follow the factor-analytic procedures used for the alcohol and marijuana studies. Instead, we decided to examine the factorial structure of the frequency of use of five classes of drugs by the people in our study: (1) "uppers" (amphetamines, methamphetamines); (2) narcotics and other street drugs (heroin, morphine, cocaine); (3) "downers" (barbiturates, tranquilizers, antidepressants); hallucinogens (LSD, psilocybin, mescaline); and (5) marijuana.[2]

---

[2]Variables were combined in order to make the drug instruments in the two years comparable.

TABLE 7.3
Rotated Factor Loadings for Frequency of Drug Use

Variables	Factors	
	I	II
Stimulants	.28	.42
Narcotics - Cocaine	.45	.05
Barbiturates - Tranquilizers	1.00	-.09
Hallucinogens	.02	.53
Marijuana	-.08	.69

Frequency of drug use was coded on a seven-point scale ranging from nonuse of the drug to use more than once a day. The correlation matrix between the frequencies of use of the five classes of drugs was factor analyzed using the maximum likelihood procedures with a two-factor solution best fitting the data ($\chi_1^2 = .50$, $p > .01$).[3] The loadings for the two-factor solution were rotated to approximate oblique simple structure using the direct quartimin method. The rotated loadings are shown in Table 7.3.

Examination of the rotated loadings indicates that the first factor contributes primarily to barbiturate use and, to a lesser extent, to narcotic and stimulant use. The second factor has high loadings for the use of hallucinogens and marijuana, with a somewhat smaller loading for the stimulant use. [While the two factors are correlated ($r = .43$) in the oblique solution, the factor separation does suggest some interesting psychological differences.] Since marijuana, hallucinogens, and, to some extent, stimulants appear to be generally used for their euphoric qualities as drugs, the second factor might be called "seeking a high."

The first factor represents the use of some potentially addictive drugs, linking together narcotics, barbiturates, and amphetamines. Neither marijuana or hallucinogenics are known to be physically addictive. Marijuana and hallucinogenics are drugs used socially—that is, experienced primarily in small groups, often at parties or other small gatherings. Narcotics and barbiturates seem to be less associated with social processes, and individuals using these drugs are probably seeking to deal with extremely negative affective states. The results of this factor analysis are similar to the factorial pattern obtained by Blum (1969) in his analysis of drug-use patterns by college students. Although Blum obtained a four-factor solution (he included several more drug classification categories, e.g., alcohol, sedatives), two of his four factors show a similar pattern of loading. Also, our results seem supportive of Carlin and Stauss' (1977) finding of recreational and self-

---

[3]In the two-factor solution, barbiturate use had an estimated initial uniqueness of less than zero. We used the suggestion of Jöreskog (1967) to accomplish the estimation in this Heywood case.

medicating patterns of substance use. Based on these studies and our own analysis, we believe there is a general drug-taking order of preference among polydrug users—that is, a general linking or patterning of different drugs, centering around a distinction between drugs used socially (Factor II), which have mind-altering effects, and drugs that have mood-altering effects such as alleviating depression or reducing tension and anxiety.

Personality and Alcohol-Use Styles

In order to examine the relationship between the 13 reasons for the consumption of alcohol and personality, a canonical correlation analysis between the alcohol-use reasons and the personality–daydreaming variables was calculated using the data from all 854 individuals who used alcohol. The overall multivariate relationship between alcohol-use variables and the personality and daydreaming scales was highly significant (χ^2_{637} = 979.96, $p < .00001$). Decomposition of the total Bartlett's χ^2 value indicates that four of the linear combinations spanning the domains have significant correlations.

Because there was more than one significant canonical correlation, the dimensions generated by standard statistical programs may not be in the most theoretically meaningful position. Canonical correlation loadings can, however, be rotated orthogonally much as factor loadings are rotated with the property that the explanatory power of the solution is maintained. In order to determine if a rotation to simple structure would increase the interpretability of the solution, the symmetric two-matrix orthosim rotation algorithm (Bentler & Huba, in press) was applied to the canonical loadings. The weights (α) given to simple structure in each of the two matrices can be manipulated. In this case, two alternate rotations were calculated. In the first rotation, the motives for alcohol use completely determined the simple structure (α = 1), whereas in the second rotation, the two domains were weighted proportionately to their importance in the total battery ($\alpha = 13/62$).

Because alternate simple-structure positions and the unrotated solution span the same geometric space, the choice between final sets of loadings rests on a comparison of the theoretical meaningfulness of the two sets of loadings. Preference for a rotated solution is predicated upon the normal assumptions underlying simple-structure rotations in factor analysis (see Bentler & Huba, in press; Thurstone, 1947), where it is recognized that a rotation of canonical loadings can often help to recover a latent structure (Bentler & Huba, in press). In examining the two rotated solutions, it seemed that the solution in which the dimensions of drug use was most consistent with the goal of these analyses was that in which the alcohol-use variables completely determined the simple structure (α = 1). Table 7.4a shows the rotated loadings, and Table 7.4b shows the transformation-adjusted canonical correlations. [It should be noted that the canonical variable loadings are the bivariate correlations

TABLE 7.4
Rotated Canonical Loadings Between
Alcohol-Use Motives and Private Personality

(a)   Rotated Loadings

Alcohol-Use Variables	I	II	III	IV
1. Just to be sociable	-.01	-.02	.02	.82
2. Hot weather	.86	.04	-.06	.01
3. Feeling under pressure, tense	.01	.82	.32	-.04
4. Pain	-.04	.20	.01	-.17
5. Hard work	.60	.03	.33	-.07
6. Having problems	.04	.27	.82	.13
7. Feeling lonely	-.01	.54	.57	-.09
8. Having nothing else to do	.27	.40	.03	.19
9. Feeling mad	-.12	.10	.53	.12
10. Just feel you have to have a drink sometimes	.09	.48	.00	.03
11. Feeling sad	.08	.29	.67	-.29
12. Not getting ahead	.11	.29	.19	.20
13. Feeling tired	-.01	.04	.26	-.09
14. Is something people do on special occasions*	-.12	-.12	-.09	.16
15. Sometimes helps you feel better*	.12	.22	.21	.03
16. Makes you less shy*	.06	.14	.09	.05
17. Makes you more satisfied with yourself*	.04	.12	.11	.02
18. Helps you relax*	.12	.22	.12	-.06
19. Helps you get along better with people*	.07	.13	.12	.06
20. Helps you forget your problems*	.06	.25	.27	-.01
21. Makes get-togethers more fun*	.18	.04	.01	.06
22. Give you more confidence in yourself*	.04	.19	.17	.01
23. Makes you feel happier*	.04	.25	.13	-.01
24. Helps you forget you're not the kind of person you'd like to be*	.01	.16	.24	.00
25. Makes you worry less about what other people think*	.05	.16	.21	.01

Private Personality Variables	I	II	III	IV
1. Sex	-.69	.10	.04	-.10
2. Daydreaming frequency	-.04	.17	.20	-.24
3. Night dreaming frequency	-.03	.09	-.10	-.23
4. Absorption in daydreaming	-.18	.36	.28	-.24
5. Acceptance of daydreaming	.11	-.02	-.18	.02
6. Positive reactions to daydreaming	.02	.19	-.13	.09
7. Frightened reactions to daydreaming	-.21	.14	.34	-.25
8. Visual imagery in daydreams	-.06	.10	.15	-.17
9. Auditory imagery in daydreams	-.14	.07	.28	-.07
10. Problem solving in daydreams	-.04	.21	.06	.01
11. Present-oriented daydreams	-.16	.17	.03	.33
12. Future-oriented daydreams	-.08	.14	-.02	.14
13. Past-oriented daydreams	.06	.02	.11	-.11
14. Bizarre-improbable daydreams	.02	-.07	.27	-.35
15. Mindwandering	-.09	.26	.36	-.02
16. Achievement-oriented daydreams	-.03	.21	.19	.15
17. Hallucinatory-vivid daydreams	-.21	.17	.35	-.06
18. Fear-of-failure daydreams	-.17	.09	.34	.00

TABLE 7.4 (*continued*)

Private Personality Variables	I	II	III	IV
19. Hostile daydreams	.05	.21	.24	.11
20. Sexual daydreams	.13	.27	.20	.10
21. Heroic daydreams	.05	.05	.11	-.06
22. Guilt daydreams	-.12	.06	.27	.00
23. Interpersonal curiosity	-.20	.10	.04	.15
24. Impersonal curiosity	.19	-.21	-.05	.00
25. Boredom susceptibility	.01	.32	.44	-.01
26. Mentation rate	.08	-.06	.06	.07
27. Distractibility	-.10	.28	.21	.17
28. Need for external stimulation	.23	.01	.10	.11
29. Self-revelation	.03	.09	.04	-.01
30. Achievement	.04	-.20	-.11	-.12
31. Affiliation	.00	-.09	.18	.28
32. Aggression	.03	.29	.13	-.04
33. Autonomy	.11	.05	-.15	-.41
34. Dominance	.25	-.19	-.11	-.04
35. Endurance	.10	-.20	-.07	-.26
36. Exhibitionism	.13	-.15	.07	.08
37. Harmavoidance	-.30	-.22	-.06	.16
38. Impulsivity	-.06	.33	.28	-.06
39. Nurturance	-.29	-.11	.20	.04
40. Order	.03	-.15	-.01	.03
41. Play	.21	-.05	.32	.07
42. Social recognition	-.11	-.16	.37	.45
43. Understanding	-.10	.00	-.35	-.14
44. Infrequency	-.04	.11	.10	-.07
45. Locus of control	.02	.38	.12	-.16
46. General sensation seeking	.21	.14	-.06	-.11
47. Thrill and adventure seeking	.17	.03	.03	-.01
48. Experience sensation seeking	.27	.33	-.10	-.23
49. Disinhibition	.54	.22	.38	-.02

(b)   Adjusted Canonical Correlations

	I	II	III	IV
I	.43			
II	.01	.39		
III	-.01	.05	.39	
IV	.01	-.02	.00	.36

*pseudo-loading

between each of the original variables and the canonical variates extracted from each domain (Cooley & Lohnes, 1971).] The loadings of the remaining 12 reasons for alcohol use were calculated on the four rotated dimensions.

Examination of the first canonical dimension indicates that the highest loadings from the first set are for the use of alcohol in connection with hot weather, hard work, and having nothing else to do. The canonical correlations with the corresponding set of daydreaming and personality variables is .43. The personality–daydreaming dimension is sex-linked with males generally scoring higher. The largest positive loadings on this dimension are for Disinhibitory and Experience Sensation Seeking and Need for External Stimulation. There is some tendency for the high scorer to report Sexual Daydreams and to have elevated needs to Dominate and Play. Such individuals have lowered needs to Avoid Harm and be Nurtured, as well as decreased numbers of Frightened Reactions to daydreams and little Interpersonal Curiosity. In general, the linear combinations linking the two domains might be interpreted as the relatively typical pattern that occurs among traditionally action-oriented, male college students. This style of alcohol use appears to be a conventional one, where alcohol serves as an essential part of social activities. The high loading of Disinhibitory Sensation Seeking argues that this form of drinking is a means of "letting go" of reality and constraints.

The second pair of canonical dimensions represents a striking contrast to the first set. Here, alcohol is used when feeling under pressure, when having problems and feeling lonely or sad, because one just feels like having a drink when there is nothing else to do, because of feelings of not getting ahead, and because it makes one feel better, feel relaxed, feel happier, and forget problems. The correlation with the corresponding private personality dimension is .39. Loading positively on the variate are: (1) an External Locus of Control; (2) Experience Sensation Seeking; (3) Absorption in Daydreaming; (4) Hostile; (5) Achievement; (6) Sexual Fantasies; (7) Impulsivity; (8) Mindwandering; (9) Aggression; (10) Distractibility; (11) Boredom Susceptibility; and (12) Disinhibitory. Loading negatively are Endurance, Harmavoidance, and Impersonal Curiosity. This pattern of rotated loadings suggests the linkage of personal frustration–dissatisfaction drinking to a private personality style characterized by a self-perception as a "pawn," manipulated by external forces (DeCharms, 1968). A diverse inner life ranging from sexual to achievement daydreams characterizes the individual highly motivated to drink by personal frustration. Such persons tend to be impulsive and aggressive. This constellation of correlations is indicative of a pattern of using alcohol to overcome frustration in a world that is not all that one fantasizes it to be.

The third set of canonical dimensions seems to represent drinking for more intense, personal, frustration reasons. The alcohol-motives variate has its high loadings for the use of the alcohol when having problems and feeling mad, sad, or lonely. Additionally, alcohol is ingested because it makes one forget problems and feel better. Alcohol is also used when feeling under pressure and tired after hard work. The corresponding private personality dimension correlates at a level of .39 with this dimension. Loading positively on the private personality dimension are the needs for Affiliation, Impulsivity, Nurturance, Play and Social Recognition, and Disinhibitory Sensation Seeking, as well as the daydreaming scales of Absorption, Frightened Reactions, Hallucinatory-Vividness, Auditory Imagery, Bizarre–Improbable quality, Mindwandering, Fear of Failure, Hostility, Guilt, and Boredom

Susceptibility. There is a negative loading on the dimension for the need for Understanding. This dimension seems much more clearly a factor associated with the use of alcohol to reduce negative affect and also with indications of neurotic types of daydreaming (Singer & Antrobus, 1963, 1972). Reported inner experiences are generally dysphoric and alcohol use is perceived as a means of reducing such negative affective experiences and expectations in the ongoing thought processes.

The fourth pair of rotated canonical dimensions again correlate moderately (.36) indicating significant levels of association. Loading on the alcohol-motives dimension is the use of alcohol to be sociable on special occasions with a tendency not to use alcohol to relieve sadness but perhaps because of feelings of not getting ahead. Variables loading on the private personality dimension are a low number of Day, Night, and Bizarre-Improbable Daydreams. For the high scorer, daydreams are Present-Oriented with few Fright Reactions and little Absorption. Needs for Autonomy and Endurance have large negative loadings on the dimension, and the needs for Affiliation and Social Recognition load positively. Experience-Sensation-Seeking tendencies appear to be low. Consequently, the pattern of loadings suggests that high motivation to consume alcohol on special occasions is a manifestation of a general personality style that is highly susceptible to group pressure to conform to the expectations of the setting to consume alcohol in order to celebrate an event.

Computation of the Stewart–Love canonical redundancy coefficient shows that 18.50% of the variation in the 13 primary alcohol-use motives can be explained from the private personality variables. Although this total redundancy is not large, the motives for alcohol use are rather heterogeneous.

Personality and Marijuana Usage Styles

A second canonical analysis was conducted in order to determine the relationship between the 11 reasons for using marijuana and the personality and daydreaming scales for the 425 subjects who used marijuana. The overall multivariate relationship between the domains was significant (χ^2_{539} = 614.5, $p < .02$), but a decomposition of Bartlett's χ^2 indicated that only the first canonical correlation was statistically significant. Table 7.5 shows the loadings of the original variables on the first canonical variable in each domain.

The marijuana dimension shows its highest loadings for the use of the drug to expand awareness, to experience new things, and to gain insight into oneself. Interestingly, there is a denial that marijuana is used under pressure from friends. The private personality dimension, which correlates .50 with an apparent enhancement of the cognitive experience dimension, through marijuana use shows positive loadings for Experience Sensation Seeking and

TABLE 7.5
Canonical Loadings Between
Marijuana-Use Motives and Private Personality

Marijuana-Use Motives	I
1. Experience something new and different	.51
2. Better insight into myself	.50
3. Get "high"	-.02
4. Satisfy curiosity	.24
5. Overcome boredom or depression	.23
6. More pep or energy	-.06
7. To relieve anxiety or tension	.14
8. To be more creative	.08
9. Relate better to others	-.01
10. Expand awareness and understanding	.63
11. Friends' pressure	-.37

Private Personality Variables	I
1. Sex	-.21
2. Daydreaming frequency	.33
3. Night dreaming	.07
4. Absorption in daydreaming	.18
5. Acceptance of daydreaming	.07
6. Positive reactions to daydreaming	.18
7. Frightened reactions to daydreaming	.05
8. Visual imagery in daydreaming	.21
9. Auditory imagery in daydreams	.19
10. Problem solving in daydreams	.23
11. Present-oriented daydreams	-.24
12. Future-oriented daydreams	.21
13. Past-oriented daydreams	.14
14. Bizarre-improbable daydreams	.16
15. Mindwandering	.20
16. Achievement-oriented daydreams	.01
17. Hallucinatory-vivid daydreams	.13
18. Fear-of-failure daydreams	-.04
19. Hostile daydreams	-.11
20. Sexual daydreams	.07
21. Heroic daydreams	.04
22. Guilt daydreams	-.10
23. Interpersonal curiosity	.35
24. Impersonal curiosity	-.03
25. Boredom susceptibility	-.02
26. Mentation rate	.17
27. Distractibility	-.07
28. Need for external stimulation	.06
29. Self-revelation	.14
30. Achievement	-.09
31. Affiliation	-.16
32. Aggression	-.10
33. Autonomy	.34
34. Dominance	-.20
35. Endurance	.04
36. Exhibitionism	-.05

TABLE 7.5 (*continued*)

Private Personality Variables	I
37. Harmavoidance	-.17
38. Impulsivity	.06
39. Nurturance	.20
40. Order	-.02
41. Play	-.26
42. Social recognition	-.35
43. Understanding	.39
44. Infrequency	.02
45. Locus of control	.11
46. General sensation seeking	.26
47. Thrill and adventure seeking	.14
48. Experience seeking	.49
49. Disinhibition	-.19

the needs for Understanding and Autonomy as well as Interpersonal Curiosity. There are high negative loadings on the dimension for the needs for Play and Social Recognition. The pattern of loadings on these two correlated dimensions point to a type of nonreckless marijuana use that is associated with general inquisitiveness and a desire for new experiences of a cognitive nature.

That the Experience-Seeking scale of the SSS was strongly associated with motivated marijuana use not only supports ancillary findings (Khavari et al., 1977; Zuckerman, 1975) but supports contentions that marijuana serves to aid those in search of new experiences (Suchman, 1968; Tart, 1970, 1971, 1975). It is also critical to note that the same variables most related to the dimension of perceived motivation for marijuana use are the same measures most related to the differentiation of the four types of substance users. This particular finding is especially illuminating of our contrasted-groups results, reported in Chapter 6.

As a final assessment of the utility of the findings, the Stewart–Love redundancy index was calculated. Approximately 2.69% of the motives for marijuana use can be predicted from the personality measures: The influence of personality on motivated marijuana use is, while statistically significant, rather small.

"Polydrug" Use and Personality Styles

A third canonical analysis, for the 185 individuals who used one or more drugs in addition to marijuana, shows that there is a significant relationship between the frequency of polydrug usage and personality and daydreaming ($\chi^2_{245} = 312.8, p < .005$); the decomposition of Bartlett's χ^2 indicates that the first two canonical correlations are significantly greater than zero.

As was the case in the study of the relationship between motives for using alcohol and private personality, more than one significant canonical dimension emerged. Consequently, the loadings were rotated to simultaneous orthogonal simple structure using the two-matrix orthosim procedure of Bentler and Huba (in press).

Two different rotations were calculated. In the first, the simple structure was determined entirely from the five drug variables (α = 1); in the second rotation, the weight given to the drug-use variables was proportional to their importance in the total battery (α = 5/54). After inspecting the two rotated solutions, it was apparent that the (α = 1) solution was most consistent with our intention of relating "simple" clusters of polydrug use to facets of private personality. Table 7.6a shows the rotated loadings in the (α = 1) solution; Table 7.6b shows the adjusted canonical correlations.

Interpreting the rotated loadings, it can be seen that the first canonical dimension in the drug-use frequency domain has its highest loading for the

TABLE 7.6

Rotated Canonical-Correlation Loadings Between "Hard"-Drug Use and Private Personality Variables for Polydrug Users

(a) Rotated Loadings	I	II
Drug-Use Frequencies		
1. Amphetamines	.66	.15
2. Narcotics - Cocaine	.15	-.31
3. Barbiturates - Tranquilizers	.76	.03
4. Hallucinogenics	-.18	.41
5. Marijuana	.12	.89
Private Personality Variables		
1. Sex	.47	-.24
2. Daydreaming frequency	-.03	-.15
3. Night dreaming frequency	.01	.03
4. Absorption in daydreaming	.13	-.27
5. Acceptance of daydreaming	-.12	-.08
6. Positive reactions to daydreaming	.10	-.16
7. Frightened reactions to daydreaming	.16	-.25
8. Visual imagery in daydreams	-.01	.02
9. Auditory imagery in daydreams	-.11	-.07
10. Problem solving in daydreams	-.08	-.27
11. Present-oriented daydreams	.02	-.20
12. Future-oriented daydreams	-.04	-.15
13. Past-oriented daydreams	.15	-.05
14. Bizarre-improbable daydreams	.01	-.10
15. Mindwandering	.07	-.11
16. Achievement-oriented daydreams	-.03	-.20
17. Hallucinatory-vivid daydreams	.24	-.16
18. Fear-of-failure daydreams	.12	.05
19. Hostile daydreams	.04	-.02
20. Sexual daydreams	.23	-.13
21. Heroic daydreams	-.04	-.16
22. Guilt daydreams	.09	-.13

TABLE 7.6 (*continued*)

Private Personality Variables

23.	Interpersonal curiosity	.02	-.22
24.	Impersonal curiosity	-.02	.27
25.	Boredom susceptibility	.23	.07
26.	Mentation rate	-.13	-.26
27.	Distractibility	.12	-.08
28.	Need for external stimulation	-.09	-.01
29.	Self-revelation	-.24	.10
30.	Achievement	-.20	-.40
31.	Affiliation	-.13	-.03
32.	Aggression	.10	.17
33.	Autonomy	.14	.13
34.	Dominance	-.06	-.24
35.	Endurance	-.05	-.16
36.	Exhibitionism	-.06	-.06
37.	Harmavoidance	-.05	-.05
38.	Impulsivity	.14	-.04
39.	Nurturance	.07	-.08
40.	Order	-.04	-.02
41.	Play	.27	.11
42.	Social recognition	-.02	-.09
43.	Understanding	-.11	-.15
44.	Infrequency	.33	.04
45.	Locus of control	.09	.14
46.	General sensation seeking	-.09	-.18
47.	Thrill and adventure seeking	.01	-.20
48.	Experience sensation seeking	-.04	.24
49.	Disinhibition	.24	.23

(b)	Adjusted Canonical Correlations		
	I	.64	
	II	-.01	.63

use of "downers" with a smaller positive loading for the use of "uppers." This dimension, then, might represent the individual's tendency to use drugs in the frequently observed upper–downer vicious cycle for study and sleep, where the chemicals are used in a complementary pattern. The second possibility is that this pattern may represent the abuse of frequently prescribed pills with high potential for physical dependency. The corresponding personality-daydreaming dimension correlates .64 with the drug-frequency dimension. The personality–daydreaming variate is sex-linked with the females scoring higher, as a group, then the males. With the exception of the need for Play, Disinhibition, and Infrequent-responding control scales, none of the personality measures load on the dimension. Daydreaming scales loading positively on the dimension include those of Hallucinatory–vividness, Sexual themes, and Boredom Susceptibility. The Self-Revelation scale has a negative loading on the dimension. There is a small positive loading for Disinhibition Sensation Seeking. This pattern is similar to that encountered in the reasons for alcohol use and probably represents the linkage of a neurotic mental style with the use of drugs to control maladaptive thoughts.

The second rotated frequency of drug-use dimension has its largest loadings for the use of marijuana together wtih a substantial loading for hallucinogenic use. This combination seems to clearly reflect the drug use associated with "obtaining a high"—that is, seeking an expanded cognitive experience. Correlated (.63) with this type of polydrug use is a private personality dimension with negative loadings for needs Achievement and Dominance. Loading positively are the Disinhibitory and Experience Sensation-Seeking scales. Loading negatively are the Absorption in Day-dreaming, Frightened Reactions to daydreaming, Problem-Solving Day-dreaming, Interpersonal Curiosity, and Mentation Rate scales from the IPI. There is a positive loading for the IPI Impersonal Curiosity scale. Overall, the pattern of results links frequency of marijuana–hallucinogenic use to a type of externally oriented individual seeking many outside stimulants because of a general cognitive experience that is devoid of directed inner activity. Such individuals tend to have low motivation to dominate or to achieve. This type of frequent marijuana–hallucinogenic user has little curiosity about others, but she or he tends to be intrigued by mechnical devices. Among polydrug users, then, there is strong indication that an impoverished inner life is related to the usage frequency of "consciousness-expanding" chemicals.

The redundancy coefficients calculated for the canonical correlation results indicated that about 17.29% of the variation in the polydrug use could be predicted from the private personality domain.

Patterns of Marijuana and Alcohol Consumption in Individuals Who Use Both

The relationships between 13 reasons for using alcohol and 11 reasons for using marijuana were studied for the subsample of 425 individuals who use both substances. The multivariate relationship between the two domains was significant ($\chi^2_{143} = 181.66$, $p < .01$), and decomposition of Bartlett's χ^2 indicated that only the first canonical correlation is significant. Table 7.7 shows the correlations between the original variables and the first canonical variate in each domain, which are correlated with a magnitude of .36. The remaining 12 alcohol-use reasons were correlated with the alcohol-use dimension.

The general configuration of loadings within each domain reveals that when emphasis is placed on the use of marijuana to cope with negative states such as depression, anxiety, and peer pressure, corresponding emphasis is placed on the use of alcohol to deal with similar negative states. Such a general pattern argues that some individuals tend to have delineated preferences for marijuana and alcohol as ways to cope with negative emotions. The redundancy analysis indicated that 4.80% of the variance in the reasons for marijuana use were accounted for by the alcohol-use motives, and

TABLE 7.7
Canonical Loadings of Marijuana-Use Motives and Alcohol-Use Motives

Marijuana-Use Motives	I
1. To experience something new and different	.53
2. To get better insight into myself	-.03
3. To get "kicks" or to get "high"	.54
4. To satisfy my curiosity about what it was like	.25
5. To overcome feelings of boredom or depression	.51
6. To give me more pep or energy	.18
7. To relieve anxiety or tension	.60
8. To be more creative	.14
9. To relate better to my friends	.09
10. To expand my awareness and understanding of things	.16
11. Friends or acquaintances pressured me into it	.35

Alcohol-Use Motives	I
1. Just to be sociable	.13
2. Hot weather	.34
3. Feeling under pressure, tense	.60
4. Pain	.38
5. Hard work	.57
6. Having problems	.48
7. Feeling lonely	.63
8. Having nothing else to do	.40
9. Feeling mad	.22
10. Just feel you have to have a drink sometimes	.33
11. Feeling sad	.66
12. Not getting ahead	.39
13. Feeling tired	.34
14. Is something people do on special occasions*	-.04
15. Sometimes helps you feel better*	.28
16. Makes you less shy*	.17
17. Makes you feel more satisfied with yourself*	.25
18. Helps you relax*	.16
19. Helps you get along better with people*	.26
20. Helps you forget your problems*	.38
21. Makes get-togethers more fun*	.05
22. Gives you more confidence in yourself*	.27
23. Makes you feel happier*	.25
24. Helps you forget you're not the kind of person you'd like to be*	.28
25. Makes you worry less about what other people think of you*	.25

*pseudo-loading

7.24% of the alcohol-use motives were accounted for by the reasons for using marijuana.

Frequency of "Polydrug" Use and Motives for Using Alcohol and Marijuana

A canonical analysis between the frequency of use of each of the five classes of drugs and the reasons for drinking and using marijuana for the 185 individuals who used each class of drugs indicated that there was not a significant multivariate relationship (χ^2_{120} = 139.98, $p > .05$).

DISCUSSION

This series of analyses was designed to supplement and extend the contrasted-groups design, so often encountered in the literature, attempting to link personality and substance use. We have tried to delineate some of the specific personality correlates of self-described reasons for using alcohol and other drugs. Our findings have shown rather clearly that the use of any particular type of substance cannot be considered a unidimensional phenomenon. Moreover, it has been demonstrated that types of substance-use patterns and motives for use correlate differentially personality and private experience. Furthermore, in many cases there are complex multidimensional relationships between substance-use patterns and personality. Consequently, although our specific interpretations may be revised as more empirical data is collected, it appears that drug and alcohol use will not be definitively linked to personality until the phenomenon of substance use is treated in a multidimensional manner. The data do indicate that, in many cases, attempts to study personality concomitants of a unidimensional drug-use continuum oversimplify the true nature of the relationships.

Of particular interest in the current analyses is the finding that many of the personality variables that best differentiate users and nonusers of a particular substance (see Chapter 6—such as Experience Sensation Seeking, Disinhibitory Sensation Seeking, Harmavoidance, Impulsivity, and need for Autonomy—are related to only some of the specific reasons for using alcohol and marijuana or the pattern of polydrug use among users. Consequently, although the results that have been presented in Chapter 6 serve to point out major private personality differences between nonusers, users of alcohol only, users of marijuana only, and polydrug users, the results of this chapter indicate that many of the daydreaming and fantasy variables not related to these gross differences are strong correlates of the selection of specific substances.

The present findings, taken together with positive results on the potential for predicting adolescent drug use from personality attributes (e.g., Chapter

6, this volume; Jessor & Jessor, 1977; Kandel, 1975b, 1978a; Khavari et al., 1977; Smith & Fogg, 1977, 1978; Wingard et al., 1979), may help to reconcile several different theoretical approaches to the influence of personality on substance use and abuse. Many writers within the substance-use area have been primarily interested in predicting a continuum of substance use from such variables as achievement (Jessor & Jessor, 1977, perceived support for deviance (Jessor & Jessor, 1977), independence (Chapter 6, this volume; Jessor & Jessor, 1977; Wingard et al., 1979), need for new experiences (Chapter 6, this volume; Khavari et al., 1977), extraversion (Khavari et al., 1977; Wingard et al., 1979), rejection of traditional social rules (Jessor & Jessor, 1977; Wingard et al., 1979) and rebelliousness (Smith & Fogg, 1977, 1978). Kandel (1978a; Kandel & Faust, 1975) has insightfully argued that drug use may follow a series of stages with different psychological processes influencing drug use at each stage, even though some relevant constructs may serve to predict what stage an individual is in, or will shift to. Some apparent nonreplicability, or shift in importance of personality-predictor variables, from one study to the next may be a function of different samples composed of highly discrepant numbers of individuals in the different drug-use stages, or with quite different motives for use of a particular drug. Such a notion is particularly important in comparing the results of investigations located in different geographical areas because of the demonstrated importance of peer cultures (Huba et al., 1979; Johnson, 1973), which may differ in suburban and metropolitan areas. We believe that it is a very direct implication of our findings that a much more fruitful approach to youthful substance use is simultaneous analysis of not only what characteristics differentiate and predict membership in some cluster of individuals with approximately the same substance-use patterns, but also which constructs are related to variations within a category in the motives for use and amount of the substance used.

The self-report nature of the current data mitigate against a strict and definitive interpretation of the overlap between substance-use motivation and the private personality domain. Further study must incorporate both other indices of motivation for use and confirmatory methodologies and longitudinal studies such as the structural-equations methods with measurement error described by Bentler (1976), Jöreskog and Sörbom (1978), and Wiley (1973). Within the current data, two different interpretations may be suggested for the pattern of results. First, it is quite possible that the dimensional structure of the substance-use reasons may be biased by current popular cultural assumptions and effects of advertising as well as educational programs. For example, one of the factors found as a motive for drinking alcohol was because of hot weather and hard work. Such a cluster of individual attributions could well have been formed by years of advertising directed toward the mass television audience extolling the benefits of beer after work and as a means to quench thirst. Nonetheless, we believe that the analyses, considered in full, argue for a second interpretation that self-attributed causes for substance use have strong psychological validity in their own right. The relationships demonstrated in different analyses would appear to indicate that overall private personality or "coping style" of the individual is intimately related to the individual's *perceptions* of her or his own substance use. Such a consistency may have the therapeutic implication that perceptions of substance use cannot be changed without changing the individual's more general style of coping.

Throughout our analyses of the reasons or motives for using various substances, two quite distinctly different types of generalized dimensions have been found. One type of dimension appears to be a general motive for using the substance to increase positive affect, or social facilitation; the second type seems to be a generalized tendency for using substances to decrease negative affects such as depression. That there are two quite distinctly different processes is supported by our finding factors representative of these generalized styles within the sets of attributed-use motives for the different substances. Even more importantly, these dimensions seem to have quite different patterns of general private personality correlates from the different facets of the research domain.

Another important aspect of the present analyses is the finding that there is a developing pattern of preference for one substance in certain situations or for certain effects among youth who use more than one drug. Although complementary patterns of use are not "strong" in the sense of sharing great amounts of variance, our canonical correlation analyses do indicate that the relationship between alcohol and marijuana is statistically robust. Furthermore, a reasonable supposition is that "drug-of-choice" patterns should not be particularly strong among individuals with only limited substance-use experience. It is likely that stylized patterns of drug preference are crystallized and ritualized through long-term use and wide experimentation with substances. Consequently, the results from the relevant canonical analyses should be taken as indication that drug preferences develop early in the individual's history of drug experience.

The final point that should be made as we conclude this chapter is a reiteration of the importance of studying the phenomenon of youthful substance use from a multivariate perspective. Just as it has proven fruitful to study phenomena such as intelligence or group cohesion from multidimensional perspectives, youthful drug use has many different points of overlap with traditional psychological processes and theories. We will not argue that our analyses establish definitive dimensions of marijuana use or polydrug use, but we can argue strongly that the results establish that certain psychological processes that are not highly related to *who will try a drug* are important in understanding who continues to use a drug and why.

8

Questionnaire, Experimental, and Qualitative Studies of Normal Daydreaming Patterns

While the major thrust of this research project was concerned with large-scale normative patterns of daydreaming and other facets of the private personality in relationship to substance use, we also sought opportunities to undertake more detailed analyses of ongoing thought in the lifestyle of the college student. This chapter discusses two related, but methodologically separable, means of probing the realm and meaning of inner experience. In the first section of the chapter, analyses conducted with our questionnaire data are described. The questionnaire data were used to examine the relationship between daydreaming, fantasy, and other aspects of private personality as well as sex and regional-background differences. In the second half of the chapter, we discuss a series of controlled experimental studies testing theoretical hypotheses about the nature of inner experience and practical applications of imagery in day-to-day life. The experimental studies were partially supported by the research grant but because of their essentially theoretical nature are described in more technical form elsewhere. Intensive interviews with a subsample of students were also conducted to determine whether values and patterns of recent and family experience could be related to daydreaming and the use of substances.

ANALYSES OF NORMATIVE PATTERNS
OF DAYDREAMING: RELATIONSHIPS TO
NEEDS, SENSATION-SEEKING TENDENCIES,
PERCEIVED CONTROL, SEX, AND BACKGROUND

As originally suggested by Singer and Singer (1972) and amplified in Chapters 2 and 3, daydreaming patterns are one facet of a total coping style that we may term the *private personality*. As shown in Chapter 5, there is a replicable, and probably invariant, set of dimensions to inner experience. Throughout this volume, we have emphasized our contention that the type of fantasies and recurrent imagery in the stream of consciousness helps to define the total person. Furthermore, it was shown that elements of, and reactions to, the stream of consciousness play a significant role in the development of motivated substance use.

Daydreaming or fantasy processes may be seen as a kind of internal stimulus field capable of evoking positive and negative emotional reactions and generally serving as an alternative to overt action. Consequently, it is necessary to systematically explore the relationship between inner experiences and more traditional views of personality. Because of the importance of daydreaming and fantasy in our conceptualization of personality and the phenomenon of substance use, it is quite necessary to ask the questions, "To what extent are daydreaming and fantasy tendencies predictable from the more traditional areas of personality measurement?", and "What aspects of daydreaming and fantasy are tightly linked to the experience of motivational tendencies, behavioral preferences, and perceived reinforcement contingencies?"

Within the scientific literature on daydreaming and fantasy, two major studies have attempted to link inner experience with patterns of social behavior commonly conceptualized as personality. These previous investigations (Giambra, 1977; Singer & Antrobus, 1972) have correlated the Imaginal Processes Inventory (IPI) with the Guilford–Zimmerman Temperament Scales (Guilford & Zimmerman, 1949). The Singer–Antrobus (1972) study also examined the relationship of the IPI scales to the California Personality Inventory (CPI; Gough, 1956). Both the Singer–Antrobus and Giambra investigations found significant patterns of overlap between the Imaginal Processes Inventory and traditional measures of personality. The original investigators concluded that these linkages were, in general, quite consistent with existing psychological theory.

Although the previous research does support our contention that daydreaming is an important facet of the private personality, there are several methodological weaknesses in the previous investigations that limit their usefulness in specifying the exact nature of these linkages. First, both studies use numerous indices from the domain of inner experience but limit scales from the area of personality to a few. The range of sampling variables and the reliance on a large number of measures from a single battery minimize generality. Second, in both of these studies, principal components analysis was used as the primary method of data reduction. As a result, a large amount of the variance in the two groups of measures has appeared on different dimensions. The finding of instrument-specific dimensions, in our view, can be interpreted as an artifact of the attempt to structure all the variance in the personality and daydreaming measures simultaneously, rather than limiting the structural analysis to only the variance in common between the two domains.

In the present study, we have used a series of canonical correlation analyses to structure the covariation in common between the traditional personality domain and the measures of inner experience in order to overcome the limitations described previously. Canonical correlation analysis has several distinct advantages over the traditionally used technique of factor analysis in attempting to explain correlations between variables in two different domains. First, emphasis is primarily placed on explaining correlations between the domains. Second, a formal testing of significance exists for each canonical correlation. Third, the multivariate null hypothesis of no relationship between the domains can be tested in a straightforward statistical manner. Thus the procedure of canonical correlation analysis provides a computational technique to answer the following question: "What personality profiles tend to be associated with what patterns of daydreaming?"

Additionally, we have sampled the personality domain, using both the extensive needs battery of Jackson (1967), as well as the additional variables of behavioral preference for activity developed by Zuckerman (1975), and the scale of perceived reinforcement described by Rotter (1966). The variable sampling was wider and more general than in the previous studies.

Method

Participants. The participants for these analyses were 1095 college students from Murray State University and Yale University. The group of respondents is the same as that described in Chapter 4 and used for the analyses presented in Chapters 5, 6, and 7. For the purpose of the present analysis, the sample was split into two halves on the basis of year of testing. In the first year, there were 590 subjects; in the second, there were 505 subjects.

Data Analysis. For the present calculations, two sets of variables were formed. In the first set of traditional personality measures, we included the 15 PRF measures of needs, the four sensation-seeking scores, and the locus-of-control scale. Additionally, dichotomous markers for the college that the individual attended (1 = Yale; 2 = Murray State) and sex (1 = male; 2 = female) were included. This inclusion of classification factors (sex and college) within the personality set was intended to force the personality dimensions to be aligned with possible classification differences in individuals. This procedure should have the effect of localizing differences due to college and sex on the personality and daydreaming variables utilized in the present analyses. The second set of variables assessing private personality were the 28 scale scores from the Imaginal Processes Inventory. As noted earlier (see Chapter 2), the IPI contains scales tapping a variety of aspects of inner experience, such as the frequency of day and night dreaming, the extent to which the individual becomes absorbed in daydreams, the types of emotional reactions to daydreams, the imagery components of inner experience, the time orientation of inner experience, and specific aspects of fantasy content such as hostility, sexual exploits, guilt, achievement, and interpersonal curiosity.

For each of the two samples, the 50 variables were intercorrelated, and the resulting product-moment coefficients were used in the canonical correlation analysis with the 22 personality-classification variables forming one set, and with the 28 IPI scales forming the second set. Canonical correlation analysis was chosen as the principal statistical method because it summarized the across-domain covariation in as few statistically reliable dimensions as possible. Because of the well-known lack of interpretability in canonical correlation solutions (Bentler & Huba, in press; Cliff & Krus, 1976; Wilkinson, 1977), the canonical loadings (see Cooley & Lohnes, 1971) for the two domains in each sample were rotated to approximate orthogonal simple structure. The rotation procedure is a generalization of Bentler's (1977) orthosim method and seeks the best simultaneous symmetric simple-structure position for two matrices (Bentler & Huba, in press). For the rotations, the two domains were weighted proportionally to the number of variables in them (α = .44). Finally, the canonical correlations in each of the two samples were adjusted for the transformations. The two sets of rotated coefficients were assessed for convergence by the use of congruence coefficients (uncentered correlations: Tucker, 1951). Canonical correlation analysis, then, determines a set of dimensions for each of two groups of variables simultaneously under the constraint that one of the dimensions from the first set is maximally correlated with one of the dimensions from the second set, and is uncorrelated with all other dimensions in either group of measures. The formal statistical test is applied to determine the number of robust dimensions. The dimensions in each set are then rotated to a simultaneous position of best simple structure using an orthogonal rotation algorithm. The final result of the analysis and rotation is two sets of within-set orthogonal dimensions, one set for each domain, which explains all of the statistically reliable covariation between the domains as present in their correlations across sets.

Since canonical correlation analysis does utilize optimization of results in maximizing the correlations across domains, a further test of the robustness of the findings was undertaken by computing the analyses separately in each of the two samples and computing indices of correlation (congruence) between the sets of dimensions so obtained (see Huba, et al., 1979, for a discussion of canonical-correlation replication strategies). Consequently, the present analyses sought to replicate the dimensions that were found. Finally, we examined the extent to which levels of functioning within one domain could be predicted from the other using an index of redundancy (Stewart & Love, 1968).

Results

In each of the two samples, it was possible to reject the hypothesis of no overlap between the domain of daydreaming and the personality-classification domain (for Sample 1, χ^2_{616} = 1971.37, $p < .0001$; for Sample 2, χ^2_{616} = 1669.68, $p < .0001$). Consequently, it is possible to conclude that there is a significant relationship between daydreaming and personality. Partialing the total χ^2 value for each of the two samples indicated that nine dimensions are necessary to fully explain the cross-domains covariation; with eight dimensions partialed, the goodness of fit tests were still significant (for Sample 1, χ^2_{280} = 327.91, $p < .05$; for Sample 2 χ^2_{280} = 356, $p < .05$), whereas with nine dimensions partialed, the tests indicated that the model could be accepted (for Sample 1, χ^2_{247} = 263.06, $p > .05$; for Sample 2, χ^2_{247} = 281.36, $p > .05$).

Unrotated canonical variables are not usually easily interpreted. Consequently, the canonical variable loadings were rotated orthogonally using the symmetric two-matrix orthosim procedure. An issue relevant to the current analyses is the number of canonical variable dimensions that should be maintained for rotation. Although there are nine significant canonical dimensions in each of the two samples, this is not to say that all nine dimensions should be rotated. It is possible that there is a smaller number of robust dimensions and that later significant canonical correlations are the result of sample specific capitalization on chance. Consequently, in order to determine the number of dimensions to maintain for rotation in the present analyses where two samples were available, we first calculated congruence coefficients between the two sets of unrotated loadings (see Wingard et al., 1979). Table 8.1 shows the congruence coefficients between the nine unrotated canonical dimensions in each of the two samples. As may be noted, the first six dimensions appear to be stable across the two samples. It was decided to retain six dimensions for the rotation.

Table 8.2 shows the congruence coefficients between the six dimensions retained in each of the two samples after rotation using the two-matrix orthosim algorithm. As may be seen, there is a larger amount of similarity

TABLE 8.1
Congruence Coefficients Between Unrotated Canonical Dimensions
for the 1973 and 1974 Samples[a]

		1974 Sample								
		I'	II'	III'	IV'	V'	VI'	VII'	VIII'	IX'
	I	-.39	.89	-.18	.27	.13	-.11	-.09	.07	-.25
	II	.16	.04	.79	-.39	-.45	.09	-.02	.14	.51
	III	-.76	-.06	.50	.30	-.25	.07	.07	.06	.12
1973	IV	.42	.19	.36	.63	.33	.36	.05	.23	-.18
Sample	V	.42	-.20	-.24	.01	-.54	-.19	.06	.13	.05
	VI	-.06	.20	.20	.25	-.23	.60	.16	.05	.25
	VII	.25	.02	.35	.16	-.04	.19	.18	.48	.12
	VIII	.18	.09	.01	.46	-.13	.21	-.28	-.33	-.17
	IX	-.08	.10	-.13	-.28	.10	-.40	.05	-.15	.30

[a]Underscored entries indicate corresponding dimensions.

TABLE 8.2
Congruence Coefficients Between Rotated Canonical Dimensions
for the 1973 and 1974 Samples[a]

		1974 Sample					
		I'	II'	III'	IV'	V'	VI'
	I	.84	-.02	.28	.08	.49	-.11
	II	-.10	.85	-.13	.03	.20	-.40
1973	III	-.08	-.35	.91	.28	-.16	.10
Sample	IV	-.19	-.33	-.06	.85	-.26	.32
	V	.06	.24	.20	.41	.74	.08
	VI	-.21	-.47	-.13	.08	.18	.88

[a]Underscored entries indicate corresponding dimensions.

between corresponding dimensions in the two samples than was apparent
from the unrotated solution. Therefore, we believe that this further evidence
shows that six stable dimensions span the domains of inner experience and
personality.

Table 8.3 shows the rotated canonical loadings for each of the two domains
in the two samples. The rotated canonical loadings for the two groups of
variables are quite similar across samples for all of the variates, and the
magnitudes of corresponding coefficients are surprisingly similar. Table 8.4
shows the canonical correlations after they have been adjusted for the
transformation.

TABLE 8.3
Rotated Canonical Loadings for Personality and Daydreaming

	I	I'	II	II'	III	III'	IV	IV'	V	V'	VI	VI'
Personality-Classification Variables												
College	0.12	-0.04	-0.24	-0.55	-0.06	0.22	0.11	-0.02	0.75	0.55	-0.15	0.07
Sex	0.84	0.71	0.15	0.10	-0.10	0.00	-0.15	-0.11	0.10	0.41	-0.03	-0.06
Achievement	-0.21	-0.10	0.18	0.08	-0.68	-0.81	0.29	0.16	-0.04	0.09	0.06	-0.01
Affiliation	0.28	0.30	0.22	-0.12	-0.21	-0.13	-0.01	0.02	0.27	0.32	0.40	0.58
Aggression	-0.08	-0.26	0.01	0.43	0.47	0.37	0.46	0.35	-0.13	0.07	0.14	0.10
Autonomy	-0.39	-0.10	0.31	0.26	0.06	-0.12	0.06	-0.20	-0.38	-0.41	-0.02	0.01
Dominance	-0.29	-0.22	0.08	0.11	-0.24	-0.47	0.52	0.38	-0.04	0.02	0.40	0.38
Endurance	-0.35	0.19	0.04	0.07	-0.56	-0.74	0.04	-0.11	0.10	-0.02	0.20	0.16
Exhibitionism	0.04	0.35	0.31	0.35	0.01	-0.23	0.71	0.53	-0.02	-0.03	0.25	0.41
Harmavoidance	0.23	0.18	-0.20	-0.28	-0.09	0.01	-0.01	0.17	0.15	0.12	-0.76	-0.62
Impulsivity	0.22	0.28	0.24	0.44	0.50	0.39	0.11	0.17	-0.06	0.10	0.37	0.44
Nurturance	0.42	0.01	0.22	0.01	-0.46	-0.22	0.02	-0.04	0.35	0.67	0.17	0.20
Order	0.06	0.01	-0.29	-0.35	-0.30	-0.27	0.06	-0.17	0.17	0.35	-0.04	-0.21
Play	0.12	0.01	0.17	-0.03	0.42	0.39	0.16	0.13	0.14	0.25	0.29	0.57
Social recognition	0.26	0.08	-0.27	-0.21	0.18	0.18	0.54	0.78	0.28	0.28	0.06	-0.02
Understanding	-0.24	-0.20	0.70	0.52	-0.31	-0.53	-0.06	-0.02	-0.11	0.10	0.01	-0.15
Infrequency	-0.26	-0.05	-0.15	0.12	0.15	0.09	-0.11	-0.05	-0.23	0.02	0.14	-0.05
Locus of control	0.16	0.17	0.11	0.27	0.48	0.40	-0.12	0.10	-0.11	-0.12	0.06	-0.07
General sensation seeking	-0.26	-0.28	0.48	0.50	0.09	-0.09	-0.06	-0.22	-0.20	-0.07	0.52	0.40
Thrill and adventure seeking	-0.15	-0.23	0.13	0.19	-0.09	-0.04	0.02	-0.12	-0.23	0.05	0.61	0.55
Experience seeking	-0.21	-0.26	0.76	0.58	0.28	0.07	-0.02	-0.20	-0.11	-0.06	0.21	0.32
Disinhibition	-0.19	-0.35	0.10	0.03	0.46	0.29	0.22	0.26	0.31	-0.08	0.25	0.51
Daydreaming Variables												
Daydreaming frequency	0.15	0.20	0.31	0.44	0.37	0.29	0.17	0.08	-0.26	-0.24	0.05	-0.09
Night dreaming frequency	0.14	0.04	0.45	0.37	0.15	-0.03	0.19	-0.12	-0.02	0.05	0.10	0.16
Absorption in daydreaming	0.32	0.15	0.33	0.44	0.27	0.28	0.14	0.22	0.10	0.20	0.07	-0.17

	I	II	III	IV	V	VI	I'	II'	III'	IV'	V'	VI'
Acceptance of daydreaming	0.14	-0.07	0.51	0.29	-0.07	-0.21	0.05	-0.07	-0.25	-0.02	-0.02	0.14
Positive reactions to daydreams	0.15	0.09	0.16	0.04	0.09	0.05	0.15	0.21	0.28	0.28	0.08	0.02
Frightened reactions to daydreams	0.19	0.12	0.20	0.20	0.15	0.24	0.08	0.27	0.17	0.29	-0.07	0.01
Visual imagery in daydreams	0.13	-0.16	0.17	0.26	0.12	0.13	0.10	0.18	0.12	0.21	0.07	0.09
Auditory imagery in daydreams	0.09	-0.16	0.30	0.30	0.09	0.07	0.02	0.12	0.11	0.20	0.13	-0.01
Problem solving in daydreams	-0.03	0.04	0.31	-0.10	-0.13	-0.12	0.15	0.18	0.41	0.24	-0.03	0.06
Present-oriented daydreams	0.17	0.24	-0.20	-0.14	-0.06	-0.03	-0.26	-0.04	0.07	0.04	0.11	0.00
Future-oriented daydreams	0.31	-0.05	0.21	0.22	-0.11	-0.18	0.39	0.28	0.05	0.38	0.03	-0.12
Past-oriented daydreams	0.16	-0.13	0.17	0.29	0.04	0.07	0.03	0.05	0.23	0.17	-0.13	-0.10
Bizarre-improbable daydreams	-0.19	-0.30	0.31	0.21	0.33	0.27	0.10	0.02	0.19	-0.03	-0.07	-0.11
Mindwandering	0.44	0.19	0.16	0.06	0.56	0.65	0.02	0.12	-0.08	0.01	0.05	0.02
Achievement-oriented daydreams	-0.13	-0.10	0.00	0.06	0.00	-0.07	0.78	0.84	0.21	0.10	0.01	0.01
Hallucinatory-vivid daydreams	0.05	-0.13	0.04	-0.02	0.17	0.23	-0.07	0.16	0.48	0.51	0.05	0.06
Fear-of-failure daydreams	-0.13	-0.06	-0.10	0.26	0.27	0.36	0.32	0.09	0.31	0.18	-0.03	-0.03
Hostile daydreams	-0.25	-0.38	-0.02	0.32	0.50	0.34	0.24	0.41	0.11	-0.05	-0.05	-0.02
Sexual daydreams	-0.13	-0.15	-0.35	0.06	0.45	0.15	0.29	0.37	0.18	-0.07	0.07	0.11
Heroic daydreams	-0.34	-0.26	-0.02	-0.06	0.00	0.05	0.02	0.33	0.18	0.11	0.15	0.22
Guilt daydreams	-0.20	0.00	-0.01	0.33	0.21	0.28	0.11	0.20	0.36	0.13	-0.07	0.16
Interpersonal curiosity	0.34	0.27	0.50	0.00	-0.23	-0.21	0.04	0.14	0.21	0.50	0.17	0.10
Impersonal curiosity	-0.68	-0.72	0.08	0.03	-0.18	-0.22	-0.01	-0.07	0.03	0.10	0.21	0.02
Boredom susceptibility	0.04	-0.05	-0.05	0.36	0.73	0.85	-0.35	0.03	0.23	-0.02	-0.09	-0.15
Mention rate	0.08	-0.03	0.18	0.12	0.00	-0.36	0.10	0.08	0.01	0.11	0.01	-0.10
Distractibility	0.49	0.20	-0.03	0.13	0.44	0.54	0.22	0.20	0.00	0.08	0.81	-0.03
Need for external stimulation	-0.02	-0.08	0.12		-0.02	-0.16		0.07	0.04	0.14		0.72
Self-revelation	0.25	0.19	0.54	0.60	-0.08	-0.10	0.07	0.01	0.13	0.32	0.34	0.20

I - VI refer to canonical dimensions in the 1973 sample.
I' - VI' refer to canonical dimensions in the 1974 sample.

TABLE 8.4
Adjusted Canonical Correlations

	I	II	III	IV	V	VI
(a) 1973 Sample						
I	.67					
II	.02	.58				
III	.03	.00	.61			
IV	-.04	.00	.02	.58		
V	.00	.04	-.02	.01	.50	
VI	-.03	.10	.01	.03	.04	.56
(b) 1974 Sample						
I	.58					
II	.02	.53				
III	.00	-.01	.66			
IV	-.01	.00	.00	.56		
V	.07	.02	-.03	.00	.52	
VI	-.02	.04	-.01	.03	.03	.57

The first dimension in the personality-classification domain has an extremely high positive loading for the sex of the participant with females scoring higher. Also loading consistently on the dimension in both samples are a high need for Affiliation, a low need for Autonomy and Endurance, and a high need for Nurturance. All the sensation-seeking scales have small, but sample-consistent, negative loadings on the dimension. Correlated with this generalized sex difference in personality dimension is a daydreaming dimension that includes positive loadings for Interpersonal Curiosity, Mindwandering, and a tendency toward Distractibility as well as sample-consistent negative loadings for Heroic and Hostile daydreams and Impersonal Curiosity. This dimension then appears to link generalized sex differences within the traditional personality domain with sex differences in inner experience tendencies. The general pattern appears almost stereotypic and might be seen as a consequence of a "traditional" sex-role socialization process.

The second dimension in the personality domain has large positive loadings for the need to Understand, Experience Sensation Seeking, and General

Sensation Seeking. Also loading on the dimension are the needs for Impulsivity and Exhibitionism with an inverse loading for Order. In the second sample, there is a tendency for the Yale students to score higher. Correlated with this general dimension of a need for external experiences is an inner experience dimension, which includes nonsample-specific positive loadings for Day and Night Dreaming Frequency, Absorption in and Acceptance of Daydreaming, Auditory Imagery, Bizarre–Improbable Daydreams, Interpersonal Curiosity, a tendency toward Self-Revelation, and a large number of Sexual Daydreams. The overall pattern suggests that a general personality dimension of seeking many varied experiences in the external environment is linked to an inner experience dimension of many experiences. That is, it appears that the same individuals who seek out new and novel environments to experience and comprehend will also tend to daydream more frequently as well as become engrossed in their daydreams. The daydreams of such an individual have a tendency to include sexual themes, to revolve around speculation about the lives of other individuals, and to include improbable associations.

The third personality dimension has large positive loadings in both samples for the needs for Aggression, Impulsivity, Play, and External Locus of Control, and Disinhibitory Sensation Seeking. There are negative loadings on the dimension for the needs for Achievement, Dominance, Endurance, Nurturance, Order, and Understanding. The high scorer on this dimension, then, would appear to be an individual who believes that the reinforcements in his or her life are controlled by forces outside control, who tends to have an impulsive behavioral style with concomitant low drives toward generalized achievement, social extraversion, and group membership. Correlated with this personality dimension is an inner experience dimension marked by positive loadings for Susceptibility to Boredom, Distractibility, and tendencies to Mindwandering, as well as a large Number of Daydreams, sometimes of a Bizarre or improbable nature. The high scorer on the dimension also reports becoming absorbed in her or his daydreams that have themes of Fear of Failure, Hostility, Guilt, and Sex. Overall, then, the highly impulsive but low-achievement and low-sociable individual tends to have a dysphoric inner experience engaged in primarily to escape boredom. This combination of personality and inner experience styles is quite possibly indicative of a coupling of behavioral and inner experience manifestations of feeling very little control over life events.

The fourth personality dimension has high positive loadings for the needs for Exhibitionism, Dominance, Aggression, and Social Recognition. Consequently, it appears that this dimension is one of generalized extraversion or social dominance. Correlated positively with this dimension is a daydreaming dimension marked in a positive manner by Achievement-Oriented, Hostile, Heroic, and Sexual fantasies in Future time frames. Consequently, the total pattern of the two dimensions seems to indicate that an individual with social presence and a tendency to dominate others while seeking their social recognition will have daydreams and fantasies of future achievement. The smaller loadings for Hostile, Sexual, and Heroic daydreams on this dimension may be interpreted as modes of attaining achievement within the current society. It is also interesting to note that the need for Achievement loads on the personality dimension with a fairly small magnitude in each of the two samples, indicating that fantasy achievement and the motivation to achieve are relatively independent phenomena only tenuously linked.

The fifth personality-classification dimension is primarily one of differences between the two colleges. In both samples, the college variable very much defines the dimension with the subjects from the rural Kentucky university tending to score higher. In the second year, sex also marks the variate, with females tending to score higher. Other variables loading on the dimension in the personality domain are a lowered need for autonomy as well as heightened needs for Affiliation, Nurturance, and Social Recognition. Correlated positively with this dimension of college differences is a daydreaming dimension in which there are positive loadings for the Tendency to Solve Problems in Daydreams, Hallucinatory Vividness of the daydreams, Interpersonal Curiosity, and Positive Reactions to Daydreams. There is a negative loading for the Frequency of Daydreaming on the dimension.

The sixth personality dimension is primarily marked by the Sensation-Seeking Scales, each of which has a positive loading. Also loading on the dimension are the needs for Play, Impulsivity, Exhibitionism, Dominance, and Affiliation. There is a negative loading for the need for Harmavoidance. Overall, this dimension appears to represent a generalized tendency toward experiencing many different social situations. The only variable that strongly marks the corresponding daydreaming dimension is the Need for External Stimulation. Consequently, it appears that the sixth pair of dimensions was primarily found because the IPI contains a scale fairly redundant with a combination of measures in the traditional personality domain. The correlations on these dimensions should be contrasted with the pattern found for the second dimension in each domain. As will be remembered, the second dimension has many of the same variables loading on it in the personality domain, but it indicates that this tendency to seek external experiences is highly correlated with the seeking of many different types of internal experiences. Therefore, the sixth pair of dimensions tends to clarify the relationship between daydreaming and the seeking of sensations: This final pair of dimensions serves to remove covariation, which would tend to confound the true relationship between the domains of inner experience and personality.

The final question that must be asked—now that it has been demonstrated that there is theoretically, as well as statistically, significant covariation between the domains of inner experience and personality—is to what extent are the two facets redundant. As a final index of the overlap of personality in daydreaming, the canonical correlation redundancy statistic suggested by Stewart and Love (1968; Gleason, 1976) was calculated. Assuming six canonical dimensions, in the first sample 12.79% of the variance in the daydreaming variables can be predicted from the personality variables, whereas 20.23% of the personality-classification variance can be predicted from the daydreaming variables. In the second sample, it was possible to predict 11.92% of the variation in the daydreaming variables from the personality measures and 19.32% of the variation in the personality-classification scales from the daydreaming indices. Alternate symmetric measures of multivariate association have been provided by Cramer and Nicewander (1979). Of the six measures they present, the most promising estimate seems to be the average squared canonical correlation coefficient. The value of this index (Cramer and Nicewander's γ_6) for the 1973 sample is .132, and the coefficient has a value of .139 for the 1974 sample. The Cramer–Nicewander coefficient, with its alternate mathematical derivation, also yields an estimate that about 14% of the variance between the two domains is in common. Therefore, it is possible to conclude that while the two domains are related in a theoretically and statistically significant manner, they certainly are not redundant and should be treated as conceptually distinct facets of personality.

Discussion

The intent of these analyses was to examine the nature of the relationships between the domains of inner experience and personality. From our statistical tests, it was possible to conclude that there are approximately nine statistically necessary dimensions spanning the two domains, of which six appear to be replicable and interpretable after rotation. Of the six interpretable pairs of dimensions, five are theoretically important.

That the two domains are related in a theoretically meaningful manner strongly supports the general model that typical patterns of motivation and inner experience arise developmentally from the same sources. Indeed, the two patterns are complimentary and nonredundant, which suggests that both must be considered in the total assessment of the individual. We do realize, of course, that such results are correlational in nature and certainly cannot demonstrate a common cause for personality and inner experience, or show that one's style of personality functioning determines one's typical stream of consciousness. In order to more fully explore the nature of the stream of consciousness and the extent to which this is related to personality style, it is necessary to examine the determinants and consequences of imagery, daydreaming, and fantasy through controlled experiments. We now discuss:

(1) a series of laboratory studies in which various conditions were experimentally manipulated; and (2) the effects of these manipulations on the stream of consciousness assessed.

EXPERIMENTAL STUDIES OF ONGOING THOUGHT

Sequences of Thought Under Natural Circumstances

As suggested in Chapter 3, we are just beginning to explore the fact that an individual's thought is not inevitably focused about very specific problems or task demands of the environment. Thought is in itself a relatively continuous process that involves rapid shifts of attention from external cues to the more elaborate processing of material generated from long-term memory.

If John walks down the street, he may pay attention to obstacles such as street lights, trash cans, or mailboxes and to oncoming passersby. At the same time, his attention may be caught by an unusual car in the street or by the glint of sunlight reflected off the glass of an office building. Concomitantly, he may be mentally rehearsing the presentation he is to make at an upcoming interview toward which he is heading.

So practiced are we in integrating visual and motor coordination for ordinary day-to-day locomotion that it requires little self-conscious commentary to maneuver on an ordinary street. Thus John can be responding privately to centrally generated images of entering the office of the prospective employer, introducing himself to the receptionist, cheerfully talking to her so that her introduction of him to the boss will itself reflect some warmth, and then greeting the interviewer with a firm handshake and a bright smile.

This relatively organized planful sequence of thought may, however, be interrupted by the honking of horns and screech of brakes as two cars narrowly avoid collision. John's eyes follow the sequence and take in its import; reassured that no one is hurt, he moves along. But before he can resume the planful thought sequence, the near accident triggers off a memory of the recent serious injury of a close friend in another automobile accident. What then follows is an extended series of memories that include how he first heard of the accident through a frantic phone call from his friend's mother and his own hasty drive to the hospital. The possibility that his friend may be crippled for life as well as the implications unfold even as he proceeds on his way toward the upcoming interview.

Examples such as this (far more beautifully represented in the work of Virginia Woolf or James Joyce) suggest aspects of a typical stream of consciousness to which we can all resonate on the basis of some introspection.

It is clear that there are rapid shifts of attention in this sequence from the external pole to the extremely internal pole of long-term memory, such as the recollection of the friend's accident or the extended fantasy of the consequences for the friend. There are also relatively rapid shifts in sequence stimulated by the necessity of processing new externally generated information and partially brought on by the very nature of thought itself or by the fact that one is continually moving down a street and receiving kinesthetic feedback from musculature.

A study (with partial support from our grant) by Dr. Kenneth Pope (1978) attempted to develop a specific methodology to discern and measure shifts of thought under various conditions. Pope sought to measure shifts in sequence of thoughts by two methods: (1) requiring an individual to talk continuously so that one could record the ebb and flow of ongoing thought (at least as reflected in speech) and count shifts in sequence; and (2) having an individual press a switch each time she or he was aware of a shift in a major sequence of thought either in the direction of attention to the external environment or to internally generated material. Thus one question asked, primarily of methodological interest, was whether shifts in sequence would be greater when one focused primarily on private thoughts without verbalizing them or when one engaged in expression of thought through continuous free-associative speech.

Another question had to do with the effect of posture on sequential processing of materials. Someone who is walking around and therefore relatively active might, of necessity, process so much novel material from the external environment and also experience enough kinesthetic feedback from musculature that basic channel space for processing private ongoing thought is reduced. In a series of studies conducted with Dr. John Antrobus, Singer (1975a, b) presented various evidence suggesting that some kinds of ongoing thought can be carried out in parallel form with the processing of externally generated information. The available channel space of the various sensory modalities involved in processing external as well as internal material is limited. An individual in a reclining posture restricts the amount of novel input because his or her eyes may be directed at blank ceiling. The reclining individual may also be restricting the amount of novel information input through kinesthetic feedback. Thus one might predict that a reclining individual would have longer sequences of thought, with less attention to the external environment and less spasmodic thinking patterns.

One might also examine the nature of thought produced by an individual concerning whether content is generated directly by external cues or derived from long-term memory, and also whether the material focuses primarily on the immediate situation of the individual, on the past or on the future. Under conditions of limited mobility, thought might reflect more content drawn from long-term memory, possibly with a future orientation, than an awareness of the immediate physical surroundings and present situation.

Still another condition examined was whether the participant was alone or in the company of another person. The experiment was conducted either with the experimenter seated in the room near the subject or with the subject alone in a small chamber. The motivational importance of the face of another person as well as the greater influence of social interaction should have some definite effects on thought sequences. Under social conditions, the individual might restrict thoughts to more present situations with more rapid sequences and shifts of attention than would be the case when alone.

The final aspect of the study involved determination of the affective reaction that individuals experienced during ongoing thought. It might be argued, as has been done by some followers of the Gestalt psychotherapy orientation, that people who function completely in relation to present experience generally feel happy. They are, by living more in the present, more likely to have a sense of joy. On the other hand, it could also be argued that the ability to shift one's attention away from the immediate present to the past or to the potential future gives an individual a scope and control over experience that may also produce more positive affective responses, especially under conditions of restricted environmental novelty or limited motor activity. In this study, an opportunity was provided to examine relationships between thought sequences, the pattern of ongoing thought, affective reactions and drug use.

Participating in the study were 90 college students from the total questionnaire study pool. Drug use was assessed by the questionnaires that students had completed 3 to 6 months earlier. In the first experiment, students either walked freely, sat, or reclined while they free associated aloud for 5 minute periods. The subjects indicated each time their thoughts shifted from an initial topic or imagery sequence and indicated when thought patterns focused on the immediate situation as opposed to past memories or future fantasies. The participants' ratings were supplemented by having the recordings of free associations rated by trained judges "blind" to the experimental conditions. In a second experiment, the subjects did not verbalize their ongoing thought but merely pressed hand-held keys indicating that they were either thinking about the immediate situation or unrelated material. The keys were depressed as long as the participant maintained one line of thought. When a thought segment shifted the key was released and pressed again when a new sequence began. Mood ratings for participants were obtained, and data on field-dependence, sensation-seeking, and daydreaming patterns as well as drug and alcohol use were available. Pope (1978) offers a detailed account of this very carefully designed and controlled study.

The data indicate that under these experimental conditions, about half of the thoughts are about experiences in the immediate present, and that about 30–40% of the time spent in thought is focused in the present. Generally, thoughts about the past or future unroll in longer sequences. Individual differences between subjects are quite great with some individuals devoting most of the time to thought unrelated to immediate circumstances. Responses to the environment produce the most shifts in thought.

The statistical analyses indicated that the number of thought shifts and the duration of present-oriented segments are highest for the "walking" condition, with the "sitting" condition intermediate and "reclining" group having the highest proportion of thought unrelated to the immediate situation. While reclining, the subjects had longer sequences of thought, the least present-oriented segments, and the least general attention to their current situation. This finding accords with earlier research reported by Berdach and Bakan (1967) and by S. Segal and Glickman (1967), which suggested that in a reclining posture people report more early childhood memories or vivid imagery.

Pope's data also indicate that when participants are in the presence of another person, their thoughts tend to shift sequence frequently and focus upon the present situation. Clearly, the stimulus of another individual leads to rapid shifts of thought and to a focusing on the present. Males seemed especially sensitive to this effect; women seemed to drift in thought even when another person was present. The button-press situation caused longer sequences of thought and less present thought than the situation of talking aloud. Presumably, translating thought into spoken form modifies the duration and deviation from present of the thought sequences.

Contrary to some clinical emphases on the present-oriented experience as a sign of contentment, the mood ratings suggested that thought of the present were correlated with unpleasant affects. The correlations between negative affect and the number and duration of present-oriented thoughts were, respectively, $r = .40$ ($p < .01$) and $r = .30$ ($p < .05$). Field dependent individuals also showed more shifts of thought, more present-oriented thought, and a longer time spent thinking about the present than those who were field independent. High experience sensation seekers also spent more time thinking about immediate circumstances. While marijuana and alcohol users showed a trend toward fewer shifts in thought and more attention to past or future, the heavy drug-use group was characterized by present-oriented thought and responses to immediate surroundings. There are indications that heavy drug users with high levels of experience sensation seeking may be considerably less likely to detach themselves from their immediate surroundings and move along the stream of thought into the past or future.

Determinants of the Content of Ongoing Thought

The study by Pope focused primarily on the structural characteristics of the ongoing thought sequence and its relation to patterns of mobility or social interaction during continuous mentation. Another question is what determines the *content* of continuous thought processes. We have already suggested that physical surroundings provide signals that may trigger either direct reaction to the novelty of these surroundings or to new information presented. The squeaking of the brakes in the earlier example or established intentions (such as the upcoming interview) may be such determinants.

What particular characteristics of an experience are likely to lead to its recurrence later in one's ongoing stream of consciousness? Antrobus et al. (1966) studied individuals who overheard a radio broadcast announcing escalation of the Vietnam War just prior to entering an experimental room to engage in a lengthy signal-detection task. The participants showed a striking increase in the number of thoughts they had unrelated to the task but related in various degrees to that surprising and disturbing information. In a series of further studies modeled on this format, Horowitz and various collaborators (Horowitz, 1975; Horowitz & Becker, 1971) examined the effects of different levels of arousal or different emotions on the kind of material that recurred in ongoing thoughts. They found that exposing individuals to frightening or distressing movies or even to sexually arousing material prior to engaging in signal-detection tasks increased the likelihood of experiencing thoughts related to the affective film material.

Still another possible content determinant of the stream of consciousness comes from theorizing and some experimental research by Klinger (1974, 1978) and Singer (1975a,b; 1978). It can be argued, as suggested in Chapter 3, that an important determinant of the recurrence of experiences is the incompleteness of a task sequence or the relationship of the experience to current concerns. It may be that the relative ambiguity of a situation that confronts one arouses the affect of interest and therefore increases the likelihood of further recurrence (Singer, 1974; Tomkins, 1962-1963).

Indeed, it might even be argued that current or unresolved concerns may be special cases of ambiguity or novelty. The activity one intends to finish but has not completed leaves one unable to make a satisfactory match between well-established schema and the intention. This failure of assimilation is associated with the arousal of the affect of interest if the degree of complexity of the material is at least moderate in amount, following Tomkins' (1962-1963) theory. Thus a cognitive affect position suggests that ambiguous material, even when it involves a low level of other types of emotional arousal, would be more likely to recur in thought than material that is fairly clear in meaning and that matches other stored information.

In two related experiments, Zachary (1978) attempted to examine the influence of type of emotional arousal and relative ambiguity of stimulus materials on recurrences of thought in the stream of consciousness. The sample of college students was drawn from the same group studied by the larger scale investigation.

In the first study, 36 male and 36 female college students each watched a film alone. Half saw a film about different varieties of flowers growing in the aboretum of a public park. It was a beautiful film whose purpose was clear and unambiguous even without a sound track. The other half of the sample watched a film in which a Japanese female played out a parable about a woman trying to come to terms with her own sense of self or identity. Using mime she carried a heavy load of baggage, misplaced it, searched frantically, and then was happily restored to it. This film, while cinematically beautiful like the first, was thematically ambiguous. Half of the subjects watching each film were presented with a detailed description of what they would be seeing beforehand. The other half of the group was simply told how long the film would run.

In effect, then, Zachary's subjects were presented with either a clear or an ambiguous film and with little or a great deal of advance information, which might lead to differential degrees of understanding and context. The two films had been pretested and differed only in the arousal of the attitudes "thoughtful," "puzzled," and "interested." The films did not differ in arousal of emotional intensity or moods such as "pleasant," "sad," or "embarrassed." Thus the critical difference between the films was that one was ambiguous, arousing only the affect of "interest" (Izard, 1977). For each film, the amount of anticipatory information was varied to see how much closure would be provided at the completion.

Following the viewing, each subject sat quietly alone in a small room. Each had been given a one-page description of the procedure in advance for "thought-sampling" and had received practice at recording into a microphone what they were thinking just when the signal musical tone was presented. Following the films, each subject completed a mood rating and then sat quietly for about 30 minutes while tones were presented at random intervals (about once every 45 seconds but ranging from 33–58 seconds). Twenty thought samples were obtained and later rated by judges for *film related content, future-oriented thoughts, present-oriented thoughts, past-oriented thoughts,* and *current concerns* related to major issues pending in the individual's life situation.

The results indicated that although neither film evoked a large number of recurring thoughts, hypothesized differences did occur. Themes from the ambiguous film presented without initial information did recur significantly more often than themes from the "flower" film or from the ambiguous film with prior information. Thus incompleteness and ambiguity can lead to recurrent material in the stream of consciousness even when there are no other major emotions, intensity, or conflicts involved in the content presented. The only affect aroused was "puzzled," which was rated highest for the ambiguous film.

The study yielded some interesting sex differences. Females generally had more evidence of future-oriented fantasy or thoughts about current problems and their implications or attempted solutions. Men had more reactions in thought to their immediate situation, such as the experiment. This pattern of current-concern–future-thought was even more apparent in women after exposure to the low-information condition.

Zachary's second experiment involved 48 male and 48 female college students. Essentially the same format was employed except that in this case *four* films were shown, two designed to arouse *negative* emotions and two designed to arouse *positive* emotions. The films also differed (based on pretesting) in *intensity* of arousal. Thus there were *Positive-High Intensity, Positive-Low Intensity, Negative-High Intensity,* and *Negative-Low Intensity* conditions. The Positive films depicted either an erotic, tender scene between lovers (High Intensity) or a cinematically beautiful depiction of free-ranging wild horses (Low Intensity). The Negative-affect films involved a demonstration of the dissection of a human cadaver (High Intensity) or a dissection of a frog (Low Intensity). The advance High- or Low-Information conditions were also employed in the study.

The results indicated that the use of generally more emotionally arousing film content led to higher rates of recurrent thoughts about the films as well as higher rates of preoccupation with current concerns. Apparently, emotional arousal is important in touching off the possibility that material will be more active in the thought stream; it also increases the likelihood of generating more preoccupation with one's major current life problems. Although the erotic film turned out to be the most likely to recur in thought, it did not differ significantly from the autopsy film. High intensity of arousal seemed more critical than positive or negative affect in producing recurrent thoughts. Although prior information about the film did not produce significant differences in recurrence of film-thoughts, there was an interaction between *Information* and *Intensity* with respect to emergence of *Current Concerns* in the thought stream. When the film's affective arousal was low and there was prior information about its content, the proportion of current concerns emerging in the postfilm period was highest. When film intensity was high and prior information *low,* there was a greater likelihood of current concerns emerging than when advance information had been provided.

Zachary also found that the degree to which an individual had recently experienced serious stress was related to recurrence of thoughts about the autopsy. There was also evidence that over time the recurrence of thoughts about the negative-affective autopsy film diminished most slowly. These data, although limited to only a brief period, are in keeping with research on stress reactions, which suggest that traumatic events persist in memory with "unbidden" or intrusive recurrences in the thought stream for months or years

(Horowitz, 1975; Janis, 1969). Again, in this study, women showed more future-oriented thought than men.

In general, then, Zachary's findings support the position that the ambiguity of material presented to a person can indeed influence the likelihood that one will later find oneself thinking about the subject. It is also clear that information causing high levels of emotional arousal will also recur in consciousness. The study is less clear about the extent to which later recurrences are a function of whether the emotions aroused are negative or positive. It might be argued that positive experiences are mentally replayed immediately afterwards less often than negative experiences are. This is certainly in keeping with most of the theories of the continuing recurrence of traumatic events (Janis, 1969). Nevertheless, we certainly do find ourselves dwelling upon happy events as well as sad ones. It is conceivable, however, that this tendency to drift into recall of pleasant events may be a conscious effort that people make in order to distract themselves from current unpleasant circumstances or from remaining fixed on unfinished tasks that cannot be immediately processed.

Unfortunately, Zachary's use of the sexual film cannot resolve the question about differential effects of positive and negative affect for later recall. Although the sexual film was certainly arousing and pleasant by contrast with the dissection material, it also is true that scenes of lovemaking presented to college students may arouse ambivalent feelings. Some individuals may actually be embarrassed (as Zachary's data clearly indicated) by the content; some may be reminded of recent unhappy outcomes in their sexual and social relationships. Interviews carried out with a group of the subjects in the larger study make it clear that potential sexual experiences are indeed a major preoccupation of students. Many find themselves thinking again and again about recent failures in attempted romantic relationships or are concerned about limitations in attractiveness to potential partners.

Zachary did not find any clear-cut relationship between the daydreaming patterns of the individuals and the likelihood of recurring thoughts. He found no interaction of predispositional tendencies with the ambiguity or emotional-arousal dimension of the experiment. As it happens, however, Zachary's sample was somewhat skewed in the direction of a more imaginative and daydreaming-oriented group and perhaps, therefore, provided relatively little variation, which might have made it possible to identify individual differences in relation to recurrence of certain types of thought content.

The data from our interviews suggest that, for college students, a good deal of the materials in dreams and daydreams is involved with the unfinished and ambiguous details of one's life. Thus, if anything, the general tone of much ongoing thought is mildly negative. As Pope's data suggest, however, the ability to detach oneself from immediate surroundings and to follow an extended thought pattern is itself more likely to be linked to a more positive mood even if the actual thought content may reflect ambiguities and incomplete activities. Interviews with students also suggest that those whose patterns reflect the "Positive–Constructive" Daydreaming style are able to transform ambiguities and unfulfilled intentions into playful fantasy with corresponding positive affect, whereas those more inclined to the "Guilt and Fear-of-Failure" pattern show an accumulation of painful imagery that can actually create a sense of pain.

Masturbation Fantasies in College Males

Popular belief is that a great deal of day-to-day fantasy and ongoing thought involves sexual preoccupation. Although the extensive research on daydreaming does not support this, it is clear that sexual fantasies have a special place in the individual's stream of consciousness. Surprisingly, there is very little systematic research evidence on the occurrence of sexual fantasy through means of recurring-thought sample techniques and also very little systematic evidence on the implications of sexual fantasy for other thought or for behavior. Hariton and Singer (1974) did report on one of the first examinations of the nature of sexual fantasy occurring in women during the act of coitus with their husbands. As yet, no reports have appeared on such fantasies in men.

In our efforts to look at the ongoing inner life of college students and the possible relation of such experience to drug use, it also seemed reasonable to consider whether we could obtain information on the patterns of fantasy that might occur during the masturbation activity of college males. The study was limited to males for various practical reasons, among them that the experimenter, in this case Campagna (1975), was a male, and initial discussions with women indicated greater resistance to obtaining this information. A sample of 102 males was drawn from the same population that had been employed in the other studies at the Ivy League college. Respondents completed a questionnaire about the patterns of their fantasies, their sexual behavior, their reactions to fantasy, and the frequency of a group of 53 daydreams that might conceivably occur during masturbation. The set of masturbation fantasies was derived from earlier pilot work.

Of the subjects, 75% reported moderately frequent levels of masturbatory activity, and 88% reported at least some masturbation on occasion. Automanipulation was the most common technique for almost all the subjects with some occasionally employing pillows, cushions, or other devices.

Of all subjects, 80% reported that they had fantasies at least occasionally while masturbating, and 75% claimed higher frequency; 32% reported fantasizing at each masturbatory occurrence. This frequency level is comparable to the only other available data (Kinsey, Pomeroy, & Martin, 1948), in which only the frequency of fantasies but not their content was obtained. Of the 53 sample fantasies presented to the subjects, 46 were reported by at least 25% of the respondents. Thus the range of masturbatory fantasies is extremely wide for a large number of subjects and include many that may actually seem disturbed to some individuals.

Campagna performed a principal-components analysis with a varimax rotation on the sexual daydreams of his respondents. A more detailed account of the results can be found in an earlier report (Campagna, 1975). In general, the findings indicated four clusters of sexual fantasy. The first factor consisted primarily of sexual memories and reminiscences of prior sexual experiences. Thus, individuals who scored high on items of this factor were likely to have a predominance of fantasies relating to thinking about a specific girlfriend or an actual recent experience they had had. Most of the sexual behavior depicted in these fantasies were fairly conventional such as, "I imagine that I am watching a very sexy woman slowly undressing." Fantasies associated with this factor tended to be shorter and less elaborate.

A second factor that emerged was characterized by daydreams that emphasized unusual or violent sexual practices. Attitudes that tend to debase or denigrate the fantasized partner load on the factor. For example, "I imagine a nude body of a woman has been beaten to death and mutiliated," or "I think about forcing myself on a woman who cries out and struggles. But I rape her anyway," were samples of fantasies loading on this factor.

The third factor involved a pattern of either passivity or anonymity and facelessness in the relationship. The fantasies were such as, "I imagine that I am having sex with a woman whose face I cannot see." In addition, there were references to passivity, prostitution, or being masturbated by a faceless woman. The fourth factor involved an increased fantasy or make-believe orientation. It included fantasies such as "I imagine that I am a rich, famous movie star and have many beautiful women beg me to have sex with them," or "I imagine that I am marooned on an island with several sexy women who want sex all the time," or "I imagine that I am an Arab sheik with many beautiful wives who worship and adore me." Thus this factor involves a more playful and imaginative orientation.

A number of nonsexual thoughts and fantasies were also included in the test battery. These tended to emerge as separate factors yielding indications of preoccupations with guilt or fear about the thoughts of others concerning the masturbatory activity. Subjects also completed the Maudsley Personality Inventory and the Mosher Guilt Inventory (Mosher, 1966). Additionally, several scales of theoretical interest from the PRF and the IPI that the participants had previously completed were included. In the group of 92 respondents to all inventories, the Guilt and Fear-of-Failure and Attentional-Control second-order factors tended to merge together on one principal component in Campagna's analysis. Negative relationships were found for acceptance of daydreaming on the dysphoric daydreaming factor; positive loadings emerged for the Maudsley Neuroticism scale and negative loadings for achievement and dominance from the PRF.

The second factor was clearly the Positive–Constructive daydreaming factor with high loadings for Future in Daydreams, Sexual Daydreams, Visual Imagery in Daydreams, Problem-Solving Daydreams, and Positive Reactions in Daydreams. While persons scoring high on this scale tended to report a great many sexual daydreams and also to score high on masturbatory daydreams, it is interesting to note that they reported less approval of heterosexual behavior for persons at their age level and also were less likely to have engaged extensively in sexual activity. A tendency for persons scoring high on this scale is to report more of the story-like masturbatory fantasies described in the previous discussion of the factors of such sexual fantasy.

A third factor that emerged was negatively linked to sex–guilt and showed in general an acceptance of sexuality and an orientation toward a variety of sexual activities, including masturbatory and homosexual behavior. The masturbatory fantasies of this group tended to involve specific experiences and were less likely to be story-like in their structural properties. It is interesting that the more elaborate make-believe quality of masturbatory fantasy does tend somewhat to go along with less actual experience in sexuality, although this result is a weak one in Campagna's data.

Campagna carried out a second study to examine the arousal effects of masturbatory fantasy. While there had been earlier theorizing that fantasy might serve a cathartic function by partially reducing aroused drive, the very fact of active fantasy during masturbation seemed to negate that. Clearly, in the data obtained by Hariton and Singer (1974) and in Campagna's questionnaire study, it was clear that individuals used fantasy for arousal purposes rather than to reduce drive. The persistence, among many clinicians and the general public of the notion that the catharsis effect is an important one, led Campagna to carry out a small experiment. One group of individuals were initially aroused by reading erotic passages from *The Happy Hooker*. The control group read prose passages. Subsequent to arousal, some of the experimental participants were given the opportunity to read further erotic passages, while others were encouraged to engage in their own private masturbatory fantasy, without any bodily activity. Subsequent reports of arousal indicated that following the use of the subject's own masturbatory fantasy, the level of arousal increased whereas the additional employment of the reading material tended to reduce arousal. Arousal dropped even further when subjects were presented with the opportunity to read nonsexual or aggressive but humorous material.

In general, therefore, the data suggest that individuals have developed and in a way practiced private sexual fantasies that can lead to high levels of personal arousal relatively quickly. Although erotic literature certainly has an effect, it does not seem to be sufficient to maintain arousal unless supplemented by more private fantasies and related material that have been associated with the reinforcement of both arousal and perhaps sexual release.

On the whole, what is striking from Campagna's study is the degree to which masturbatory fantasy is relatively circumscribed in its pattern and function. It seems to be related to two particular sets of circumstances, times, and places in which masturbation is possible and has already been practiced. It also is clear that there are rather strong individual styles in the development of such fantasy. One might surmise that those individuals who fantasize predominantly acts of sadism, violence, or bizarre behavior may be more prone to potential sexual difficulties, although there is no clear evidence from the available data to support this. It also seems likely that those students who have become heavily involved in sexual activity are more likely to support the more traditional patterns of masturbatory fantasy, whereas those to whom much sexual experience still remains in itself a fantasy are more free-ranging in the type of material they provide in their daydreaming. This finding suggests that actual experience does determine the pattern of sexual fantasy and, quite possibly, may restrict and modify the full range of adult fantasies. Although no systematic major findings emerged for drug- or alcohol-use patterns, there were clear indications that those who used drugs and alcohol with some regularity were more likely to be those who were more sexually active and whose masturbatory patterns were linked to more realistic fantasies.

Daydreaming Patterns and Social Competence

The data we present now are part of a larger study (Powell & Singer, unpublished) designed to examine the structural properties of imagery and fantasy in relation to simulations of drug or alcohol use. The imagery evoked in fantasy use of drugs or alcohol was also related to differential patterns of performance in a role-playing method for estimating *social competence* developed by Powell (1971). Powell has argued that Piaget's stages of cognitive development are insufficient to deal with additional changes in the structure of intellectual growth and that an important feature of development is the elaboration of competencies in social interactions. Powell has further argued that cognitive capacities for effective social interaction mature during adolescence. Powell's method for evaluating social competence makes use of role-playing techniques in which the subject portrays a character like a clerk who must persuade a customer to make an improbable purchase. The customer is in all cases a confederate who offers obstacles to the clerk–subject. In this partially unstructured situation, the shifts in emphasis, the reasoning ability, and the apparent empathic capacity for sensitivity to the customer demonstrated by the clerk–subject are all scored to measure social competence.

It seemed likely that there ought to be a relationship between social competence and other measures of ego development such as that proposed by Loevinger (1976). Loevinger has made use of a sentence-completion format scored to measure ego development. This stage theory proposes that children begin with a presocial level of development, move on through an impulsive, then self-protective, conformist, conscientious-conformist, conscientious-individualistic, autonomous, and finally to an integrated stage of development. Powell and Singer were interested in the possibility that one could relate actual role-playing social competence with the level of development on the Loevinger scales following suggestions developed by the work of Frank (1978).

Of particular significance for the present monograph was the second phase of the study. Powell and Singer sought to determine to what extent we could learn something about the nature of students' expectations of drug and alcohol experience through role-playing being under the influence of alcohol or of drugs. In the experiment, therefore, a subject was introduced into a waiting room and encouraged to relax. After initial relaxation, the participant was encouraged to generate intense imagery of either being inebriated or of being under the influence of a drug. Most students chose marijuana since few had any experience with any other substances. Half of the subjects underwent the drug-imagery experience first. Following a period of further free imagery during which mood and imagery ratings were obtained, they underwent the Powell social competence role-playing task. In a second situation, individuals generated the alcohol inebriation imagery before the social competence task. Powell and Singer were interested in this particular substudy in learning whether the carry-over of a particular mood—created by intense imagery simulating the actual experience that the students had or expected to have under the influence of drugs or alcohol—would affect their social competence performance.

Extensive ratings of imagery were obtained in the waiting room prior to and then following the drug and alcohol simulation. Since some data are still subject to extensive analysis, we report only the main initial findings here.

The spontaneous thoughts of each participant, as reported in the thought-sampling procedure, were related to the patterning of emotionality produced during the imagined drug and alcohol role-playing situations. In general, the data suggest that occurrence of reported imagery is linked positively to intensity of emotional response ($r = .32$, $p < .05$), positive affective state ($r = .48$, $p < .05$), and especially to strong visual components ($r = .70$, $p < .05$), or tactile components in imagery ($r = .50$, $p < .05$). Among the sensory modalities, only touch showed consistent positive relations to other imagery modalities especially under the condition of simulated drug or alcohol use.

In the attempted simulation of drug and alcohol conditions, it was clear that students represented the two conditions as very different. Alcohol was portrayed as disinhibitory and also as an active process more likely associated with somewhat positive emotions. Drug use was depicted as a more passive, attentive, and cognitively disorganized. Although there was a trend for greater visual, taste, and olfactory imagery to be associated with drug use in contrast with the more kinesthetic imagery associated with the alcohol experience, the affects linked to the drug experience were lack of interest and fear, whereas those linked to the alcohol experience suggested a greater sense of physical and psychological comfort along with greater anxiety, sadness, and anger.

There was a significant correlation between social competence and the type of imagery experienced just before entering into the social competence task. If subjects had been involved in the alcohol imagery, they tended to perform somewhat better in the social-competence situation than when they had been imagining themselves under the influence of drugs. The correlation between types of imagery prior to undergoing the social-competence task and scores in social competence was $r = .24$ ($p < .05$). In other words, when the subjects imagined themselves deeply involved in drug use and then after a few minutes went in to undergo a social-competence task of trying to sell to a recalcitrant customer, they performed less adequately and were given ratings of lower social competency. The correlation between Loevinger's scale of development and performance on social competence was $r = .31$ ($p < .05$).

In general, partially based on experience and also reflecting to a certain extent expectations of how one behaves under the type of substance used, there are different patterns of imagined affect as well as actual role-playing performance. Clearly, the students perceive the alcohol situation as a socially oriented, extraverted one, whereas the drug experience is primarily a self-oriented, introverted experience more linked to apathy and anxiety. The alcohol experience contains more forceful emotions such as anger, sadness, and a generally greater sense of comfort and appropriateness. Getting themselves into the mood of these chemically induced states had subsequent consequences on performance so that the more extraverted alcohol stance led to more effective role-playing of the salesman, while the more introverted drug-use stance led to shyness and rigidity in the attempt to persuade another.

Unfortunately, there was insufficient variability in drug-use frequency among the subjects participating in the experiment to permit us to relate the imagery and role-playing behavior to drug and alcohol use. Most of the subjects were moderate users of marijuana and alcohol, and this simply did not provide enough variation within the sample to permit meaningful analyses.

This type of research is at best viewed as exploratory. More extensive and carefully controlled studies of individuals' expectations and ongoing images about the nature of drug and alcohol use are needed. Studies that link patterns of ongoing thought—and expectations about the possible effects of drug or alcohol use—with such manifestations as social competence could help us to understand better how private experiences interrelate systematically to affective social behavior in the presence or absence of regular substance use.

The results do, however, bear on the questionnaire finding that in the college youth there are indications of the stylization of preferences for alcohol over marijuana in different situations for those individuals who use both substances. As methodologies for laboratory studies such as the Powell–Singer simulation are developed further, it should be possible to ascertain nonquestionnaire means of assessing the importance of such preferences and stylization.

Training and Levels of Empathy

Still another experimental study carried out within the framework of the present study of college adults was directed by Frank (1976, 1978). This study considered the possible beneficial effects on students of specific training in the uses and awareness of private fantasy.

Frank identified three levels of empathy or, in effect, prediction of others' experiences. On the one hand, one could talk of *behavioral* prediction, in which case one might show fairly good accuracy in describing how another person would behave or at least in predicting another person's self-description of his or her behavior. A second level of empathy might be termed the *subjective* level, in which an individual shows a capacity to identify the emotions that another is experiencing or to identify the nonverbal cues presented by facial expression and related gestural behaviors. A third level may be termed the *cognitive–structural* level, in which an individual can interpret symbolic and implied meaning from others. Frank's conceptualization was similar to that recently given by N. Feshbach (1978).

In an extremely complicated experiment, Frank proposed to test the possibility that specialized training in awareness of one's own fantasies and in recognition of the variety and range of other's fantasies could help college students be especially successful in coping with each of the levels of empathy described previously.

A group of students employed in our research were assigned to either a *Behavior-Discussion* group, a *Fantasy-Experience* group, or a *Fantasy-Discussion* group. The first group received careful training in the contingencies of behavior with a view to discerning how one could eliminate unwanted behaviors by studying sequences of overt acts and their reinforcement consequences. The second group simply came together to share dreams and daydreams and to engage in group fantasy activities without any attempt at interpretation or commentary. The third group carried out much the same process as the second except that there was much greater effort to understand and share understandings of the nature of the experience so that a more cognitive component was involved in the training.

It was hypothesized that the first type of training would be especially valuable in leading to behavioral predictions but would not be especially useful in predicting empathic performance at the upper two levels as measured by the instruments. The second group was felt to be especially useful in helping individuals to develop the second level of empathy—that is, the ability to identify emotional reactions of others at the nonverbal level. The third group was felt to be more appropriate for training individuals to identify implied meanings.

In addition to the three training groups, there was a fourth group employed as an untreated control group. These individuals were students who were primarily interested in theater and had begun training themselves quite on their own in awareness of ongoing fantasy experiences. Thus this group might be called a *Fantasy-Interest* group who had established their own self-directed training program.

Following 10 training sessions spread over 5 weeks, subjects were first given a measure called the "Accurate Predictions of Attitudes Test," which was designed to measure the first level of empathy. They received a test of implied meanings developed by Sundberg (1966), a measure developed by Selman (1976) to measure interpersonal concepts, and finally, the PONS, a measure of nonverbal communication employing films of people reflecting different emotional states (Rosenthal, Hall, DiMatteo, Rogers, & Archer, 1979).

After the completion of the testing phase, participants were encouraged 5 weeks later to maintain a continuous daydreaming log. Over a week's time, the students were taught to "sample" their three most vivid fantasies six different times during a particular day. They kept index cards and rated their fantasies on descriptive categories along five-point scales. These categories included: (1) modalities such as *visual, auditory, bodily concerns;* and (2) the specific affects associated with *imagery, fear, distress, surprise, interest, shame, joy, contempt,* and *anger.*

In accordance with Frank's predictions, participants in the Behavior-Discussion and Fantasy-Discussion groups made more accurate prediction of their partner's self-descriptive behaviors than did participants in the Fantasy-Experience or control groups ($t = 3.35$, $df = 102$; $p < .001$). Thus Frank was able to conclude that training in objective reality-oriented observation, as well as in social inference, facilitates the subjects' capacity to predict how others will behave at the level of overt behavior.

With respect to the test for implied meaning, the subjects in the pure Fantasy-Experience and the Fantasy-Interest groups performed best. The Fantasy-Discussion group did not do as well ($t = 3.05$, $df = 102$, $p < .01$). The implication of this result was that the more cognitive components of the fantasy training may have interfered with the more direct experiencing of meanings in other emotional responses. Frank, incidentally, also found that women were significantly better in identifying implied meanings than men. With respect to social reasoning and the more advanced cognitive level of functioning, the subjects in the Fantasy-Discussion group on the whole performed better than did participants in the other groups (t = 3.75, df = 100, $p < .01$).

With some qualifications, it seemed clear that 10 training sessions of the type described by Frank (1978) are quite effective in helping college students to increase their capacity to empathize with others along the dimensions suggested. It is particularly important for us to recognize that awareness of private fantasy, as well as learning about the comparable fantasies of others, may be useful in enhancing one's ability to sense underlying meanings in others' communications and also in identifying specific emotional expressiveness by others.

Frank (1978) obtained data from daydreaming logs scored for content and affect variables that subjects maintained following group participation. She found rather interesting consequences of the different training conditions on subsequent fantasy. Those who were in the Fantasy-Experience group exhibited a tendency to more future-oriented fantasy. They also reported higher levels of achievement-oriented daydreams, less guilty daydreams, and less bodily concerns, but somewhat more fantasy about failures. They also had fantasies reflecting loneliness. The Fantasy-Discussion group showed more tendency toward a wider emotional range in the daydreams, more negative as well as positive affective states. These participants showed somewhat less self-focused images.

The group that did not have formal training but was in effect self-trained, the Fantasy-Interest group, also had a greater number of affective responses in fantasy, and a somewhat more negative and perhaps less mystical pattern. It should be kept in mind, however, that this group was, in effect, not an intervention group, and therefore the correlation may simply be reflecting long-range patterns for them.

Frank also found some very interesting relations between the ongoing daydreaming log patterns and the way individuals performed on the various criterion measures of the study. Thus, persons whose daydream modalities were primarily visual also tended to do better in the measure of sensitivity to implied meanings (r = .26, $p < .05$) and to some degree better on nonverbal sensitivity (r = .21, $p < .05$) and behavioral prediction (r = .18, $p < .05$). Individuals whose recurring fantasies tended to be more focused on physical characteristics or their bodies or on objects in their environment tended on the whole to show negative relationships to all empathy measures. It is worth noting that those individuals whose daydream content showed considerable positive attitudes toward others also proved to do well on the PONS, the measure of identification of emotions through nonverbal communication. Individuals with negative fantasies about other people tended to produce more negative reactions in the PONS and a poorer total score on the scale.

In general, the Frank study indicates clearly that awareness of one's ongoing fantasies and special training in such awareness can have behavioral implications. The domain of imagined experience of an interpersonal nature does have rehearsal properties. It does seem to be related to one's capacity: (1) to anticipate actual social interactions; (2) to enhance the fundamental skill of sensing others' meanings or emotions; and (3) to some degree, even with additional focus training, to predict self-descriptions of overt behavior. Again, the data suggest that whereas ongoing fantasy may not always be pleasant, those individuals who have more positive styles of fantasy relationships to others may be more empathic. It is possible that more extensive emphasis on training individuals for self-awareness, and acceptance and enjoyment of their own fantasy capacities, may smooth the way toward more effective relatedness with others. It is quite possible that such training could reduce some of the more negative private experiences that do seem to be linked to the choice to use alcohol as our earlier chapters suggested.

Intensive Interview Data

Intensive interviews were carried out with approximately 40 students at the two institutions. The interviews were semistructured and involved questions about important recent events; persons who had been especially influential in the individual's life; attitudes toward morality, sex, and drug use; and the meaning of the transition to college life. Subjects talked relatively freely and provided a considerable amount of personal detail.

Examination of the interviews, however, does not add substantially to the generalizations drawn from the large-scale quantitative data. Thus it is clear that most the students are relatively accepting of the use of alcohol and marijuana. A few indicate that they have been influenced since arriving at college in the direction of such use, but the majority point primarily to high-school influence. Indeed, one student now reports his own concern that his younger brother at 15 has been "tripping" with "acid." The most characteristic indication of differences between students emerged for those few individuals who reported that they were using drugs heavily, chiefly marijuana but occasionally LSD or other "hard" drugs. The students showed a less focused orientation about their college careers and less clarity about their involvement with other students. Indeed, what emerges from these reports of the heavier drug users is an increased focus of their whole attention on the nature of the drug experience and a blurring of focus with respect to other elements of college life. One seems to see a kind of identity formation developing around drug use in contrast with the identity of some of the students around career choices or others around deepening their inter-personal relationships. This particular finding, however, must be considered within the context that drug use had severe legal penalties at the time the data were collected. The preoccupation with drugs, then, may be a typical reaction to stringent social controls. The interviews do seem to point out, however, that drug use is part of a more generalized search for identity.

Since most of the interviewees were beginning freshmen, we still see the persistence of many attitudes that they brought with them from their homes. As Klos (1977) has suggested in his work on adolescent autonomy, there are strong indications that parental values and influences are still dominant in thoughts and attitudes. Peer-group effects are beginning to be felt, and some of the students report with a kind of amazement their awareness of the diversity of experiences available to them. This is especially true of the Ivy League students, many of whom were being exposed to a much greater cultural diversity among classmates than they had among their high-school friends. Despite these peer-group effects, there is still a very strong concern about traditional morality and especially a heightened religiosity. A variety of traditional Christian influences remained among these students; although a few had begun to question some tenets of their faith, a surprising number seemed to be moving in the direction of deepening religious commitment. Indeed, some who actually had moved away from religion during high school were now moving back.

The students' major preoccupations that occur in fantasy, as suggested earlier, dealt with career possibilities. A minority of students seemed to have clearly focused goals around professional attainment. The majority of those interveved were rather vague about their plans, although a sizable minority were business-oriented and viewed their education as leading in that direction. In the case of the females, career goals seemed much less focused than might have been expected in a period of supposedly heightened liberation; rather, women seemed much concerned with the nature of their relationships with other women and with finding deeper intimacy with men. Only a few students had any continuing strong interest in purely intellectual, social change or scientific interests. By far the greatest emphasis in discussions was upon social relationships. The Yale men and women in general had somewhat greater similarities in value and motivational patterns. Indeed, although sex differences along the traditional lines of the male as achiever or aggressor and the woman as nurturer and affiliator do emerge, they were far less prominent for Yale students than for those from Murray State. By comparison, the Kentucky students were far more "supermale" and "South-ern Belle" in their orientations than one might expect from reading national magazine literature.

Conclusions

In general, the experimental studies open the way for a number of intriguing new methodological approaches. It is clear that we can explore ongoing thought and its relation to affect, and that imagery and role-playing simulations can open the way for new avenues in studying role expectations in college students as they may bear on substance use or other private activities. It is likely that persisting levels of dysphoric private experience may play a part in increasing the likelihood that some students will be especially vulnerable to group pressures for drug or alcohol exploration and use. It remains to be seen whether the data that suggest links of greater awareness of or acceptance of fantasy to empathy and social competence may be practically useful in averting the likelihood of substance abuse or vulnerability to excesses in drinking and drug taking.

9 Summary and Conclusions

In the preceding sections of this volume, attention has been focused narrowly upon presenting our major theoretical ideas, data-collection strategies, analyses, and results. Our major intent in employing this strategy was to be as detailed as possible so that the reader who disagrees with our general conclusions will have major summaries of the data available for alternate interpretation. The thrust of this final chapter is more speculative. The chapter has three objectives. First, the major results of the volume are summarized in a more integrated manner. Second, the analytic procedures used to probe within the empirical data are discussed so that the reader is aware of how various choices necessary for successful multivariate analysis of such a complex phenomenon were made. Third, in a more speculative vein, the focus of the interpretation is widened beyond the pages of tables previously presented, and the major implications of the work for a variety of areas are discussed. Specifically, interpretations of the results in terms of their relevance to general theories of personality and inner experience, general theories of youthful drug use, psychotherapy, and intervention strategies, and future work on youthful drug taking are discussed.

SUMMARY AND CRITIQUE OF THE COLLEGE DRUG STUDY

Sample Characteristics

In Chapter 4, the prevalence of drug-taking behavior among collegians was studied. Additionally, the most frequent self-described reasons for using various substances were presented. It was concluded that the college samples were roughly comparable in typical usage rates for various substances to other recent investigations of youthful drug use. Although it was recognized that the college samples studied certainly cannot be described as random cross sections of youth in general, the broad comparability was interpreted as indication that the more specific results are probably generalizable to a sizable segment of the youthful population.

The descriptive analysis of motives for use allowed a characterization of the samples as youth with limited drug-taking experience. Furthermore, use was primarily for recreation or exploratory purposes. The modal pattern is one of beginning drug experimentation resulting from curiosity or the recommendation of friends. The descriptive results further indicate that a relatively small segment of the substance users ingest drugs either to escape from pressing problems or to "drop out."

In several ways, the results from the simple descriptive analysis can be perceived as partial validation for our overall theoretical orientation in studying drug use as a specific form of more generalized "exploration" behavior. Descriptions of the duration of use as well as reasons given for the use do not suggest that the typical user in our sample has either an extremely maladaptive substance-use pattern or a need to use the drug obsessively to cope with normal stresses. Rather, there is indication that these individuals try drugs out of curiosity, because drugs might induce a new set of cognitions, or because the drug experience might make social situations seem less stressful and more natural. College students, confronting decisions that will shape their adult lives, seem to turn to drugs in order to experience new alternatives and possibilities or possibly to make the transition to the responsibilities of adulthood smoothly. Furthermore, the nonchronic use of drugs by most of the students seems intended to provide a means of social lubrication or release from the implicit tensions of surviving the college experience.

Organization of Private Personality

In Chapter 5, the notion that drug use may cause a "reorganization" of personality structure was taken quite literally and was tested in a rather direct manner. In retrospect, the test was probably a "severe" operationalization of the speculation of various writers in the drug literature; the term "reorganization" may mean to some simply that average differences occur in personality dimensions between users and nonusers. At any rate, the strong test of personality reorganization devised for the current data was to assess whether or not there was a different set of underlying factors for the same measures of personality in groups defined by drug-use pattern. Factor patterns for the domains of inner experience and motivational tendencies were calculated separately for groups of nonusers, alcohol-only users, marijuana-only users, and polydrug users. The results presented in the numerous tables of Chapter 5 make it quite clear that no radical differences appear between groups in the underlying pattern of psychological relationships.

Stated in a different way, the analyses of Chapter 5 sought to determine if the basic "traits" that underlie responses on motivation and inner experience measures were the same for groups of drug users and nonusers. Had we found such differences, it would have been reasonable to argue that the personality style of the drug user is qualitatively different from that of the nonuser. Differences in the domain of inner experience would have suggested that the daydreams and fantasies of drug users take on different forms and are controlled by different dynamics than those of their nonuser peers. In neither the case of motivation nor inner experience were we able to find substantial differences in the underlying pattern and presumed internal causes for the scale responses. Consequently, it has been concluded that although there may be quantitative (or mean) differences between users and nonusers on different aspects of personality functioning, the overall quality of the private personality is about the same, within precision error attributable to sampling influences for the groups. This demonstration that personality functioning is of the same nature for users and nonusers is the first one in the literature on drug use. Consequently, one very direct implication of this result is that, in the absence of further data in other domains of personal functioning, theoretical speculation about the personality differences between users and nonusers of drugs should be limited to possible changes in average level of functioning either attributable to the drug use or as a potential etiological factor.

Since the methodology used to test the hypothesis of personality reorganization is not standard, several technometric issues should be discussed. First, if the loadings for the factors obtained in the different groups had been independently rotated to some simplicity (or "simple-structure") criterion, estimates of factor stability would not be as high. Although, as pointed out earlier, it may be argued that alignment rotations can capitalize on chance in placing factor matrices in comparable position, independent simple-structure rotations will also capitalize on chance in pushing matrices toward some mathematically defined criterion of simplicity. In aligning the matrices to some randomly generated positions, it was shown that the common positions chosen were far superior than some random set of hypotheses about how the factors should be structured. Second, since the time of the publication of the original analyses (Huba, Segal, & Singer, 1977a, b), newer methodologies have been developed in the COFAMM (Confirmatory Factor Analysis with Model Modification; Sörbom & Jöreskog, 1976) model, which allow constraining equal factor pattern matrices in several groups. These newer models will allow further testing of personality reorganization in different drug-use groups, but the method also requires a much stronger theoretical set of hypotheses than could be generated for the current measures. In any case, it still remains to be seen if the newer COFAMM method has sufficient utility as a *data-analysis* strategy as well as a statistical procedure (see McGaw & Jöreskog, 1971, for an example of disregarding the statistical testing aspects of the model). The present analyses do indicate, within most accepted criteria of scientific accuracy, that there are no gross reorganizations of personality as a result of experimenting with psychoactive drugs. Furthermore, the consistency was manifested in spite of our decision to try to avoid interpretation difficulties by holding the various factors at unit length in each group (or to factor correlations rather than covariances); in several ways, we have minimized the amount of congruence that might be found.

After determining that the same common private personality system was applicable to the different groups of drug users and nonusers, we then inquired whether or not there were mean level differences in personality functioning. Such an analysis presupposes the finding of Chapter 5 that there is a common personality structure and mechanism for different types of individuals.

Level of Private Personality Functioning

In Chapter 6, the mean scores on the various individual constructs in the domain of private personality were examined for the nonuser, alcohol-only, marijuana-only, and polydrug-use groups. In order to guard against possible vagaries in the multivariate analyses, two replications within each sex were utilized to determine which of the 48 private personality measures were consistently different among the criterion groups. It was found that the four groups of users could be reliably differentiated on the scales of Experience Seeking, Disinhibition, Thrill–Adventure, and General Sensation Seeking. Furthermore, there were consistent differences in the needs for Autonomy, Harmavoidance, Impulsivity, Order, Play, Social Recognition, and Understanding. Finally, the degree of Auditory Imagery reported for Daydreams, the Need for External (as opposed to internal) Stimulation, and Self-Revelation tendencies separated the groups.

When all private personality measures were considered simultaneously, most of the variables significantly different between the groups *univariately* were found to be highly related to the best additive, linear discriminant combination of scale scores in the battery. That is, when the single optimal way of separating the groups *multivariately* was determined, the same measures were highly related to the combination. This result, in and of itself, is not surprising; the multivariate analyses do serve, however, to ensure that the more easily interpreted univariate analyses do not unduly capitalize on chance.

As a final empirical step, drug-use category was predicted from the scores in the test battery. Since the equations were derived from the same samples to which they were applied, it is not possible to argue that the classification findings will be as unbiased as they would be if the weights were applied to independent samples. On the other hand, the extent to which individuals can be successfully categorized yields, at the minimum, a rough index of psychometric importance and meaningfulness. Overall, it was determined that about 60% of the participants could be successfully classified into the correct drug-use category on the basis of the total array of personality scores. A slight penalty for prediction was applied by assuming that the a priori probability of membership in any of the four groups was equal. Balancing the "help" given by using the same samples to derive and to which to apply the equations against the "penalty" applied by keeping a conservative a priori estimate of group membership, the estimate of around 60% correct classification from the domain of private personality is a reasonable figure that is indicative of the theoretical import of the domain for the phenomenon of drug use.

After examining the relationship of the entire set of private personality measures to the drug-use categories, an assessment was made to determine whether the best personality predictors of drug use in one sample are the same as those for another sample. Results from both a total stepwise discriminant analysis for each sample and best-predictors analyses were disappointing. With the exception of the Experience and General Sensation-Seeking scales, the variables seemed to enter the functions somewhat arbitrarily. On the other hand, the full functions generalize quite well, and the pattern of loadings is highly similar in all four college samples. Consequently, it seems reasonable to argue that the lack of generality found in the stepwise analyses is more attributable to the method of data analysis than to replication problems. We then conclude that the full discriminant functions were relatively invariant in the college samples.

Several methodological comments should be made about the analyses presented in Chapter 6. First, the discriminant analyses in both full and stepwise forms assumed that a meaningful way of classifying drug use was in the four groups: nonusers, alcohol-only, marijuana-only, and polydrug. Such classification is crude, and within any one category, frequent users of the substance are equated with individuals with minimal experience. It might be argued that more encouraging classification results would ensure from a more fine-grained classification of the various types of substance users; it is our impression that this argument is true, although there would be the concomitant risk of lower generality to other samples. Further separation of the groups would probably lead the analytic techniques to capitalize on sample-specific sources of covariation between usage and private personality, which are irrelevant to the overall theoretical context. The classification scheme used for these analyses corresponds roughly to either Kandel's (1975a; Kandel & Faust, 1975) stages or the factors (see Blum, 1969) frequently found for adolescent drug-use data. Additionally, it should be noted that an examination of the variances within groups in these analyses found that the dispersion indices were approximately equal. It is possible to infer from the inspection of within-group variances that the categories have about the same degree of coarseness. Such a finding further argues that the drug-use groups correspond to broad but "real" classes of individuals.

A second methodological issue implicit in the Chapter 6 analyses is that we have assumed that the groups of drug users are best differentiated using a *weighted linear combination;* that is, weights have been derived to be applied to the original measures under the constraint that the final sum is an additive combination of the original measures multiplied by the weights. The loadings discussed in data interpretation are a consequence of the weights and the correlations among the personality measures. Dunnette (1975) has argued that measures may combine in various nonadditive ways in order to separate drug-use groups. Such results in general personality and cognitive-abilities research, however, have typically been illusory (Wiggins, 1973), and the current analyses have focused on the more simple, additive linear combination. While our results cannot be used to argue that additive models are the best single approach in the absence of specific theory that predicts interactions, it does seem desirable to limit large-scale exploratory investigations such as the present one to the robust and parsimonious main-effects model.

In order to integrate the results from Chapter 6, it is necessary to rely heavily upon the theoretical conception outlined in Chapter 2. As will be remembered, the theoretical framework adopted considers preferred behavioral actions to be the outermost shell, with inner experiences forming the central core. Again it will be remembered from Chapter 2 that it is expected that the outermost shell is both most responsive to the environment and simultaneously most often expressed as behavior. This outer shell of behavior preference also modifies and shapes how needs and inner experience tendencies will be expressed as behavior.

The mean differences among groups seem quite interpretable in the context of layers of private personality. As noted in Chapter 6, the variables representing preferred behavioral actions or sensation-seeking tendencies at the outermost surface of private personality were most related to drug-taking. Furthermore, these variables have the strongest degree of association with the drug-use categories.

At a moderately inner level of private personality, those needs that can be satisfied by drug use, or more easily expressed under the influence of one or more psychoactive substances, are related to the use of the various substances. Specifically, needs such as autonomy, social recognition, and exhibitionism can be met *within the current culture* by using drugs in a context where peers are aware of the usage. Other needs such as risk-taking (not avoiding harm) and impulsivity reflect characteristics of the drug-taking act in a culture in which many substances can cause physical harm and their use is punished by legal retribution. Each of these measures is more moderately related to the substance-use categorization than the preferred behavioral actions cell. These attenuated relationships are supportive of the general theoretical orientation, since it should be argued that behavioral preference will moderate how a need is expressed in behaviors and what the circumstances will be.

Finally, the measures of inner experience at the core level of private personality were, for the most part, not related to drug use. We assume that this is partially because the expression of fantasized events is moderated by the needs of the individual, preferred modes of action, and situational constraints. The additional analyses from Chapter 8, however, make it clear that there is enough association between inner experience measures and variables assessing needs and preferred behavioral actions to infer that the inner experiences can modify needs and preferred behavioral modes.

In summary, it seems to us that in spite of the fact that we have had many years to rationalize the results since the original analyses were completed, the overall pattern of which aspects of the private personality are most different among substance users and nonusers is best explained in the context of the private personality model.

Private Personality and Motives for Drug Use

Given the finding of mean differences in level of personality functioning, the way in which private personality indicators are related to various motives for, and consequences of, drug use were examined in Chapter 7. In the discriminant analyses, it was demonstrated that certain aspects of private personality explain the major differences *between* types of users and nonusers. In generalized form, the discriminant results are probably best conceptualized as being most related to the state of *initiation into drug use*. On the other hand, it might be asked how marijuana users differ from *one another in major ways* and, furthermore, how their different patterns of usage are reflective of more basic personality styles. The analyses of Chapter 7 were explicitly intended to address exactly these issues. Furthermore, we believe that the results generated from those analyses may be best conceived of as mechanisms for the *continuation* (see Huba et al., 1980; Lettieri, 1978) of substance use.

Several general results from Chapter 7 are of interest before presenting more specific findings. First, in contrast to the results of the discriminant analyses, it was found that inner experience measures are highly related to *certain forms* of self-described alcohol, marijuana, and polydrug use. Furthermore, the overall pattern of many major analyses suggests that the general personality style of the individual is quite concretely related to the manner in which substance use will be (or will not be) engaged in as the individual incorporates drug taking into a more general coping style.

The first set of analyses presented in Chapter 7 examined the factor pattern of groups of self-reported motives underlying alcohol and marijuana use for those individuals who used the substances. In both sets of analyses, it was possible to conclude that several major factors could be found. The first factors were concerned with the use of the drug to enhance feelings of positive affect and provided social facilitation and cognitive expansion. In concert with the other findings in the study, this factor might also be seen as partially reflective of the degree to which individuals use the substances and alcohol as part of their exploration of self-identity. The second theme that arose from both analyses was the use of psychoactive substances to cope with depressed feelings.

Both major themes of self-perceived substance use were found to be related to private personality styles. Although the strength of the relationships found did not indicate that the personality styles were synonymous with the substance-use styles, there is enough overlap to consider the pattern of drug use to be indicative of underlying personality themes. Particularly interesting is the fact that patterns of personality such as the seeking of understanding, the need for autonomy, and the preference for new experiences are related to the use of drugs for expansion and exploratory purposes. These major sets of relationships were found for both the drinking of alcohol and the smoking of marijuana.

The theme of using alcohol and marijuana to overcome feelings of anxiety, depression, low self-esteem, and inadequacy was also found to be related in a rather fundamental manner to the private personality measures. It is noteworthy that although markers of inner experience did not significantly differentiate drug users from their nonuser peers, these variables were related to the differentiation of users of a particular substance. Thus one of the major concomitants of alcohol use to alleviate feelings of depression, is a set of inner experience variables indicative of various guilty–dysphoric themes. Consequently, although we do find that drug users do not have inner experiences that are strikingly different from those of nonusers, certain individuals with a history of using the substance may extend the use to the self-medication of dysphoric themes. Marijuana also seems to be used in a similar manner, and some individuals seem to have developed a preference for using that substance for many of the same reasons.

In studying the use of "hard," more illegal drugs, we felt it necessary to make use of the frequency-use data for these substances in lieu of more detailed motives. We have assumed implicitly that the different "hard" drugs are used for different reasons in concordance with the "psychopharmacological" model presented in Chapter 1. Although such an assumption may seem to some unwarranted, the general pattern of results obtained when analyzing the polydrug users is quite consistent with that generated from the marijuana- and alcohol-use motives. Again, different constellations of personality variables seem to be related to different types of substance use.

Several methodological issues must be raised about the analyses upon which the arguments of Chapter 7 depend. First, the multivariate procedures of principal components factor analysis and canonical correlation analyses were used with dichotomous indicators of reasons for using marijuana and alcohol. Difficulties with using dichotomous variables are well discussed by Comrey (1978); in the current case, various safeguards were employed to partially negate some of the major objections against such analyses. It is important to note, however, that the major effect of the use of dichotomous markers will be to attenuate the relationships between variables. For the factor analyses of drug-use reasons, it is possible that the attenuated correlations served to "split" factors and increase the number of dimensions that were found necessary to accept as sufficient. Furthermore, the instructional set given to our subjects for some of the social-facilitation items precluded those variables from loading highly on the dimensions determined primarily from the depression items.

For the canonical correlation analyses, the use of dichotomous indicators served to attenuate the size of the relationships among private personality and perceived motives for alcohol and marijuana use. That is, we suspect that interval-scaled measures of alcohol- and marijuana-use motives would yield more substantial estimates of the overlap between domains. Our original belief in designing the drug-study questionnaire was that individuals would have great difficulty rating the magnitude of motives for use and would therefore give more valid responses using a simple checklist. Consequently, dichotomous measures were used for alcohol- and marijuana-use motives. In retrospect, we still believe that this domain may not be amenable to reliable ratings in a traditional "Likert-type" manner, but the possible theoretical importance of the current analyses suggests that a more detailed and complex method of scaling perceived motives for drug use may yield estimates of greater redundancy with private personality. Such a scaling task must be reserved for future studies.

The second major methodological issue concerns our use of canonical correlation analysis as a major analytic tool. As noted in the introduction to Chapter 8, many investigators seeking the linkages between two conceptually distinct domains have traditionally combined the variables in one large principal components or factor analysis. Given that two moderately related sets of measures (with the "moderate" association partially a function of test reliability!) may share only 15–20% of their variance, it is not surprising that such researchers have often found that the two domains are explained by "different," "orthogonal" principal components. In Chapters 7 and 8 analyses, the variance in common between domains has been the focus, and the intent has been to simplify a large set of small but reliable correlations. In all cases we have studied, it has been possible to reject *statistically* the hypotheses of no significant multivariate correlation and to make estimates of the amount of multivariate redundancy.

A related and third methodological issue for Chapter 7 is the fact that we rotated the canonical-correlation dimensions. In all cases, the rotation of the loadings has served to simplify the interpretation of the results and make them more theoretically meaningful. The decision to rotate the loadings is predicated upon the methodological work of Cliff and Krus (1976) and Bentler and Huba (in press), which shows that rotation of canonical-correlation loadings may serve to recover input latent structure much better than the traditional unrotated matrices. A salient issue that should be noted is that the rotations in no way destroy the explanatory properties of the solution (see Bentler & Huba, in press, for a proof), and the procedure is analogous to the typical rotation of factor loadings. In all areas, the simple symmetric solution (Bentler & Huba, in press) was used.

We have probed the relationship among the private personality measures and the motives for substance use. Methodologically, we would recommend that future investigations employ interval-scaled measures of motives and similar analytic procedures to those used here. Throughout the analysis of the reasons for using a substance, it was found that the linkages between personality and the major motives for using a drug are rather complex, although it has been possible to simplify the interpretation of the analyses through appropriate rotations. It seems very clear from the analyses presented that private personality plays a major role in the maintenance of substance use of particular types in addition to the influence in determining which youth will initiate drug use.

The argument that private personality variables are important for maintaining specialized types of use has a very clear implication that the usage pattern may become part of the day-to-day personality expression of the individual. For certain types of personalities, the use of one or more drugs becomes "personalized" in one or more settings such as parties. For other individuals, use of alcohol or other substances may become a means of combating negative feelings about oneself or anxieties caused by external stressors. It should furthermore be pointed out that there are no strong indications within the current data that these linkages between substance use and forms of personality functioning are abnormal.

The results that link private personality with substance use in order to achieve certain desired effects should be perceived as exploratory. In most cases, the structure of the linkages has been examined and found sufficiently robust to merit theoretical speculation about the causes for such relationships. On the other hand, the analyses testing the association of private personality styles and reasons for substance use were first conceptualized within the study as ancillary to the more primary intent of finding private personality differences among groups of users and nonusers.

Consequently, although these results are suggestive and moreover appear to be "meaningful," the interpretation has admittedly been post hoc, and further studies must be undertaken to replicate the basic findings and determine more precisely their theoretical significance. At the present time, we can conclude from these data that there appear to be major affective components to the maintenance of substance use among a group of nonaddicted, relatively normal youth. Furthermore, the perceived gains of substance use appear to be related in a compensatory manner to more fundamental private personality traits.

IMPLICATIONS FOR THEORIES OF DRUG USE

In this volume, we have studied what might be called a "normal" pattern of drug use by a group of fairly well-adjusted individuals, who are by now taking their places in adult society. Many of these individuals experimented with drugs during their youth, and undoubtedly, many of these same individuals will continue to use drugs at least moderately for recreational purposes. Almost all of the college students in our studies first used drugs in the 1970s, when: (1) experimentation with alcohol was a normative precollege behavior; (2) use of marijuana was decriminalized in some states and ignored by the legal system in others; and (3) the "protest" or "flower" generation had faded from the forefront of media accounts about American life. In summary, then, the youth in these samples became late adolescents at a time when knowledge about psychoactive chemicals was widespread and certain forms of illegal drug use were not statistically deviant behaviors.

For the samples, experimentation with psychoactive chemicals and initiation into the drug-taking behaviors for various forms of substances were certainly not controlled by some single personality trait that might be deemed indicative of an "addictive" or "preaddictive" personality style. Rather, markers of many different traits were related to the simple categorization of drug-use pattern in a "never-tried/tried" fashion. Among the collegians, the strongest single predictors of psychoactive drug experimentation was a generalized propensity toward such disparate behaviors as enjoying modern art, sampling new and varied foods, and traveling through strange areas. Simply put, the best single predictor of drug-use initation was a tendency to seek out many new and varied experiences. Indeed, to put this finding in another context, it was our impression as we studied the items on the Experience Seeking scale that the behaviors contributing to a high score are those that many of our professional colleagues would like to have attributed to them! Overall, it does not appear that there is any implication of "deviance" accounting for the finding of a very strong relationship between initiation status and experience seeking; rather, it appears that this result can only be understood as indicative that experimentation with psychoactive substances is a means for youth in our society to fulfill wishes for gaining new experiences of a nontraditional type.

We perceive what passes for theory in the field of youthful drug use to be oriented in a direction diametrically opposed to that taken by our study and supported by our results. Throughout our analyses and interpretation, we have found that those psychological processes associated with substance use seem to be ones that might be conceptualized as "normal." Furthermore, it seems that many of the more extreme tendencies such as the heightened need for autonomy associated with polydrug use, in particular, may be explained parsimoniously by examining aspects of the current society.

The general approach currently dominant within the field is one that might be called the "new deviance theory" or the "neodeviationist" viewpoint. Jessor and Jessor (1977) invoke concepts such as problem behavior, sanctions for deviant behavior, and support for deviant behavior in their integrated attempt to show that drug taking is controlled by the same psychological mechanisms that explain other "problem" behaviors such as minor difficulties with the legal system and nonvirginity. Kandel (1978a) discusses initiation into peer cultures that espouse drug use and further argues that individual difference variables such as rebelliousness and depression predispose an individual toward substance use.

As pointed out earlier in Chapter 1, several writers (e.g., Mellinger, 1978; Suchman, 1968; Wingard et al., 1979) have argued that many of the behaviors and generalized individual differences subsumed implicitly as "traits" in the neodeviationist viewpoint are indeed values and attitudes. Certainly, it must be remembered that to the extent that certain behaviors, values, and attitudes are not those of the majority culture, more generalized forms of maladjustment may develop among "deviant" individuals because of external pressures; such "secondary" deviance (see Becker, 1963) should not necessarily be attributed to the individual exhibiting it. Furthermore, there is some tendency to view the individual who partakes in one salient atypical behavior in a very negative manner. Consequently, to the extent to which the act of drug taking is a priori considered to be "deviant" behavior by the society, it is likely that individual drug takers will manifest signs of psychological maladjustment; to the extent to which the act of drug taking is a priori considered to be a deviant behavior by researchers, it is likely that individual drug takers will be found to have high levels on traits related (at the level of *face validity*) to the rejection of traditional society.

In the current test battery, the focus has been on psychological measures with external records of reliability and validity. As compared to the typical drug study, the measures employed here have been more adequately validated, and the labels given to the psychological dimensions are more in line with consensual psychological interpretations of meaning. Furthermore, in general, the scales have less conceptual slippage from the terms such as "autonomy," "social recognition," and "experience seeking" employed by the typical behavioral scientist—which is another way of saying that because there has been an emphasis on using externally validated personality instruments in this investigation, we believe that our results are more synonymous with the definitions for the constructs than those employed in various neodeviationist studies. Consequently, although we have found that individuals who use drugs are more autonomous than individuals who do not, the construct of need for autonomy subsumes the rebelliousness construct frequently employed elsewhere. Similarly, the various indicators of inner experience subsume the "depression" indicators used in other studies of youthful drug use.

In many ways, the personality indicators in our study yield results consistent with those touted by the neodeviationist workers. On the other hand, it has been consistently argued that the results generated here do not indicate that the typical college drug user has a maladjusted personality style. How can two conclusions so dissimilar be consistent with one another? The apparent similarity in results and dissimilarity in interpretation can be attributed to three factors: (1) sampling issues; (2) nonconsistent definitions of psychological constructs; and (3) the inclusion of a "mixed bag" of personality constructs in the present study.

The difference between our sample and that used in Jessor and Jessor's (1977) high-school study, Kandel's (1978a) high-school study, and Smith and Fogg's (1977, 1978) longitudinal project has been underscored by Mellinger (1978). As Mellinger notes, the individual allowed entry into college, particularly a selective institution, has already passed through several stages designed to eliminate individuals who do not have the necessary psychological characteristics to survive in a highly competitive academic environment. Such individuals typically will not be those who frequently "drop out" from reality for weeks at a time while in a drug-induced stupor. Similarly, those individuals will typically not be supporting drug "habits" through larceny, burglary, or prostitution. Similarly, those individuals will typically not have less than average intelligence and may not be subject to blind impulse. As a group, then, it is likely that the college samples are relatively low risk to develop destructive patterns of substance use. This is, of course, not to argue that some of these individuals will not develop future problems traceable to experience with psychoactive substances, but to note that many of these individuals are capable of exercising the necessary restraint to ensure that drug use will not pass beyond stages of experimentation or recreational use. In the studies in which neodeviationist explanations have appeared tenable (Jessor & Jessor, 1977; Kandel, 1978a; Smith & Fogg, 1978), the populations under study were both younger in age and less selected.

The second point of difference between studies is in the definition of psychological constructs. Most of the current psychological studies include measures of such constructs as achievement (or ambition), autonomy (or rebelliousness), extraversion (or sociability), social recognition (or needs to belong in groups or susceptibility to "deviance") and similar constructs. At the present time, we are not sure if the construct measures used in those different studies are entirely interchangeable and redundant with the construct measures used in our studies. Most of the "drug" projects have used much shorter scales of their psychological dimensions, and many of these studies have chosen to incorporate "project-specific" measures of consensual constructs. In using project-specific scales, one sacrifices the fairly rich nomological networks of the current scales and opens the possibility that the project specific measure of the construct may not correlate highly with more consensual measures. Additionally, it appears to use that many of the neodeviationist projects incorporate "narrow-band" rather than "broad-band" measures of certain dimensions. For example, in the 20 items contained on the PRF personality need scales used, quite a large domain of possible situations in which the need may be manifested are assessed. This wide sampling of constructs is in opposition to the more limited scales employed in the studies of Kandel (1978a) and the Jessors (1977).

The final point of difference—our sampling of a more comprehensive personality domain—is by far the most critical reason why it is possible to interpret our "similar" findings in a dissimilar manner. In isolation, the high correlation of the need for autonomy with increasing levels of drug use might be interpretable as a generalized rebelliousness tendency. Our battery, however, has also included measures of the seeking of many varied experiences such as traveling, attending "wild" parties, sampling new foods, mountain climbing, skin diving, and seeing "sexy" movies. Preference for many new, thrilling, and disinhibiting experiences is a stronger concomitant of drug use than the need for autonomy. Therefore, although it may be argued that autonomous needs are expressed in the drug-taking act, these needs may also be channeled into other forms of new, exciting, or disinhibiting experiences. Because of this pattern of correlations, it has been possible to ascertain that autonomy strivings are almost a prerequisite for engaging in many different behaviors that contain elements of risk. These different behaviors appear to be parts of a more general constellation of behaviors tried in order to test the full range of possibilities available for an adult life style. The strong relationship of various drug-use experimentation forms to this constellation suggests that youth perceive that drugs can either make mundane activities "new" and exciting, or that the drug use experience is perceived as providing a new experience, or both.

A major implication of the present result is that it is going to be necessary in future theorizing to delineate qualitatively different forms of drug use and to study the psychomechanics within each type. For the generally intact, generally intelligent, generally "normal" group of individuals we have studied, drugs appear to have a functional significance as "rituals" marking transitions from a dependent adolescence to an independent young adulthood. The same individuals most likely to try drugs are those individuals who wish to try other forms of nontraditional behaviors, many of which are *legal* but practiced by a small percentage of all adults. Indeed, it might be argued that the infrequent legal behaviors (mountain climbing, skin diving, parachute jumping) these youth wish to try are, on the basis of their lower baseline of occurrence than marijuana usage, more deviant. Consequently, if we are to invoke a concept such as rebelliousness to explain the drug taking of youth similar to those we have studied, it is necessary to expand the concept of the construct to include wishing to try many different types of nontraditional activities in addition to using drugs. The individuals studied here certainly cannot be characterized as "junkies" or "addicts," and it seems a mistake to invoke concepts that connote deviance in order to try to explain their drug-taking behavior.

IMPLICATIONS FOR DRUG USE TREATMENT AND INTERVENTION

The results of our analysis have several implications for intervention and treatment strategies designed to remedy drug-related problems, particularly in those instances where no physical addiction or dependency is involved. It has been repeatedly pointed out throughout the preceding chapters that not all drug use needs to be considered as drug abuse. Furthermore, our data indicate that drug experimentation may be normative and even normal, behavioral exploration for youth. Perceiving drug use as drug abuse, as discussed more fully in Chapter 1, has a profound impact on legal, social, psychological, and treatment approaches to the use of drugs. Such a situation is particularly crucial, because those who have traditionally assumed the primary role in treating drug-related problems—psychiatrists—have themselves received little formal training in drug use and abuse and therefore respond to such behaviors on the basis of attitudinal factors (Einstein, Quiones, & Lavenhar, 1972). If all forms of drug use are thus equated to drug abuse, it follows that treatment will emphasize abstinence and will focus on improving or restoring effective psychosocial functioning. Although the merits of abstinence are open to debate, it is nevertheless important to ascertain why such a goal should be chosen, particularly when abstinence may be at variance with the person's own perception of self-understood reasons for using drugs, particularly when to the individual's frame of reference, drug taking does not constitute deviant behavior. As Cohen (1971) has indicated, it is time to begin to consider drug use as a social *norm*. Drugs have become such an integral part of our youthful culture that they represent a naturalness not necessarily related to personality disturbance or deviance. Focusing only on deviant behavior explanations may have dysfunctional priorities when such a viewpoint is applied to intervention and treatment goals.

Consistently, our analyses have found that youthful drug taking is an expression of certain aspects of personality. Furthermore, it was shown that an individual's perceptions of the drug taking are once more related to personality. Repeatedly, though, it has been emphasized that the current findings do not support a conception of a "deviant personality style" related to youthful drug-taking behavior nor do the same findings argue for a simple personality cause of most types of drug taking. Rather, we have found that many different traits and characteristic behaviors typical of what may be called a general life style form a constellation with drug-taking behavior. Based on this premise, an important therapeutic implication is that if the individual is to discontinue the use of a substance, changes in general life style may be at least as important as realignment of personality functioning.

Within such a framework, our findings take on special relevance. We have shown that reasons (or motives) for using various substances are, to a large degree, attributable to different generalized motives. The first general theme appears to be a motive to use drugs to increase positive affect; the second dimension is a superordinate tendency to use drugs to combat feelings of negative affect. That these are two quite distinctly different processes is supported by our finding of essentially uncorrelated factors representative of these generalized styles within the sets of attributed use motives for the different substances. Furthermore, the dimensions seem to have quite different patterns of general personality and private experience correlates. Consequently, such results argue that individualized treatment must centrally consider why the individual uses drugs and what the perceived gains are if there is to be some change in behavior.

In the case where drugs are used chiefly to obtain positive affective experiences, to bring about the experience of a "high," or to increase social facilitation, it seems appropriate to pursue alternatives to such use within a group of activities ranging from providing exciting activities to decreasing shyness around others. In this manner, the therapist does not have to directly try to alter personality but indeed can try to provide substitute behaviors and relaxation techniques to achieve the satisfaction currently achieved by ingesting substances. Cohen (1971, 1973) has been a strong advocate of this viewpoint, contending that "major inroads on drug abuse cannot be made by stressing the undesirability of drugs. It can only be done by offering *more desirable alternative involvements*—activities, life styles, and satisfaction which are more rewarding than drug experiences and incompatible with dependence on chemicals [1973, p. 2]." Thus it seems logical to begin to think along such lines, particularly when motives for drug use are strongly interrelated to sensation-seeking tendencies (Kilpatrick et al., 1976). Sensation seekers, as reported by Segal (1973b), may be motivated to obtain an optimal state of arousal without fear or distress. In the context of drug use, the drug experience itself is what is important, and drugs are perceived and experienced with respect to the degree of arousal that they can induce. If this need for arousal or stimulation is an indication of a personality style, then it would appear that high sensation seekers would not be good candidates for traditional counseling, because such individuals do not generally manifest introspective tendencies. Focusing on behavior changes through substitution would seem to hold greater promise than concentrating on achieving individual personality change.

In those cases where drug use may be linked primarily to a desire to relieve or self-medicate unpleasant affect, traditional forms of clinical intervention may be more appropriate. In such instances, maladaptive learning patterns that link drug use to a reduction of undesirable states must be broken, particularly when the individual is in risk of either becoming addicted to the substance or is placed in a state of psychological conflict because of the social context of the drug-taking behavior. Therapeutic intervention would have to take the form of either learning new associated behaviors for the self-control of negative affective states or relief from the underlying psychological distress. In any case, the initiation of such intervention can only begin after the nature of the drug-taking behavior is clearly understood.

The major conclusion to be drawn from this discussion of treatment and intervention is that it is not generally beneficial to perceive a variety of drug users as belonging to homogeneous groups and then to subject them to uniform treatment approaches. Successful alleviation of drug-taking behavior is most likely to occur when specific patterns of drug use and motives for use are considered in the context of the total coping and personality strategy of the individual. It seems to us that a further typologizing of drug use, as well as the significance of drug use for each of these types of individuals, is necessary to successfully design different types of innovative intervention strategies *for the individual user.*

IMPLICATIONS FOR PERSONALITY THEORY AND RESEARCH

It has become increasingly clear to investigators in the psychology of personality that emphasis on either the unique individual consistency of persons or on the special properties of social situations in which they find themselves is not adequate for the development of a scientific theory of personality. The interactionist point of view (Magnusson & Endler, 1977) represents an important step toward developing procedures for looking systematically at the ways that established traits and situational demands interact to produce a unique response or recurring behavior pattern. We have chosen in this work to place most of our emphasis on the individual personality and especially on the private pole of personality, specifically on these memories, wishes, expectancies, fantasies, and thoughts that are not necessarily revealed to others except under special circumstances.

A close reading of recent interactionist literature suggests that although increasing attention is paid to trait consistency, there has still been a relative neglect of the more "internalized" features of experience and, in effect, covert behavior. As our findings in the experimental research of Chapter 8 suggest, there is a tremendous amount of ongoing thought and covert information processing that characterizes the human being in the waking state and, almost certainly, during sleep as well. The free-ranging possibilities provided by thought in the form that Freud called "experimental action" makes it unlikely to expect to find a direct correlation between all thought and specific actions. The elaborate realm of private daydreams and speculative fantasies about one's own or other's future constitutes a domain of experience and in a sense an alternative environment that must inevitably remain somewhat separate from observable actions.

Perhaps it is because of this necessary gap between thought and overt behavior that psychologists determined to operationalize their discipline have tended to ignore private experience and indeed have even neglected to consider the imagery capacities of individuals as part of newly emergent cognitive theories (Holt, 1964; Shepard, 1978; Singer, 1966). One way of looking at the results reported in this volume is to recognize that we have made at least a small step toward bridging the gap between anecdotal and introspective accounts of private fantasies, expectancies, and daydreams and the direct actions of individuals. Our results, we believe, make it clear that sets of private intentions and motivational hierarchies as well as general and specific daydream patterns are predictive of overt behavior. Ultimately, if personality psychologists have the means, they will have to explore extensively recurrent patterns of the private fantasy of individuals and experienced intentions or expectancies and then relate these to the objective character-istics of a variety of social situations as well as to the cognitive attributions made to such situations by individuals. Our own fantasy can extend to the day when personologists will have available to them systematic factor structures for a variety of social settings in which individuals in a given culture may find themselves. One could next include in a prediction equation descriptive data of the private personality orientation of the individual, for example, his or her scores on the three major factors of daydreaming, scores on anticipations and expectations or motive orderings such as are measured in the Personality Research Form and, finally, data on subjects' perceptions of the *meanings* of different situations. Such an approach suggests that interaction research will require multivariate, predictive, large-scale statistics rather than the analysis of variance methods that have been primarily favored by the interactionists in the mid-1970s.

As Bowers (1977) has written:

Historically the situationist's failure to recognize the importance of intrapsychic organization as a stabilizing influence on behavior has its counterpart in the dynamic psychologist's underestimation of how the environment can modify a person's ongoing behavior. Fortunately, both traditions seem to be alerted to the crackers in their bed and a reconciliation of sorts may be in the offing [p. 75].

In conclusion, we feel that the present volume represents a contribution to this general movement by emphasizing the extent to which it is possible to explore in detail various elements of the private personality using reasonably objective and reliable methods of data collection and data analysis that reflect reasonable scientific sophistication.

PATTERNS OF DAYDREAMING

In this volume, we have sought to carry much further than was possible before an examination of the patterns of private experience as reflected in daydreams and related phenomena, available essentially only through personal report. Our findings reflect a great deal of consistency with the earliest studies of daydreaming through questionnaire methods and interviews (Singer & Antrobus, 1963, 1972). At the deepest level of statistical analysis, we consistently find three major dimensions that seem to characterize self-reports of ongoing thought by adults:

1. One pattern clearly represents a more positive, exploratory, and fanciful or playful orientation of thought, the kind of "garden-variety" daydream that all of us recognize with its wishful or often planful quality.

2. The second dimension is characterized by a strongly negative affective tone even though some of the fantasies linked to this dimension may be wishful or achievement-oriented. The major dominating patterns of fantasy of the second dimension seem to involve speculations about guilty or hostile and aggressive behaviors as well as fantasy expectations of failure.

3. The third dimension seems in some sense not really one of daydreaming or fantasy but almost an expression of a difficulty in controlling one's thoughts and in developing elaborate inner speculations. Thus, this last dimension reflects aspects of mindwandering, distractibility, and boredom, as well as occasional fleeting, frightening, or anxious fantasies.

In effect, these results suggest that all of us vary in some degree in the awareness of experiences along each of the three dimensions. It seems likely that some individuals, whether constitutionally or as a result of socialization experiences, gradually come to emphasize one or two of the dimensions more than others. We need much more research identifying individuals who show differing patterns across these three major dimensions in order to examine their overt behavior or their style of situational interpretations. Nevertheless, it seems apparent that individuals who show a great deal of positive and vivid imagery daydreaming are likely to be somewhat more positive in their general mood and to be able to use this fantasy realm in a variety of ways for self-entertainment and possibly for effective life planning. The dysphoric guilt-oriented fantasy dimension seems somewhat more characteristic of males in our society and, in its extreme form, may become the basis for obsessional rumination and depressive moods. As our data from the college samples suggest, this dimension may also be linked to an inclination to try to escape from such thoughts by alcohol ingestion. What seems most likely, however, is that all of us show some reasonable combination of both general types of fantasy behavior, the positive–fanciful and the guilty–dysphoric. The most problematic individuals are those who have especially strong predilections in the style reflected by the third dimension, the difficulty in controlling their own thoughts.

Again it is important to recognize that all three of these dimensions and the more specific factors that make them up at the first-order level reflect a range of ways in which human beings vary in patterns of private experience. It remains to be seen whether we can identify sets of situations or social demands that might yield differential patterns of emphasis on one or another of these dimensions in individuals. Thus it is conceivable that under conditions of high pressure or external demand, an individual may become more aware of the thoughts and inner experiences reflective of our distractibility dimension. Under conditions of a relatively redundant, un-demanding environment, one may become more aware of fantasies and thoughts more reflective of the positive–vivid daydreaming dimension. Clearly also we would have to take into account in studying such situational variations the long-standing predisposition of the individual to favor one or several of these daydreaming dimensions.

In general, it is clear that the daydreams of the individual, or at least the pattern of such activity, represent perhaps the deepest level of behavior and the one most remote from direct action. Our findings at least with respect to prediction of drug use would suggest that the most conscious intentional features of the private personality as reflected in the preferred motives or activity preferences of the Personality Research Form and the Sensation-Seeking Scales are closer to actual overt responses and choice behaviors in our college sample. Nevertheless, our data also indicate that the fantasy life of the individual is not by any means completely separate from such overt choices and socially observable response patterns. These findings, together with results from the experimental studies, emphasize the importance of a continuing inner source of stimulation in the form of private images and interior monologues.

It is important to stress that although we have chosen in the present study to limit our emphasis to studies with college students, other research suggests that essentially the same patterns of daydreaming emerge whether we study children as young as 6 to 8 (Rosenfeld, 1978) or a sample of adults ranging from late adolescence through old age (Giambra, 1974, 1977). Rosenfeld (1978), for example, rewrote items of the Imaginal Processes Inventory in a form suitable for administration to children in the 1st through 3rd grades. She found through factor analysis that she could identify three factors: (1) a negatively toned aggressive fantasy style (roughly comparable to the guilty–dysphoric factor but in such young children lacking the heavy self-recrimination component); (2) a factor involving fanciful, vivid high intensity daydreams; and (3) a factor that reflected a kind of positive, active, and intellectual style of fantasy. It remains to be seen whether we can track changes in the organization of these patterns through the earlier years until adolescence by which time essentially the patterns we describe in the present volume seem crystallized.

A series of studies by Starker (1979) extends the studies of daydreams to more clearly pathological populations. Starker and Singer (1975a, b) examined the daydreaming patterns of psychiatric patients, and Starker subsequently followed up these studies with other groups and with individuals with sleep disturbance and depression. Starker (1979) writes:

> Taken together the... studies outlined clearly argue against the notions that psychotic patients experience rich, elaborate fantasy lives to which they retreat under pressure and that a particularly vivid fantasy life is a regular feature of the disorder. Rather they indicate relatively little baseline difference in fantasy and imagery between normals and psychotics, with two exceptions: psychotic patients have a greater tendency to block inner experience, and hallucinatory schizophrenics have a tendency to experience reduced vividness and controllability of imagery where emotionally charged interpersonal content is involved. Both of these exceptions suggest the operation of a powerful defense mechanism in psychosis whereby the normal imagery and fantasy process is disrupted or inhibited [p. 28].

Starker also summarizes other research that calls attention to the fact that the guilty–dysphoric pattern of daydreaming may create a cycle of depressive response to the point in which, without the alternative of positive fantasy that may break up the loop and change mood (Schultz, 1978), the ultimate resolution may have to be the intervention of "mood elevating drugs, psychotherapy and social support systems" (Starker, 1979, p. 29). Indeed, Starker's results from still another study that he cites suggest a tie between insomnia and a predominance of guilty–dysphoric daydreaming patterns. In general, Starker (1979) concludes that: "The myth of the fantasy-ridden psychotic patient 'living in his own world' is seriously undermined and increasingly supplanted by the idea that psychosis involves the severe disruption of the rich, varied fantasy life that constitues an important resource for healthy individuals [p. 30]."

We should also call attention to the relationship of our results to the more general cognitive–affective theory that is emerging in the field of personality (Izard, 1977; Singer, 1974; Tomkins, 1962–1963). Our study of the private personality suggests that patterns of fantasy and private thought seem to be closely tied to particular kinds of emotional reactivity. It seems likely that the rapidity with which novel experiences or thoughts can be assimilated into established memory schema may be related to the evocation of positive or negative affective reactions. Persisting fantasies of guilt or potential failure may evoke the affects of anger or despair just as much as unpleasant social experiences. The very lack of a developed capacity for self-modulating fantasy may drive some young people toward extreme sensation seeking, whether in action or in drug abuse. Our findings with respect to reasons for drug use and their relation to private experiences suggest that some patterns of fantasy as well as drugs may be enhancing of positive experiences, whereas others may be indulged in primarily to reduce negative affect or to blot private experience that has a negative tone to it. The questionnaire methods we have used have not made it possible to highlight the important role of the affects as much as would be desirable. This is a task for future research. Nevertheless, it is clear that we must pay much more careful attention to the subtle ways in which our dimensions of private experience reflect an alternative stimulus field with novel or repetitive information that must be processed and that can generate powerful affective reactions.

It seems likely to us that individuals who lack a well-developed capacity for self-entertainment through fantasy or for shifting from unpleasant thoughts to playful positive images may be especially susceptible to resorting to drugs or alcohol on a regular basis to reduce negative affect by blotting out thought or to produce novelty when they cannot spontaneously generate a lively "inner" environment. Where drugs or alcohol are used primarily to provide a positive affective experience in a social situation with peers, there seems less likelihood of a powerful psychological dependence. This seems the case today with the near-normative use of marijuana and beer. The more ominous situation—of resort to multidrug use and liquor as a means of reducing negative affect associated with an inner sense of emptiness, despair or guilt— is more likely to lead to psychological dependence on these substances. A preventive approach, we believe, must include at least some systematic efforts for enhancing the ability of children and adolescents to employ their imaginative potential for planning, playful fantasy, and the development of imagery of self-efficacy (Bandura, 1977). Our exploration of the inner lives of so many hundreds of young adults points up the great range of imagination and also the widespread individual differences in the enjoyment and, apparently, effective use of this basic human capacity. Perhaps we need to pay much more systematic attention to exploring the different ways in which young people approach their own private experiences, whether with denial, avoidance, or shame or with delight and controlled playfulness. The human imagination may be still a relatively "underdeveloped" resource for creative and adaptive living.

SOME FINAL WORDS:
COLLEGE YOUTH IN THE 1970S

The implementation of a research program involving hundreds of young men and women, most of them beginning their college careers, full of anticipation, hope, and wild surmise has been an exciting, challenging opportunity. We and our research assistants were privileged to read their accounts in questionnaires and interview protocols of some of their innermost fantasies and aspirations. We are wistfully aware that our emphasis in this volume on normative data, methodological precision, and technical and theoretical questions in psychological science has precluded our presenting detailed case material and has, indeed, omitted a sense of the liveliness and variety of the qualities of our youthful participants. Drug ingestion, drinking, and day-dreaming have occupied only a small part of the complex lives of the students at Murray State and Yale. They have been attending classes, adjusting to new living circumstances, making new friends, joining clubs and fraternities, playing at sports, singing in choruses, or working at odd jobs to support themselves at school. They have begun to move into intimate and sexual relationships in an atmosphere at once more free than ever existed before for college youth and also more anxiety-provoking because of the increasing self-assertion of women and the absence of established conventions. To capture the complexity of the daily lives of these young Americans as they move through the college system toward the mainstream of adult life in the 1980s requires a far greater combination of research resources and, perhaps, literary imagination than was available to us.

We can say, somewhat speculatively, that the college students we studied represent a major transitional group. They are the first wave of young people who reflect the shift from the turbulent '60s with civil rights movements and the Vietnam War as tremendous influences toward the security-conscious, politically cynical, self-oriented '70s. When these students were freshmen and sophomores in college, the Southeast Asia War ended in obvious defeat for their country, and the President of the United States, the key figure in the nation usually assumed to be above scandal and corruption, was driven from office in disgrace. The great opportunities for a variety of interesting career lines for college students that had characterized the '50s and '60s began to contrast sharply in the economic "stagflation" of the '70s. The great archetypes of potential social change and of idealistic commitment for students were crumbling as Russia, China, and other symbols of the Socialist perfectibility of humankind were unmasked as bureaucratic and power-oriented, while the democratic–capitalist symbols of America and Western Europe suffered from economic difficulties and contracting opportunities, seemingly helpless victims of a few despotic oil-rich and socially backward nations.

The young people we studied seemed uncertain, doubtful, and cynical about broader values on the whole. They were turning increasingly toward an education that would provide them with financial security and an adequate private life, capable of providing the leisure and luxury daily represented on the television sets, which undoubtedly formed a major source of their imagery and fantasy. We mention television because it is increasingly clear that this talking box, watched as it is 3 to 4 hours daily by children from 3 years of age to adolescence, is a major source of input into the consciousness of a whole generation. Can we be sure that the rapid pace with which TV material is presented, the sudden shifts of sequence, and the bombardment of commercial messages have not played some part in producing a kind of passivity, an expectation of entertainment from "outside," that has eroded some of the active and imaginative trends in young adults? Is sensation seeking, which we find in our research to be so strongly linked to substance use, a reflection already of a generation whose consciousness was formed in front of the television set? That certainly is a question for future investigation in this area.

A certain conservatism and self-protection has been evident in the youth we studied during the past few years. Murray State University, certainly little in evidence on the national scene, appeared briefly in the news as the first college to invite Lt. Calley, convicted of killing women and children in the My Lai massacre, as a guest speaker. At this writing, the Yale University Political Union is negotiating with Richard Nixon about a speaking engagement on campus.

What will become of our study participants as we move into the 1980s? The ethical requirements of confidentiality for our student samples (especially because of their frank answers about drug use) have precluded our maintaining records that would permit any continuing contacts. Despite the many fears about college youth becoming "hopheads" or indecisive lost souls because of their interests in drugs, we found on the whole that such concerns have been unfounded. Although a sizable number of our participants have indeed experimented, especially with marijuana, drugs played only a minor role in the various influences and challenges that confronted these young people. Our peek into the fantasies and aspirations of our college students suggests that they are indeed wide-ranging and still hopeful of interesting lives ahead. Wherever they are, we wish them well.

APPENDIX:
Generalizability Research
on Other Youthful Samples

The bulk of our analyses in college samples suggests a link between the domains of private personality and the use or nonuse of psychoactive substances. Because the relationships found are within the context of samples of college youth who have passed through several stages designed to eliminate less intelligent and motivated or economically disadvantaged individuals, the issue of generality to other types of people must be of concern. We have conducted several preliminary studies of noncollege youth to ascertain the generality to other individuals within the same age bracket. This appendix briefly discusses a series of analyses undertaken to determine whether comparable results would be obtained in samples of youthful individuals undergoing training in the U.S. Navy at the time of testing.

SAMPLES

Three samples were collected through contact with Navy officials. The first two (160 males and 65 females) were in training at the U.S. Naval Training Center in Orlando, Florida. The third sample consisted of 125 advanced recruits enrolled at the Naval Air Technical Training Center in Millington, Tennessee. The individuals tested were generally comparable in age to the college samples obtained from the two colleges, with the mean ages for the Memphis male, Orlando male, and Orlando female samples being 19.06, 18.82, and 19.61 years, respectively. The three samples were also primarily white, with less than 15% minority individuals in any sample. Individuals were from a large geographical area. Testing was conducted in the spring of 1974.

INSTRUMENTS

The Sensation-Seeking Scale, the Locus-of-Control Scale, and the Drug and Alcohol Research Form were administered to the three Navy samples in the same form as received by the college students. Navy subjects completed a longer form of the Personality Research Form (PRF), which included six additional content scales and a control scale for social desirability responding. Due to time constraints, it was not possible to administer the Imaginal Processes Inventory to all participants, and consequently it has not been used in analyses reported here.

STATISTICAL ANALYSES

Following the derivation of the four drug-use groups in a manner analogous to that used in the college samples, separate discriminant analyses were computed for each of the three Navy samples. The independent variables were the total set of personality dimensions scored from the PRF, SSS, and LC items, resulting in the attempted discrimination of the four groups from 27 private personality measures. The analyses and mode of presentation parallel those used previously (see Chapter 6).

DRUG USE LEVELS

Table A.1 shows the number of respondents who belong to the four drug-use groups. There is no significant difference between the three Navy samples in the incidence of membership in the categories ($\chi^2_6 = 8.18$, $p > .05$).

TABLE A.1
Drug Classifications for Three Navy Samples[a]

Sample	Nonuser	Alcohol Only	Marijuana Only	Polydrug
Memphis Male	7 (5.6)	35 (28.0)	35 (28.0)	48 (38.4)
Orlando Male	8 (5.0)	31 (19.4)	41 (25.6)	80 (50.0)
Orlando Female	6 (9.2)	17 (26.2)	11 (16.9)	31 (47.7)

[a]Value given is number of respondents; number in parentheses is percentage of sample.

TABLE A.2
Drug Categorization of Navy and College Samples[a]

Sample	Nonuser	Drug Category Alcohol Only	Marijuana Only	Polydrug
(a) Males				
College	59 (11.8)	155 (31.2)	162 (32.5)	122 (24.5)
Navy	51 (5.3)	66 (23.1)	76 (26.7)	128 (44.9)
(b) Females				
College	144 (24.1)	210 (35.2)	135 (22.6)	108 (18.1)
Navy	6 (9.2)	17 (26.2)	11 (16.9)	31 (47.7)

[a]Value given is number of respondents; number in parentheses is percentage of sample.

Although our major intent in this appendix is not to compare levels of drug use among the college and Navy samples, a rough analysis of differential usage rates is necessary. Table A.2 shows the number of male and female college and Navy respondents in the four categories. Patterns of drug use are distributed differently for male ($\chi^2_3 = 38.10$, $p < .0001$) and female ($\chi^2_3 = 32.45$, $p < .001$) college and Navy participants. In particular, for both males ($z = 5.90$, $p < .001$) and females ($z = 5.56$, $p < .0001$), there is a higher level of polydrug use among the Navy samples. For both males ($z = -3.03$, $p < .01$) and females ($z = -2.72$, $p < .01$), a significantly smaller percentage of Navy recruit respondents fall in the nonuser classification. Consequently, the Navy results must be interpreted as conducted within a group of individuals with greater drug-use experience.

RESULTS

Overall, it was not possible to show that the four drug-use groups could be successfully differentiated on the total array of 27 private personality variables when all scales are considered simultaneously for the male samples. For the Memphis males, Wilks' λ was .41 ($\chi^2_{81} = 96.31$, $p = 11$), whereas λ was .50 ($\chi^2_{81} = 99.68$, $p = .08$) for the Orlando male samples. Although they are not statistically robust at the conventional statistical reliability level of .95, the two male sample multivariate tests are close to significance. On the other hand, even with the small number of observations ($N = 65$) for the Orlando female sample, the multivariate association between groups and private personality was statistically robust (λ = .11, χ^2_{81} = 106.62, p = .03). Overall, though, we interpret the lack of significant multivariate effect for the male samples to be a function of the lowered statistical power caused by the small groups and the inclusion of a number of scales that were not expected to differ between drug categories on the basis of the college results. Nonetheless, in spite of the marginal significance of the overall discriminant analyses attributable to power, a comparison of the discriminant-function loadings shown in Table A.3 to the coefficients for the college samples given in Chapter

TABLE A.3
Correlations of Original Variables With
the Discriminant Variable in Three Navy Samples

Variable	Memphis Males	Orlando Males	Orlando Females
Abasement	.22	-.02	.05
Achievement	.17	.15	.05
Affiliation	-.24	.03	.11
Aggression	.00	-.49	-.29
Autonomy	-.14	-.39	-.24
Change	-.17	-.07	-.27
Cognitive Structure	.10	.32	.02
Defensive Structure	-.04	-.21	-.22
Dominance	.12	-.06	-.39
Endurance	.31	.06	.05
Exhibitionism	-.34	-.24	-.32
Harmavoidance	.19	.35	.27
Impulsivity	-.47	-.37	-.28
Nurturance	.15	.05	.01
Order	.18	.26	.06
Play	-.34	-.55	-.11
Sentience	.07	-.04	-.14
Social Recognition	.15	.00	.09
Succorance	-.15	-.06	-.10
Understanding	.27	.20	-.35
Infrequency	-.22	-.10	-.11
Social Desirability	.06	.22	.14
Locus of Control	-.26	-.17	-.03
General Sensation Seeking	-.36	-.33	-.36
Thrill Seeking	-.26	-.35	-.32
Experience Seeking	-.41	-.67	-.47
Disinhibition	-.50	-.61	-.57

TABLE A.4
Means and Univariate *F* Ratios of Variables
Significantly Different Between Drug-Use Groups

Sample	Nonuser	Alcohol Only	Marijuana Only	Polydrug	F
Need for Autonomy					
MM[1]	10.71	9.34	9.20	10.23	1.05
OM[2]	7.38	8.29	8.34	9.67	3.36**
OF[3]	5.17	8.35	6.45	8.84	2.50*
Need for Harmavoidance					
MM	7.41	9.6	8.71	8.19	1.21
OM	11.25	8.61	8.17	7.96	2.62*
OF	12.50	9.53	10.27	8.00	1.95
Need for Impulsivity					
MM	9.00	8.71	9.20	10.83	3.91**
OM	6.63	8.84	9.59	9.74	2.66*
OF	8.67	10.29	9.09	11.58	1.79
Need for Order					
MM	10.29	12.00	11.54	10.69	1.07
OM	12.87	12.61	11.68	11.24	1.29
OF	14.17	10.94	11.55	11.19	1.04
Need for Play					
MM	11.14	11.37	11.63	12.85	1.90
OM	8.63	11.42	12.37	12.65	6.31***
OF	12.00	12.41	12.18	12.90	.23
Need for Social Recognition					
MM	10.42	11.06	11.43	10.25	.85
OM	11.00	11.39	10.95	11.24	.12
OF	12.00	9.71	12.55	10.35	1.70
Need for Understanding					
MM	14.28	11.51	10.00	10.60	3.45***
OM	13.38	12.58	11.85	12.04	.88
OF	11.50	12.47	12.55	14.61	2.30*
General Sensation Seeking					
MM	12.00	10.34	11.80	12.23	3.31**
OM	10.25	11.29	11.17	12.43	2.52*
OF	9.33	11.76	11.73	13.77	3.18**
Thrill and Adventure Seeking					
MM	9.71	8.69	9.37	9.96	1.47
OM	7.87	9.97	9.95	10.58	2.59*
OF	8.17	9.76	10.27	11.45	2.40*

228

Experience Seeking					
MM	6.57	7.31	7.83	8.48	2.80**
OM	5.50	6.06	7.56	8.65	9.60***
OF	3.50	6.65	6.82	8.94	6.72***
Disinhibition					
MM	3.57	6.17	6.46	7.21	6.34***
OM	3.63	5.32	6.27	6.94	6.90***
OF	2.67	3.47	4.18	6.39	7.23***

   * p < .10

  ** p < .05

 *** p < .01

[1]Memphis Males

[2]Orlando Males

[3]Orlando Females

6 shows that approximately the same dimension of difference between drug groups has been found.

Table A.4 shows the mean scores on a selected set of personality scales for the four drug-use groups in each sample. The variables were selected for relevance because the college analyses (Chapter 6) concluded that these variables significantly discriminated drug-use groups in at least one sample of each sex.

As a measure of the generalizability of the discriminant function loadings, we calculated the factor similarity coefficients between the values obtained in Table A.3 for the Navy samples and those presented for the college sample in Table 6.1. The 20 loadings for the variables in common between the two sets of analyses were used. The factor similarity coefficients (Tucker, 1951) represent an unstandardized correlation between the discriminant vectors. To then summarize the overall pattern of similarity, we submitted the seven sample factor similarity coefficient matrix to a principal components analysis. The first eigenvector was 6.03 accounting for about 86% of the similarity among samples. Loadings on the first unrotated principal component indicate about how similar the results in the different samples were. The loadings on the first component were .85 for Memphis males, .91 for Orlando males, .88 for Orlando females, .96 for 1973 males, .96 for 1974 males, .96 for 1973 females, and .98 for 1974 females. We interpret this further analysis as indicating that about the same dimension of overall individual differences among substance-use groups exists within the noncollege samples.

As may be seen from Table A.4, the two most important univariate variables—Experience Sensation Seeking and Disinhibition—in the college sample analyses are different between substance use groups for all Navy samples. The other sensation-seeking measures—Thrill-Adventure Seeking and General Sensation Seeking—yield more mixed results, but the trends within the two Orlando samples are in the right direction and significant.

Considering the PRF variables, the results upon replication are again mixed but, when not statistically significant at conventional levels, are almost invariably in the correct direction. Heightened Autonomy strivings are associated with polydrug use in the two Orlando samples but not in the Memphis sample. High levels of the need for Harmavoidance are associated with drug nonuse for the two Orlando samples. Impulsivity is associated with increasing levels of drug use, although the results are only marginally significant for the two Orlando groups. The need for Order does not seem associated with drug use for the noncollege participants, and the need for Play is only related to drug use for the Orlando male group. In contrast to the college results, the need for Social Recognition is not related to drug-use classification. Finally, the need for Understanding is inversely related to drug use among the Memphis male sample and is positively related for the Orlando female sample.

DISCUSSION

The present findings indicate that certain major results reported in Chapter 6 are readily generalizable to groups of noncollege youth. It was previously shown that users of drugs and alcohol are best differentiated on those aspects of the private personality that assess sensation-seeking tendencies. In the three Navy recruit samples, it has been found that Experience Sensation and Disinhibition scales discriminate significantly among different drug user and nonuser groups.

Some discrepancies between the current results and those obtained for the college samples can be attributed to slight methodological differences. One change involved the slightly different test battery used in the Navy studies. The deletion of the 28 IPI scales and the addition of seven PRF scales may have slightly altered major discriminant-function loadings. Furthermore, as pointed out earlier, the rates of drug use and nonuse are distributed somewhat differently for the college and Navy samples. Finally, there was a potential sacrifice in statistical power due to the relatively small Navy samples.

In general, however, it appears that even those variables that did not pass the conventional significance test at the .95 confidence level yielded a general pattern of results consistent with that expected after studying the college samples. Indeed, given the differences in the environments of the Navy recruits and the college students, it is somewhat striking that there are not more differences between populations in the personality correlates of drug use. Moreover, given the personality correlates found, it seems possible to explain the relatively high base rate of psychoactive drug-use experience among the Navy recruits by the situational demands they face. Navy personnel, living in a highly structured situation, have relatively fewer degrees of freedom to obtain new and varied experiences on a day-to-day basis. Drug and alcohol use thus may be pursued not only more actively but because such experiences are one of the major ways of finding variety and novelty within a structured military environment for the individual who does not turn "inside" to fantasies and daydreams for novelty and excitement. Consequently, we believe that it is the combination of the general personality styles manifested by individuals prone to experiment with drugs and the relatively impoverished environment that interact to cause such high rates of drug use.

The finding that basic personality dimensions identified for college students are also intimately related to substance use for youth not in the college environment argues for the robustness of the results and the necessity of considering personality factors in the etiology of youthful drug use. Furthermore, it seems reasonable to surmise that means of the same personality dimensions may be related to drug use for many different types of youth.

References

Abelson, H., Cohen, R., & Schrayer, D. *Public attitudes toward marijuana, Part I.* Princeton, N.J.: Response Analysis Corporation, 1972.

Abelson, H., Cohen, R., Schrayer, D., & Rappaport, M. *Drug experience, attitudes, and related behavior among adolescents and adults.* Princeton, N.J.: Response Analysis Corporation, 1973.

Allport, G. W. *Pattern and growth in personality.* New York: Holt, Rinehart & Winston, 1961.

Antrobus, J. S. Information theory and stimulus-independent thought. *British Journal of Psychology,* 1968, *59,* 423–430.

Antrobus, J. S., Singer, J. L., Goldstein, S., & Fortgang, M. Mindwandering and cognitive structure. *Transactions of the New York Academy of Science,* 1970, *32* (2), 242–252.

Antrobus, J. S., Singer, J. L., & Greenberg, S. Studies in the stream of consciousness: Experimental enhancement and suppression of spontaneous cognitive processes. *Perceptual and Motor Skills,* 1966, *23,* 399–417.

Austin, G. A., Johnson, B. D., Carroll, E. E., & Lettieri, D. J. *Drugs and minorities.* Rockville, Md.: National Institute on Drug Abuse, 1977.

Ausubel, D. Psychopathology and treatment of drug addiction in relation to the Mental Hygiene Movement. *Psychiatric Quarterly Supplement,* 1948, *22,* 219–250.

Bailey, J. P., Jr., & Guertin, W. H. Test item dependence of several oblique factor solutions. *Educational and Psychological Measurement,* 1973, *40,* 611–619.

Bandura, A. The self-system in reciprocal determinism. *American Psychologist,* 1978, *33,* 344–358.

Becker, H. S. *Outsiders: Studies in the sociology of deviance.* New York: Free Press, 1963.

Becker, H. S. Consciousness, power and drug effects. *Journal of Psychedelic Drugs,* 1974, *6,* 67–76.

Bem, D. J., & Allen, A. On predicting some of the people some of the time: The search for cross-situational consistencies in behavior. *Psychological Review,* 1974, *81,* 506–520.

Bem, S. L. The measurement of psychological androgyny. *Journal of Consulting and Clinical Psychology,* 1974, *42,* 155–162.

Bentler, P. M. *Response variability: Fact or artifact?* Unpublished doctoral dissertation, Stanford University, 1964.

Bentler, P. M. Multistructure statistical model applied to factor analysis. *Multivariate Behavioral Research*, 1976, *11*, 3–25.

Bentler, P. M. Factor simplicity index and transformations. *Psychometrika*, 1977, *42*, 277–295.

Bentler, P. M. The interdependence of theory, methodology, and empirical data: Causal modeling as an approach to construct validation. In D. Kandel (Ed.), *Longitudinal research on drug use: Empirical findings and methodological issues*. Washington, D.C.: Hemisphere, 1978.

Bentler, P. M. Multivariate analysis with latent variables: Causal modeling. *Annual Review of Psychology*, 1980, *31*, 419–456.

Bentler, P. M., & Bonett, D. G. Significance tests and goodness of fit in the analysis of covariance structures. *Psychological Bulletin*, 1981, in press.

Bentler, P. M., & Eichberg, R. H. A social psychological approach to substance abuse construct validity: Prediction of adolescent drug use from independent data sources.In D. J. Lettieri (Ed.), *Predicting adolescent drug abuse: A review of issues, methods, and correlates*. Rockville, Md.: National Institute on Drug Abuse, 1975.

Bentler, P. M., & Huba, G. J. Simple minitheories of love. *Journal of Personality and Social Psychology*, 1979, *37*, 124–130.

Bentler, P. M., & Huba, G. J. Symmetric and asymmetric rotations in canonical correlation analysis: New methods with drug variable examples. In N. Hirschberg (Ed.), *Multivariate methods in the social sciences: Applications*. Hillsdale, N.J.: Lawrence Erlbaum Associates, in press.

Bentler, P. M., Lettieri, D. J., & Austin, G. A. *Data analysis strategies and designs for substance abuse research*. Rockville, Md.: National Institute on Drug Abuse, 1976.

Berdach, E., & Bakan, P. Body position and free recall of early memories. *Psychotherapy*, 1967, *4*, 101–102.

Blum, R. H. *Students and drugs*. San Francisco: Jossey-Bass, 1969.

Bowers, K. S. There's more to Iago than meets the eye: A clinical account of personal consistency. In D. Magnusson & N. S. Endler (Eds.), *Personality at the crossroads*. Hillsdale, N.J.: Lawrence Erlbaum Associates, 1977.

Brantley, W. G. Marijuana trends at a state university in the deep south. *Journal of Alcohol and Drug Education*, 1975, *20*, 53–60.

Brecher, E. M. *Licit & illicit drugs*. Boston: Little, Brown, 1972.

Breger, L., Hunter, I., & Lane, R. W. *The effect of stress on dreams*. New York: International Universities Press, 1971.

Brill, N. Q., Compton, E., & Grayson, H. M. Personality factors in marijuana use. *Archives of General Psychiatry*, 1971, *24*, 163–165.

Broadbent, D. E. *Perception and communication*. New York: Pergamon, 1958.

Browne, M. W. Oblique rotation to a partially specified target. *British Journal of Mathematical and Statistical Psychology*, 1972, *25*, 207–212.

Burkhart, B. R., Schwarz, R. M., & Green, S. B. Relationships between dimensions of anxiety and sensation seeking. *Journal of Consulting and Clinical Psychology*, 1978, *46*, 194–195.

Cahalan, D., Cisin, I. H., & Crossley, H. M. *American drinking practices*. New Brunswick, N.J.: Rutgers Center of Alcohol Studies, 1969.

Campagna, A. *Masturbation fantasies in male college freshmen*. Unpublished doctoral dissertation, Yale University, 1975.

Carlin, A. S., & Stauss, F. F. Descriptive and functional classification of drug abusers. *Journal of Consulting and Clinical Psychology*, 1977, *45*, 222–227.

Cattell, R. B. The scree test for the number of factors. *Multivariate Behavioral Research*, 1966, *1*, 140–161.

Chambers, C. D., Inciardi, T. A., & Siegal, H. A. *Chemical coping: A report on legal drug use in the United States*. New York: Spectrum, 1975.

Clausen, J. A. Social patterns, personality and adolescent drug use. In A. H. Leighton, J. A. Clausen, & R. N. Wilson (Eds.), *Explorations in social psychiatry*. New York: Basic Books, 1957.

Cliff, N., & Krus, D. J. Interpretation of canonical analysis: Rotated vs. unrotated solutions. *Psychometrika*, 1976, *41*, 35–42.

Cohen, A. Y. The journey beyond trips: Alternatives to drugs. *Journal of Psychedelic Drugs*, 1971, *3*, 16–21.

Cohen, A. Y. *Alternatives to drug abuse: Steps toward prevention*. Rockville, Md.: National Institute on Drug Abuse, 1973.

Comrey, A. L. Common methodological problems in factor analytic studies. *Journal of Consulting and Clinical Psychology*, 1978, *46*, 648–659.

Cooley, W., & Lohnes, P. *Multivariate data analysis*. New York: Wiley, 1971.

Couch, A. S., & Kenniston, K. Yea-sayers and nay-sayers: Agreeing response set as a personality variable. *Journal of Abnormal and Social Psychology*, 1960, *60*, !51–174.

Cramer, E. M., & Nicewander, A. W. Some symmetric, invariant measures of multivariate association. *Psychometrika*, 1979, *44*, 43–54.

Cronbach, L. J., & Meehl, P. E. Construct validity in psychological tests. *Psychological Bulletin*, 1955, *52*, 281–302.

Csikszentmihalyi, M. *Beyond boredom and anxiety*. San Francisco: Jossey-Bass, 1975.

Csikszentmihalyi, M. Attention and the holistic approach to behavior. In K. S. Pope & J. S. Singer (Eds.), *The stream of consciousness*. New York: Plenum, 1978.

Darlington, R. B. Multiple regression in psychological research and practice. *Psychological Bulletin*, 1968, *69*, 161–182.

DeCharms, R. *Personal causation*. New York: Academic Press, 1968.

Dember, W. N. Motivation and the cognitive revolution. *American Psychologist*, 1974, *29*, 161–168.

Dixon, W. J. (Ed.). *BMDP: Biomedical computer programs*. Berkeley: University of California Press, 1975.

Dunnette, M. D. Individualized prediction as a strategy for discovering demographic and interpersonal/psychological correlates of drug resistance and abuse. In D. J. Lettieri (Ed.), *Predicting adolescent drug abuse*. Rockville, Md.: National Institute on Drug Abuse, 1975.

Edwards, A. L. *Edwards Personal Preference Schedule*. New York: Psychological Corporation, 1959.

Edwards, A. L., & Abbott, R. D. Relationships among the Edwards Personality Inventory scales, the Edwards Personal Preference Schedule, and the Personality Research Form scales. *Journal of Consulting and Clinical Psychology*, 1973, *40*, 27–32.

Edwards, A. L., Abbott, R. D., & Klockars, A. J. A factor analysis of the EPPS and the PRF. *Educational and Psychological Measurement*, 1972, *32*, 23–29.

Einstein, S., Quiones, M., & Lavenhar, M. Treating the drug abuser: Relevant and irrelevant factors. In W. Keup (Ed.), *Drug abuse: Current concepts and research*. Springfield, Ill.: Thomas, 1972.

Endler, N. S., & Magnusson, D. (Eds.). *Interactional psychology and personality*. Washington, D.C.: Hemisphere, 1976.

Fagerberg, S. A comparative study of drug use patterns in three academic settings: University, community college, and high schools. *Journal of Alcohol and Drug Education*, 1975, *20*, 27–34.

Fein, G., & Antrobus, J. S. *Daydreaming: A Poisson process*. Manuscript in preparation, 1979.

Ferraro, D. P., & Billings, D. K. Marihuana use by college students: Three-year trends, 1970–1972. *International Journal of the Addictions*, 1974, *9*, 321–327. (a)

Ferraro, D. P., & Billings, D. K. Illicit drug use by college students: Three-year trends, 1970–1972. *International Journal of the Addictions,* 1974, *9,* 879–883. (b)

Feshbach, N. D. Studies of empathic behavior in children. In B. A. Maher (Ed.), *Progress in experimental personality research* (Vol. 8). New York: Academic Press, 1978.

Frank, S. *Fantasy and internalized role-taking.* Unpublished doctoral dissertation, Yale University, 1976.

Frank, S. Just imagine how I feel: How to improve empathy through training in imagination. In J. L. Singer & K. S. Pope (Eds.), *The power of human imagination.* New York: Plenum, 1978.

Freud, S. [*Creative writers and daydreaming*]. In J. Strachey (Ed. and Trans.), *The standard edition of the complete psychological works of Sigmund Freud* (Vol. 9). London: Hogarth, 1962. (Originally published, 1908.)

Giambra, L. M. Daydreaming across the life span: Late adolescent to senior citizen. *Aging and Human Development,* 1974, *5,* 118–135.

Giambra, L. M. A factor analytic study of daydreaming, imaginal process, and temperament: A replication of an adult male life-span sample. *Journal of Gerontology,* 1977, *32,* 675–680.

Ginsberg, I. J., & Greenley, J. R. Competing theories of marijuana use: A longitudinal study. *Journal of Health and Social Behavior,* 1978, *19,* 22–34.

Glatt, M., & Hills, D. Alcohol abuse and alcoholism in the young. *British Journal of Addictions,* 1968, *63,* 183–191.

Gleason, T. S. On redundancy in canonical analysis. *Psychological Bulletin,* 1976, *83,* 1004–1006.

Globetti, G. Young people and alcohol education—abstinence or moderate drinking. *Drug Forum,* 1972, *1,* 269–272.

Goode, E. *Deviant behavior: An interactionist approach.* Englewood Cliffs, N.J.: Prentice-Hall, 1978.

Gorsuch, R. L. *Factor analysis.* Philadelphia: Saunders, 1974.

Gorsuch, R. L., & Butler, M. C. Initial drug abuse: A review of predisposing social psychological factors. *Psychological Bulletin,* 1976, *83,* 120–137.

Gough, H. G. *California Psychological Inventory.* Palo Alto, Calif.: Consulting Psychologists Press, 1956.

Gough, H. G., & Heilbrun, A. B. *The adjective check list manual.* Palo Alto, Calif.: Consulting Psychologists Press, 1965.

Gray, J. A. A neuropsychological theory of anxiety. In C. Izard (Ed.), *Emotions in personality and psychopathology.* New York: Plenum, 1979.

Grinspoon, L. *Marijuana reconsidered.* Cambridge, Mass.: Howard Press, 1971.

Grossman, J. C., Goldstein, R., & Eisenman, R. Openness to experience and marijuana use: An initial investigation. *Proceedings of the 79th Annual Convention of the American Psychological Association,* 1971, *6,* 335–336. (Summary)

Guilford, J. P., & Zimmerman, W. S. *The Guilford-Zimmerman Temperament Survey: Manual.* Beverly Hills, Calif.: Sheridan Supply Co., 1949.

Gusfield, J. The structural contest of college drinking. In G. L. Maddox (Ed.), *The domesticated drug: Drinking among collegians.* New Haven, Conn.: College and University Press, 1970.

Hakstian, A. R., & Abell, R. A. A further comparison of oblique factor transformation methods. *Psychometrika,* 1974, *39,* 429–444.

Hamilton, D. L. Personality attributes associated with extreme response style. *Psychological Bulletin,* 1968, *69,* 192–203.

Hariton, E. B., & Singer, J. L. Women's fantasies during sexual intercourse: Normative and theoretical implications. *Journal of Consulting and Clinical Psychology,* 1974, *42,* 313–322.

Harman, H. *Modern factor analysis.* Chicago: University Chicago Press, 1967.

Hebb, D. O. The American revolution. *American Psychologist,* 1960,*15,* 735–745.

Hogan, R., Mankin, D., Conway, J., & Fox, S. Personality correlates of undergraduate marijuana use. *Journal of Consulting and Clinical Psychology,* 1970, *35,* 58–63.

Holroyd, K., & Kahn, M. Personality factors in drug use. *Journal of Consulting and Clinical Psychology,* 1974, *42,* 236–243.

Holt, R. Imagery: The return of the ostracized. *American Psychologist,* 1964, *19,* 254–264.

Horn, J. L. *Comments on the many faces of alcoholism.* Paper presented at the NATO International Conference on Experimental and Behavioral Approaches to Alcoholism, Norway, 1977.

Horn, J. L., & Knapp, J. R. On the subjective character of the empirical bases of Guilford's structure-of-intellect model. *Psychological Bulletin,* 1973, *80,* 33–43.

Horn, J. L., & Wanberg, K. W. Symptom patterns related to excessive use of alcohol. *Quarterly Journal of Studies on Alcohol,* 1969, *30,* 35–58.

Horn, J. L., & Wanberg, K. W. Dimensions of perception of background and current situation of alcoholic patients. *Quarterly Journal of Studies on Alcohol,* 1970, *31,* 633–658.

Horn, J. L., & Wanberg, K. W. Females are different: On the diagnosis of alcoholism in women. In M. E. Chafetz (Ed.), *Proceedings of the first annual Alcoholism Conference of the National Institute on Alcohol Abuse and Alcoholism.* Rockville, Md.: U.S. Department of Health, Education and Welfare, 1973.

Horowitz, M. J. Intrusive and repetitive thought after experimental stress. *Archives of General Psychiatry,* 1975, *32,* 1457–1463.

Horowitz, M. J. *Stress response syndromes.* New York: Aronson, 1976.

Horowitz, M. J., & Becker, S. The compulsion to repeat trauma. *Journal of Nervous and Mental Diseases,* 1971, *153,* 32–40.

Huba, G. J. A computer program for restricted oblique Procrustes rotation to a primary factor pattern matrix. *Behavior Research Methods and Instrumentation,* 1975, *7,* 688.

Huba, G. J. Daydreaming. In R. H. Woody (Ed.), *Encyclopedia of clinical assessment.* San Francisco: Jossey-Bass, 1980.

Huba, G. J., & Hamilton, D. L. On the generality of trait relationships: Some analyses based on Fiske's paper. *Psychological Bulletin,* 1976, *83,* 868–876.

Huba, G. J., Segal, B., & Singer, J. L. The consistency of daydreaming styles across samples of college male and female drug and alcohol users. *Journal of Abnormal Psychology,* 1977, *86,* 99–102. (a)

Huba, G. J., Segal, B., & Singer, J. L. Organization of needs in male and female drug and alcohol users. *Journal of Consulting and Clinical Psychology,* 1977, *45,* 34–44. (b)

Huba, G. J., Wingard, J. A., & Bentler, P. M. Beginning adolescent drug use and peer and adult interaction patterns. *Journal of Consulting and Clinical Psychology,* 1979, *47,* 265–276.

Huba, G. J., Wingard, J. A., & Bentler, P. M. Framework for an interactive theory of drug use. In D. J. Lettieri (Ed.), *Theories of drug use.* Rockville, Md.: National Institute on Drug Abuse, 1980.

Humphreys, L. G., Ilgen, D., McGrath, D., & Montanelli, R. Capitalization on chance in rotation of factors. *Educational and Psychological Measurement,* 1969, *29,* 259–271.

Ikard, F. F., & Tomkins, S. S. The experience of affect as a determinant of smoking behavior: A series of validity studies. *Journal of Abnormal Psychology,* 1973, *81,* 172–181.

Isaacs, D. *Cognitive style in daydreaming.* Unpublished doctoral dissertation, City University of New York, 1975.

Izard, C. *Human emotions.* New York: Plenum, 1977.

Izard, C. E., & Tomkins, S. S. Affect and behavior: Anxiety as a negative affect. In C. Spielberger (Ed.), *Anxiety and behavior.* New York: Academic Press, 1966.

Jaccard, J. J. Predicting social behavior from personality traits. *Journal of Research in Personality,* 1974, *7,* 358–367.

Jackson, D. N. *Personality research form*. Goshen, N.Y.: Research Psychologists Press, 1967.

Jackson, D. N., & Guthrie, G. M. Multitrait–multimethod evaluation of the Personality Research Form. *Proceedings of the 76th Annual Convention of the American Psychological Association*, 1968, *3*, 177–178. (Summary)

Jackson, D. N., & Morf, M. E. Testing the null hypothesis for rotation to a target. *Multivariate Behavioral Research*, 1974, *9*, 303–309.

James, W. *Principles of psychology*. New York: Holt, 1890. (Reprinted, 1950.)

Janis, I. L. (Ed.). *Personality: Dynamics, development, and assessment*. New York: Harcourt, Brace, Jovanovich, 1969.

Janis, I., & Mann, L. *Decision making*. New York: The Free Press, 1977.

Jennrich, R. I. Stepwise discriminant analysis. In K. Enslein, A. Ralston, & H. S. Wolf (Eds.), *Statistical methods for digital computers* (Vol. III). New York: Wiley, 1977.

Jennrich, R. I., & Sampson, P. F. Rotation for simple loadings. *Psychometrika*, 1966, *31*, 313–323.

Jessor, R. Predicting time of onset of marijuana use: A developmental study of high school youth. In D. J. Lettieri (Ed.), *Predicting adolescent drug abuse: A review of methods, issues, and correlates*. Rockville, Md.: National Institute on Drug Abuse, 1975.

Jessor, R., Graves, T., Hanson, R., & Jessor, S. *Society, personality, and deviant behavior*. New York: Holt, Rinehart & Winston, 1968.

Jessor, R., & Jessor, S. L. *Problem behavior and psychosocial development*. New York: Academic Press, 1977.

Johnson, B. D. *Marijuana users and drug subcultures*. New York: Wiley, 1973.

Johnston, L. D., O'Malley, P. M., & Eveland, L. K. Drugs and delinquency: A search for causal connections. In D. B. Kandel (Ed.), *Longitudinal research on drug use*. Washington, D.C.: Hemisphere, 1978.

Jöreskog, K. G. Some contributions to maximum likelihood factor analysis. *Psychometrika*, 1967, *32*, 443–482.

Jöreskog, K. G. A general approach to confirmatory maximum likelihood factor analysis. *Psychometrika*, 1969, *34*, 183–202.

Jöreskog, K. G. Simultaneous factor analysis in several populations. *Psychometrika*, 1971, *36*, 409–426.

Jöreskog, K. G. Structural analysis of covariance and correlation matrices. *Psychometrika*, 1978, *43*, 443–478.

Jöreskog, K. G., & Sörbom, D. *LISREL IV: Analysis of linear structural relationships by the method of maximum likelihood*. Chicago: National Educational Resources, Inc., 1978.

Julien, R. *A primer of drug action*. San Francisco: Freeman, 1975.

Kaiser, H. F. The varimax criterion for analytic rotation in factor analysis. *Psychometrika*, 1958, *23*, 187–200.

Kandel, D. B. Inter- and intragenerational influences on adolescent marijuana use. *Journal of Social Issues*, 1974, *30*, 107–135.

Kandel, D. B. Stages in adolescent involvement in drug use. *Science*, 1975, *190*, 912–914. (a)

Kandel, D. B. Some comments on the relationship of selected criteria variables to adolescent drug use. In D. J. Lettieri (Ed.), *Predicting adolescent drug abuse: A review of issues, methods, and correlates*. Rockville, Md.: National Institute on Drug Abuse, 1975. (b)

Kandel, D. B. Convergences in prospective longitudinal surveys of drug use in normal populations. In D. B. Kandel (Ed.), *Longitudinal research on drug use: Empirical findings and methodological issues*. Washington, D.C.: Hemisphere, 1978. (a)

Kandel, D. B. *Longitudinal research on drug use: Empirical findings and methodological issues*. Washington, D.C.: Hemisphere, 1978. (b)

Kandel, D. B. Similarity in real-life adolescent friendship pairs. *Journal of Personality and Social Psychology*, 1978, *36*, 306–312. (c)

Kandel, D. B., & Faust, R. Sequences and stages in patterns of adolescent drug use. *Archives of General Psychiatry*, 1975, *32*, 923–932.

Kandel, D. B., Kessler, R. C., & Margulies, R. Z. Antecedents of adolescent initiation into stages of drug use: A developmental analysis. In D. B. Kandel (Ed.), *Longitudinal research on drug use: Empirical findings and methodological issues*. Washington, D.C.: Hemisphere, 1978.

Keniston, K. *Youth and dissent*. New York: Harcourt, Brace, Jovanovich, 1970.

Khantzian, E. J., & Treece, C. J. Psychodynamics of drug dependence: An overview. In J. D. Blaine & D. A. Julius (Eds.), *Psychodynamics of drug dependence*. Rockville, Md.: National Institute on Drug Abuse, 1977.

Khavari, K. A., Mabry, E., & Humes, M. Personality correlates of hallucinogen use. *Journal of Abnormal Psychology*, 1977, *86*, 172–178.

Kilpatrick, D. G., Sutker, P. B., & Smith, A. D. Deviant drug and alcohol use: The role of anxiety, sensation seeking, and other personality variables. In M. D. Zuckerman & C. D. Spielberger (Eds.), *Emotions and anxiety: New concepts, methods, and applications*. Hillsdale, N.J.: Lawrence Erlbaum Associates, 1976.

Kinsey, A. C., Pomeroy, W. B., & Martin, C. E. *Sexual behavior in the human male*. Philadelphia: Saunders, 1948.

Klinger, E. *Structure and functions of fantasy*. New York: Wiley, 1971.

Klinger, E. Utterances to evaluate steps and control attention distinguish operant from respondent thought while thinking out loud. *Bulletin of the Psychonomic Society*, 1974, *4*, 44–45.

Klinger, E. Modes of normal conscious flow. In K. S. Pope & J. L. Singer (Eds.), *The stream of consciousness*. New York: Plenum, 1978.

Klos, D. S. *Relationship values: Highpoints and lowpoints in the interactions of 18-to-30 year olds with their parents and close friends*. Unpublished manuscript, Williams College, 1977.

Kohn, P. M., & Annis, H. M. Personality and social factors in adolescent marijuana use: A path-analytic study. *Journal of Consulting and Clinical Psychology*, 1978, *46*, 366–367.

Kramer, J. C. Introduction to the problem of heroin addiction in America. *Grassroots*, 1972 (May supplement).

Lawley, D. N. The estimation of factor loadings by the method of maximum likelihood. *Proceedings of the Royal Society of Edinburgh*, 1940, *60*, 64–82.

Lawley, D. N., & Maxwell, A. E. Factor analysis as a statistical method. New York: American Elsevier, 1971.

Lefcourt, H. M. *Locus of control: Current trends in theory and research*. Hillsdale, N.J.: Lawrence Erlbaum Associates, 1976.

Lettieri, D. J. (Ed.). *Predicting adolescent drug abuse: A review of issues, methods, and correlates*. Rockville, Md.: National Institute on Drug Abuse, 1975.

Lettieri, D. J. Theories of drug abuse. In D. J. Lettieri (Ed.), *Drugs and suicide: When other coping strategies fail*. Beverly Hills, Calif.: Sage, 1978.

Lewin, K. Das Problem der Willenmessung und das Grundgesetz der Association. *Psychologisches Forschung*, 1922, *1*, 191–302.

Lewin, K. *A dynamic theory of personality*. New York: McGraw-Hill, 1935.

Lewis, D. L. Color it black: The failures of drug abuse policy. *Social Policy*, 1976, *6*, 26–32.

Loevinger, J. *Ego development: Conceptions and theories*. San Francisco: Jossey-Bass, 1976.

Magnusson, D., & Endler, N. S. (Eds.). *Personality at the crossroads*. Hillsdale, N.J.: Lawrence Erlbaum Associates, 1977.

McAree, C., Steffenhagen, R., & Zheutlin, L. Personality factors in college drug users. *International Journal of Social Psychiatry*, 1969, *15*, 102–106.

McClelland, D. C. *Personality*. New York: Holt, Rinehart & Winston, 1958.

McClelland, D. C. *The achieving society*. Princeton, N.J.: Van Nostrand, 1961.

McClelland, D. C. *Power: The inner experience*. New York: Irvington, 1975.

McClelland, D. C., Davis, W. N., Kalin, R., & Wanner, E. *The drinking man: Alcohol and human motivation*. New York: Free Press, 1972.

McClelland, D. C., & Steele, R. Motives for drug-taking among college men. In D. C. McClelland, W. N. Davis, R. Kalin, & E. Wanner (Eds.), *The drinking man: Alcohol and human motivation.* New York: Free Press, 1972.

McGaw, B., & Jöreskog, K. G. Factorial invariance of ability measures in groups differing in intelligence and socioeconomic status. *British Journal of Mathematical and Statistical Psychology,* 1971, *24,* 154–168.

McGuire, J., & Megargee, E. Personality correlates of marijuana use among youthful offenders. *Journal of Consulting and Clinical Psychology,* 1974, *42,* 124–133.

Meichenbaum, D., Henshaw, D., & Himmel, N. Coping with stress as a problem solving process. In W. Krohne & L. Laus (Eds.), *Achievement stress and anxiety.* Washington, D.C.: Hemisphere, 1979.

Mellinger, G. D. Use of licit drugs and other coping alternatives: Some personal observations on the hazards of living. In D. J. Lettieri (Ed.), *Drugs and suicide: When other coping strategies fail.* Beverly Hills, Calif.: Sage, 1978.

Miller, G. A., Galanter, E. H., & Pribram, K. *Plans and the structure of behavior.* New York: Holt, Rinehart & Winston, 1960

Miller, T. *Some characteristics of two different ways of listening.* Unpublished doctoral dissertation, New York University, 1972.

Mischel, W. *Personality and assessment.* New York: Wiley, 1968.

Mischel, W. *Introduction to personality.* New York: Holt, Rinehart & Winston, 1971.

Morrison, D. F. *Multivariate statistical methods* (2nd ed.). New York: McGraw-Hill, 1976.

Mosher, D. The development and multitrait–multimethod matrix analysis of three measures of guilt. *Journal of Consulting Psychology,* 1966, *30,* 25–29.

Mulaik, S. A. *The foundations of factor analysis.* New York: McGraw-Hill, 1972.

Murray, H. A. *Explorations in personality.* New York: Wiley, 1938.

National Commission on Marijuana and Drug Abuse. *Marijuana: A signal of misunderstanding.* Washington, D.C.: U.S. Government Printing Office, 1972.

National Commission on Marijuana and Drug Abuse. *Drug use in America: Problem in perspective.* Washington, D.C.: U.S. Government Printing Office, 1973.

National Institute on Alcohol Abuse and Alcoholism. *Alcohol and health (DHEW Pub. No. (HSM) 73-9031).* Washington, D.C.: U.S. Government Printing Office, 1971.

Nehemkis, A., Macari, M. A., & Lettieri, D. J. *Drug abuse instrument handbook.* Rockville, Md.: National Institute on Drug Abuse, 1976.

Neisser, U. *Cognitive psychology.* New York: Appleton-Century-Crofts, 1967.

Nesselroade, J. R., & Baltes, P. B. Higher order factor convergence and divergence of two distinct personality systems: Cattell's HSPQ and Jackson's PRF. *Multivariate Behavioral Research,* 1975, *10,* 387–407.

Oakland, J. A. Note on the social desirability response set in Singer's Daydreaming Questionnaire. *Psychological Reports,* 1968, *22,* 689–690.

Page, H. Studies in fantasy—daydreaming frequencies and Rorschach scoring categories. *Journal of Consulting Psychology,* 1957, *21,* 111–114.

Paivio, A. On the functional significance of imagery. *Psychological Bulletin,* 1970, *73,* 385–392.

Paivio, A. *Imagery and verbal processes.* New York: Holt, Rinehart & Winston, 1971.

Piaget, J. *Play, dreams and imitation in childhood.* New York: Norton, 1962.

Pihl, R. O., & Spiers, P. Individual characteristics in the etiology of drug abuse. In B. A. Maher (Ed.), *Progress in experimental personality research.* New York: Academic Press, 1978.

Platt, J. J., & Labate, C. *Heroin addiction: Theory, research and treatment.* New York: Wiley, 1976.

Pope, K. S. How gender, solitude, and posture influence the stream of consciousness. In K. S. Pope & J. L. Singer (Eds.), *The stream of consciousness.* New York: Plenum, 1978.

Pope, K. S., & Singer, J. L. Determinants of the stream of consciousness. In G. Schwartz & D. Shapiro (Eds.), *Consciousness and self-regulation: Advances in research* (Vol. 2). New York: Plenum, 1978. (a)

Pope, K. S., & Singer, J. L. (Eds.). *The steam of consciousness.* New York: Plenum, 1978. (b)

Pope, K. S., & Singer, J. L. The waking stream of consciousness. In J. Davidson & R. Davidson (Eds.), *The psychobiology of consciousness.* New York: Plenum, 1979.

Powell, P. *A study of social cognition and role-playing based upon the works of Jean Piaget and Ralph H. Turner.* Unpublished doctoral dissertation, University of Chicago, 1971.

Rapaport, D. On the psychoanalytical theory of motivation. In R. Jones (Ed.), *Nebraska Symposium on Motivation.* Lincoln: University of Nebraska Press, 1960.

Ray, O. *Drugs, society, and human behavior.* St. Louis, Mo.: Mosby, 1972.

Richards, L. G., & Blevens, L. B. *The epidemiology of drug abuse.* Rockville, Md.: National Institute on Drug Abuse, 1977.

Robins, L. N. The interaction of setting and predisposition in explaining novel behavior: Drug initiation before, in, and after Vietnam. In D. B. Kandel (Ed.), *Longitudinal research on drug use: Empirical findings and methodological issues.* Washington, D.C.: Hemisphere, 1978.

Rodin, J., & Singer, J. L. Eyeshift, thought, and obesity. *Journal of Personality,* 1977, *44,* 594–610.

Rosenfeld, E. *The development of an imaginal processes inventory for children.* Unpublished doctoral dissertation, University of Illinois at Chicago Circle, 1978.

Rosenthal, R., Hall, J. A., DiMatteo, R. M., Rogers, P. L., & Archer, D. *Sensitivity to nonverbal communication: The PONS test.* Baltimore, Md.: Johns Hopkins University Press, 1979.

Rotter, J. Generalized expectancies for internal versus external control of reinforcement. *Psychological Monographs,* 1966, *80*(Whole No. 609).

Rychlak, J. R. *Introduction to personality and psychotherapy: A theory construction approach.* Boston: Houghton Mifflin, 1973.

Sadava, S. W. Research approaches in illicit drug use: A critical review. *Genetic Psychology Monographs,* 1975, *91,* 3–59.

Schacter, S., & Singer, J. E. Cognitive, social and physiological determinants of emotional state. *Psychological Review,* 1962, *69,* 379–399.

Schank, R. R., & Abelson, R. P. *Scripts, plans, goals, and understanding.* Hillsdale, N.J.: Lawrence Erlbaum Associates, 1977.

Schmid, J. L., & Leiman, J. M. The development of hierarchical factor solutions. *Psychometrika,* 1957, *22,* 53–61.

Schultz, D. Imagery and the control of depression. In J. L. Singer & K. S. Pope (Eds.), *The power of human imagination.* New York: Plenum, 1978.

Schur, E. M. The addict and social problems. In S. Clog & R. Edgerton (Eds.), *Changing perspectives in mental illness.* New York: Holt, Rinehart & Winston, 1969.

Seeman, W. The Freudian theory of daydreams: An operational analysis. *Psychological Bulletin,* 1951, *48,* 369–382.

Segal, B. *A questionnaire of drug and alcohol use.* Unpublished manuscript, Murray State University, Murray, Ky., 1973. (a)

Segal, B. Sensation seeking and anxiety: Assessment of responses to specific stimulus situations. *Journal of Consulting and Clinical Psychology,* 1973, *41,* 135–138. (b)

Segal, B. *Alcohol Drug Research Survey (Revised).* Unpublished manuscript, Murray State University, Murray, Ky., 1974.

Segal, B. *Sensation seeking and drug use.* Paper presented at the annual meeting of the American Psychological Association, San Francisco, August 1977.

Segal, B., & Merenda, P. F. Locus of control, sensation seeking, and drug and alcohol use in college students. *Drug Forum,* 1975, *4,* 349–369.

Segal, B., & Singer, J. L. Daydreaming, drug and alcohol use in college students: A factor analytic study. *Addictive Behaviors,* 1976, *1,* 227–235.

Segal, S. J. *Imagery: Current cognitive approaches.* New York: Academic Press, 1971.

Segal, S. J., & Fusella, V. Influence of imagined pictures and sounds on detection of visual and auditory signals. *Journal of Experimental Psychology*, 1970, *83*, 458–464.

Segal, S. J., & Glickman, M. Relaxation and the Perky Effect: The influence of body position and judgments of imagery. *American Journal of Psychology*, 1967, *60*, 257–262.

Selman, R. Toward a structural analysis of developing interpersonal relationship concepts: Research with normal and disturbed preadolescent boys. In A. Pick (Ed.), *Tenth Annual Minnesota Symposia on Child Psychology*. Minneapolis: University of Minnesota Press, 1976.

Shaffer, L. F. *The psychology of adjustment*. Boston: Houghton Mifflin, 1936.

Shepard, R. N. The mental image. *American Psychologist*, 1978, *33*, 125–137.

Sherif, M., & Sherif, C. *Social Psychology*. New York: Harper & Row, 1969.

Siess, T. F., & Jackson, D. N. Vocational interests and personality: An empirical investigation. *Journal of Consulting Psychology*, 1970, *17*, 27–35.

Singer, J. L. *Daydreaming*. New York: Random House, 1966.

Singer, J. L. Research applications of the projective techniques. In A. Rabin (Ed.), *Projective techniques in personality assessment*. New York: Springer, 1968.

Singer, J. L. Drives, affects and daydreams: The adaptive role of spontaneous imagery or stimulus-independent mentation. In J. S. Antrobus (Ed.), *Cognition and affect: The City University Symposium*. New York: Little, Brown, 1970.

Singer, J. L. (Ed.). *The child's world of make-believe: Experimental studies of imaginative play*. New York: Academic Press, 1973.

Singer, J. L. *Imagery and daydream methods in psychotherapy and behavior modification*. New York: Academic Press, 1974 (a)

Singer, J. L. Daydreaming and the stream of thought. *American Scientist*, 1974, *2*, 417–425. (b)

Singer, J. L. *The inner world of daydreaming*. New York: Harper & Row, 1975. (a)

Singer, J. L. Navigating the stream of consciousness: Research in daydreaming and related inner experience. *American Psychologist*, 1975, *30*, 727–738. (b)

Singer, J. L. Imagination and fantasy play in early childhood: Some educational implications. *Journal of Mental Imagery*, 1977, *1*, 127–144. (a)

Singer, J. L. Ongoing thought: The normative baseline for alternate states of consciousness. In N. E. Zinberg (Ed.), *Alternate states of consciousness*. New York: Free Press, 1977. (b)

Singer, J. L. Experimental studies of daydreaming and the stream of thought. In K. S. Pope & J. L. Singer (Eds.), *The stream of consciousness*. New York: Plenum, 1978.

Singer, J. L., & Antrobus, J. S. A factor analytic study of daydreaming and conceptually-related cognitive and personality variables. *Perceptual and Motor Skills*, 1963, *17*, 187–209.

Singer, J. L., & Antrobus, J. S. *Manual for the Imaginal Processes Inventory*. (copyright 1970). Available from Educational Testing Service, Princeton, N.J. 08540.

Singer, J. L., & Antrobus, J. S. Daydreaming, imaginal processes, and personality: A normative study. In P. Sheehan (Ed.), *The function and nature of imagery*. New York: Academic Press, 1972.

Singer, J. L., & McCraven, V. Some characteristics of adult daydreaming. *Journal of Psychology*, 1961, *51*, 151–164.

Singer, J. L., & McCraven, V. Patterns of daydreaming in American subcultural groups. *International Journal of Social Psychiatry*, 1962, *8*, 272–282.

Singer, J. L., & Singer, D. G. Personality. *Annual Review of Psychology*, 1972, *23*, 375–412.

Smith, G. M., & Fogg, C. P. Psychological antecedents of teenage drug use. In R. G. Simmons (Ed.), *Research in community and mental health: An annual compilation of research* (Vol. 1). Greenwich, Conn.: JAI, 1977.

Smith, G. M., & Fogg, C. P. Psychological predictors of early use, late use, and non-use of marijuana among teenage students. In D. B. Kandel (Ed.), *Longitudinal studies on drug use: Empirical findings and methodological issues*. Washington, D. C.: Hemisphere, 1978.

Sörbom, D. A general method for studying differences in factor means and factor structure between groups. *British Journal of Mathematical and Statistical Psychology,* 1974, *27,* 229–239.

Sörbom, D., & Jöreskog, K. G. *COFAMM: Confirmatory factor analysis with model modification.* Chicago: National Educational Resources, Inc., 1976.

Starker, S. Daydreaming styles and nocturnal dreaming. *Journal of Abnormal Psychology,* 1974, *83,* 52–55.

Starker, S. Fantasy in psychiatric patients: Exploring a myth. *Hospital & Community Psychiatry,* 1979, *30,* 25–30.

Starker, S., & Singer, J. L. Daydreaming and symptom patterns of psychiatric patients. *Journal of Abnormal Psychology,* 1975, *84,* 567–570. (a)

Starker, S., & Singer, J. L. Daydream patterns and self-awareness in psychiatric patients. *Journal of Nervous and Mental Diseases,* 1975, *161,* 131–137. (b)

Steffenhagen, R. A., McAree, C. P., & Zheutlin, L. S. Social and academic factors associated with drug use on the University of Vermont campus. *International Journal of Social Psychiatry,* 1969, *15,* 92–96.

Steffenhagen, R., Schmidt, F., & McAree, C. *Emotional stability and student drug use.* Unpublished manuscript, University of Vermont, 1971.

Stewart, D., & Love, W. A general canonical correlation index. *Psychological Bulletin* 1968, *70,* 160–163.

Straus, R., & Bacon, S. D. *Drinking in college.* New Haven, Conn.: Yale University Press, 1953.

Stricker, L. J. Personality Research Form: Factor structure and response style involvement. *Journal of Consulting and Clinical Psychology,* 1974, *42,* 529–537.

Suchman, E. A. The hang-loose ethic and the spirit of drug use. *Journal of Health and Social Behavior,* 1968, *9,* 146–155.

Sundberg, N. D. A method for studying sensitivity to implied meanings. *Gawein,* 1966, *15,* 1–8.

Tart, C. T. Marijuana intoxication: Common experiences. *Nature,* 1970, *226,* 701–704.

Tart, C. T. *On being stoned.* Palo Alto, Calif.: Science and Behavior Books, 1971.

Tart, C. T. *States of consciousness.* New York: Dutton, 1975.

Tart, C. T. Putting the pieces together: A conceptual framework for understanding discrete states of consciousness. In N. E. Zinberg (Ed.), *Alternate states of consciousness.* New York: Free Press, 1977.

Tatsuoka, M. M. *Multivariate analysis.* New York: Wiley, 1971.

Thurstone, L. L. *Multiple factor analysis.* Chicago: University of Chicago Press, 1947.

Tomkins, S. S. *The thematic apperception test: The theory and technique of interpretation.* New York: Grune & Stratton, 1947.

Tomkins, S. S. *Affect, imagery, and consciousness* (Vols. I & II). New York: Springer, 1962–1963.

Tomkins, S. S. Psychological model for smoking behavior. *American Journal of Public Health,* 1966, *12,* 17–20. (a)

Tomkins, S. S. Theoretical implications and guidelines for future research. In B. Mausner & E. Platt (Eds.), *Behavioral aspects of smoking: A conference report. Health Education Monographs,* 1966 (Supplement No. 2), 35–48. (b)

Tomkins, S. S. Script theory: Differential magnification of affects. In *Nebraska Symposium on Motivation.* Lincoln: University of Nebraska Press, 1979.

Tucker, L. R. *A method for synthesis of factor analysis studies* (Rep. No. 984). Personnel Research Section, Department of the Army, 1951.

Tucker, L. R., & Lewis, C. A. A reliability coefficient for maximum likelihood factor analysis. *Psychometrika,* 1973, *38,* 1–10.

Van de Geer, J. P. *Introduction to multivariate analysis for the social sciences.* San Francisco: Freeman, 1971.

Victor, H., Grossman, J., & Eisenman, R. Openness to experience and marijuana use in high school students. *Journal of Consulting and Clinical Psychology,* 1973, *41,* 78–85.

Weckowicz, T., & Janssen, D. Cognitive functions, personality traits, and social values in heavy marijuana smokers and nonsmoker controls. *Journal of Abnormal Psychology,* 1973, *81,* 264–269.

Weil, A. T. The marriage of the sun and moon. In N. E. Zinberg (Ed.), *Alternate states of consciousness.* New York: Free press, 1977.

Weinberger, D. A., Schwartz, G. E., & Davidson, R. J. Low anxious, high anxious, and repressive coping styles: Psychometric patterns and behavior and physiological responses to stress. *Journal of Abnormal Psychology,* 1979, *88,* 369–380.

Wiggins, J. S. *Personality and prediction: Principles of personality assessment.* Reading, Mass.: Addison-Wesley, 1973.

Wikler, A. *Opiate addiction.* Springfield, Ill.: Thomas, 1953.

Wiley, D. The identification problem for structural equation models with unmeasured variables. In A. S. Goldberger & O. D. Duncan (Eds.), *Structural equation models in the social sciences.* New York: Seminar, 1973.

Wilkinson, L. R. Response variable hypotheses in the multivariate analysis of variance. *Psychological Bulletin,* 1975, *82,* 408–412.

Wilkinson, L. R. Confirmatory rotation of MANOVA canonical variates. *Multivariate Behavioral Research,* 1977, *12,* 487–494.

Wingard, J. A., Huba, G. J., & Bentler, P. M. The relationship of personality structure to patterns of adolescent drug use. *Multivariate Behavioral Research,* 1979, *14,* 131–143.

Wurmser, L. Mr. Pecksniff's horse? (Psychodynamics in compulsive drug use). In J. D. Blaine & D. A. Julius (Eds.), *Psychodynamics of drug dependence.* Rockville, Md.: National Institute on Drug Abuse, 1977.

Zachary, R. *Cognitive and affective determinants of ongoing thought.* Unpublished doctoral dissertation, Yale University, 1978.

Zinberg, N. E. (Ed.). *Alternate states of consciousness.* New York: Free Press, 1977.

Zinberg, N. E., & Weil, A. A comparison of marijuana smokers and non-users. *Nature,* 1970, *226,* 119–123.

Zuckerman, M. The sensation seeking motive. In B. A. Maher (Ed.), *Progress in experimental personality research* (Vol. 7). New York: Academic Press, 1974.

Zuckerman, M. *Manual and research report for the sensation seeking scale.* Unpublished report, University of Delaware, 1975.

Zuckerman, M. Development of a situation-specific trait–state test for the prediction and measurement of affective responses. *Journal of Consulting and Clinical Psychology,* 1977, *45,* 513–523.

Zuckerman, M., Bone, R., Neary, R., Mangelsdorff, D., & Brustman, B. What is the sensation seeker? Personality trait and experience seeking correlates of the sensation-seeking scales. *Journal of Consulting and Clinical Psychology,* 1972, *39,* 308–321.

Zuckerman, M. *Sensation-Seeking.* Hillsdale, N.J.: Erlbaum Associates, 1979.

Author Index

Subject Index